Lecture Notes in Economics and Mathematical Systems 469

Springer
Berlin
Heidelberg
New York
Barcelona
Hong Kong
London
Milan
Paris
Singapore
Tokyo

Michael P. Vogel

Environmental Kuznets Curves

A Study on the Economic Theory and Political Economy of Environmental Quality Improvements in the Course of Economic Growth

Springer

Author

Michael P. Vogel
Institute of Theoretical Economics
University of Kiel
Wilhelm-Seelig-Platz 1
D-24098 Kiel, Germany

Library of Congress Cataloging-in-Publication Data

Vogel, Michael P., 1967-
Environmental Kuznets Curves : a study on the economic theory and political economy of environmental quality improvements in the course of economic growth / Michael P. Vogel.
p. cm. -- (Lecture notes in economics and mathematical systems, ISSN 0075-8442 ; 469)
Includes bibliographical references.
ISBN 3-540-65672-3 (softcover : alk. paper)
1. Pollution--Economic aspects--Mathematical models.
2. Environmental economics--Mathematical models. 3. Economic development--Mathematical models. I. Title. II. Series.
HC79.P55V64 1999
333.7--dc21 99-19796
CIP

ISSN 0075-8442
ISBN 3-540-65672-3 Springer-Verlag Berlin Heidelberg New York

Typesetting: Camera ready by author
SPIN: 10699916 42/3143-543210 - Printed on acid-free paper

This book is dedicated

to my parents,

who still don't know what Environmental Kuznets Curves are,

and to Tina,

the most wonderful determinant of the quality of my environment.

Acknowledgements

Environment to each must be
all there is, that isn't me.
The universe, in turn, must be
all that isn't me AND ME.

R. Buckminster Fuller[1]

The text of this book has been accepted by the Faculty of Economic and Social Sciences of the University of Kiel, Germany, as a doctoral thesis in Theoretical Economics. It won the Faculty's 1998 Erich Schneider Memorial Award.

In the course of the three years which it took me to complete this piece of research, many people have contributed to it, or supported me in one way or another. I want to take this opportunity to express them my gratitude and appreciation.

First of all, I wish to thank my supervisor, Professor Horst Herberg, for many fruitful discussions, his constructive criticism, and his general support of my project. I also benefitted a lot from his courses in Advanced Mathematics and Microeconomics, and from the work environment he provided me with. As well, I would like to thank my co-supervisor, Professor Rolf Langhammer (Kiel Institute of World Economics), for many useful tips, reading recommendations, and his interesting course in Development Economics.

Deeply indebted I am to Klaus Wälde (now World Bank) for coaching and mentoring me at the earlier stages of my thesis. I also greatly enjoyed our continuous intensive exchange and discussion of ideas. For their critical remarks and suggestions, as well as for their helpfulness, I am further grateful to Frank Bulthaupt, Uwe Rentmeister, Frank Stähler, Feng Wei, Gerald Wogatzki, and the other participants of the Seminar in Theoretical Economics.

A number of academic teachers contributed to this book in more indirect ways: Professor David Pearce (University College London) made me familiar with the concept of Environmental Kuznets Curves; Malcolm Pemberton (University College London) and Professor Michael Rauscher (now

---

[1] From the poem "Cosmic Plurality" in: Fuller (1983), p. 37.

University of Rostock) introduced me to the world of dynamic optimisation; to Professor Wilfed Beckerman (Balliol College, Cambridge/U.K.) I owe my first insights into environmental ethics; and Professor Wolfgang Deppert (University of Kiel) inspired me with his courses in Theory of Science and Systems Theory.

For their help and the good co-operation I thank Gaby Bünz, Anita Hartz, and the library staff of the Kiel Institute of World Economics.

A very special mention deserve Ariane, Jan, Kirsten, Ole, Tim, Tini and of course Tina for their invaluable moral support and the great time they gave me in Kiel.

Finally, the people to whom I owe the most are my parents. In order to avoid a long „Without them..." enumeration at this point, I simply wish to thank them for all they have done for me.

Hamburg, September 1998

Contents

Chapter 1 Introduction

Whatever I dig from thee, Earth, may that have quick growth again. O purifier, may we not injure thy vitals or thy heart.

Hymn to the Earth, Atharva Veda, 3000 B.C. [2]

The past three decades have seen the emergence of a tremendous body of literature on the relationship between growing economic activity and the state of the environment. Without looking at any data, the very flood of papers, articles and books alone already refutes the conjecture that this relationship could be simple, unambiguous, or fully understood. On the contrary, the great bandwidth of results presented suggests a most intricate and diverse link between economic growth and the environment, turning broader generalisations made on empirical grounds into a daring enterprise. In any case, the neo-Malthusian "Garbage in and garbage out"[3] view which was widespread in the early 1970s, and still has its advocates, has not been supported by the evidence provided.

Apart from the complexity of the matter itself, the weak empirical foundations of this field - due to lacking or patchy data series, measurement standardisation problems, and disagreement about what actually to measure - are a second important reason for the extremely diverging conclusions arrived at by researchers.

The third major source of dissent as regards the growth-environment nexus, and perhaps the least obvious for "outsiders" and laymen, are the different world views, values, and paradigms underlying the respective works. Heilbroner (1973), p. 39, writes that "every social scientist approaches his task with a wish, consciously or unconsciously, to demonstrate the workability or unworkability of the social order he is investigating." This might be particularly true for the scientists working on the growth-environment relationship whose results have often been unbalanced and were employed

---

2 Quoted by King and Schneider (1991), p. 154.

3 Baumol and Oates (1979), p. 133, quoting a reviewer of "The Limits to Growth" [Meadows et al. (1972)]. The quotation refers to the so-called materials balance argument which holds that economic growth is associated with increasing material input, throughput, output, and ultimately waste or emissions.

either to support and strengthen the existing order of, say, capitalism and liberalism which seem to favour economic growth, or to attack the existing order, and to propose alternative ones. So whether economic growth is bad for the environment is not only a scientific but also a very political issue.

1.1 Why Does the Environment Matter?

Obviously, the environment matters, for otherwise it would not make it into the headlines of newspapers, the programmes of political parties, or the research agendas of scientists. But why does it matter? The way people tend to answer this question will be illustrated by means of an example. Suppose that measurements indicate a rising concentration of heavy metals in a river which provides the local population with drinking water and food. Heavy metals such as lead, cadmium, arsenic, mercury or nickel are often discharged by industry, mining, and agriculture. They bioaccumulate in human bodies, but also in fish and shellfish, thus entering the food chain. These metals are associated with high health risks both for humans and for animals [Grossman and Krueger (1995), pp. 358-359]. Should the concentration of heavy metals be reduced, possibly to zero? Most people would agree; but why? Is it because they attach a high value to human health? Do they want the animals to be saved? Or do they regard the unnatural presence of heavy metals in the river as morally reprehensible?

The first motive will meet by far the broadest support since maximising human wellbeing is a generally accepted objective in decision making. If it is the only or the overriding objective, then the decision maker adopts a human-based or *anthropocentric-utilitarian* position. It means that beings or things only have a value if it is attributed or assigned to them by humans, who are the starting point of any ethical reasoning (the so-called moral reference class). Value in any anthropocentric ethics is therefore a *subjective* conception: it depends solely on those who assign it. Returning to the above example, the people who live from the river will probably place a very high value on water quality improvements, whereas others who are neither personally concerned by the contaminated river, nor informed about the problem will hardly care about reductions in the heavy metal concentration. Finally, for the owner of the factory that pollutes the river, a better water quality will even have a negative value if she or he has to finance it.

The second motive, namely to reduce the heavy metal load of the river in order to protect animal life, can be justified by the same anthropocentric argument. Since fish and shellfish are the local people's source of food, they have a *use value* for humans. But anthropocentric positions have often been criticised for their "speciesism", that is, their unjustified preference of humans over other species. Instead, it is argued that all living beings capable of sensing pleasure or pain should be given a moral standing. Already Jeremy Bentham, one of the founders of utilitarianism, wrote in 1780: "The question is not, can they reason? Nor, can they talk? But, can they suffer?" [Economist (1991), p. 30; see also O'Neill (1997), p. 129]. Such a position is called *non-anthropocentric utilitarianism*. Höffe (1993) emphasises that the criterion of sentience has been advocated by so many philosophers in the present and past that it can hardly be called heterodox anymore [pp. 206-207]. The value conception of non-anthropocentric utilitarianism is still *subjective*, but with a moral reference class which is larger than in anthropocentric utilitarianism.

The third motive for reducing the heavy metal concentration, finally, expresses the view that all the constituent parts of the biosphere, including whole ecosystems, have the natural right to exist and flourish. This view is referred to as *ecocentric-preservationist*. Different from utilitarian positions with their subjective value conception, ecocentrism assumes that nature has an intrinsic absolute or *real* value which is independent from the existence of humans or any other moral reference class. It is sometimes even asserted that the value of human beings is only relative, depending on their relative contribution to biosphere integrity [Pearce and Turner (1990), pp. 228-234]. However, the conception of real environmental values raises severe philosophical problems. "What makes it hard to establish these real values is the *realism* rather than the *ecocentrism*, a metaphysical difficulty that cannot be overcome ... Appeals to a position which, if true, would have strong implications will establish nothing at all if the truth of the position cannot be shown" [O'Neill (1997), p. 128; italics in the original].

Apart from the different shades of utilitarianism and ecocentrism there are still many other positions in environmental ethics. However, the important lesson to be learnt here is that a question like "Is Growth Bad for the Environment?"[4] remains meaningless unless a particular ethical position is assumed, for "bad" is a value judgement which must refer to some moral

---

[4] The full title of the paper by van Marrewijk et al. (1993) reads: "Is Growth Bad for the Environment? Pollution, Abatement, and Endogenous Growth".

reference class or standard. The most broadly accepted moral reference class in Western societies is the class of humans, implying that the environment is considered *instrumental* for human wellbeing, and any impact on the environment that alters its state to the worse for humans is now by definition "bad for the environment" because it is bad for humans. Environmental protection effectively means protection of the human existence and wellbeing.

The present study will be positive in character, which means that it deals with what is (or what is thought to be), rather than what should be. Hence the analysis needs to reflect the predominant view. Therefore *an anthropocentric position will be adopted*. This position will become particularly obvious in chapter 2 where environmental quality improvements will be valued in economic terms, based on the utility which households (humans) directly and indirectly derive from it.

The meaning of "environment" has not been clarified yet. A reasonably operational anthropocentric definition is offered by Radetzki (1992), p. 122, which reads: "environment is broadly defined to comprise all the physical aspects that shape the human habitat." Hence the environment is a physical concept. The same will be assumed to apply to "environmental quality", "pollution", and "emissions". Environmental quality is taken to be a measure of the absence of pollution.

Pollution in the sense of this study is caused only by man-made or anthropogenic emissions, and it is to be understood in a *broad* sense, covering not only aspects such as the unnaturally high concentrations of heavy metals in water or of carbon dioxide (CO_2) in the atmosphere, but more generally all undesired consequences of human interference with the environment including barrier effects due to road building, biodiversity loss resulting from deforestation, or soil erosion and desertification following land conversion. This broad definition of pollution implies that road building, deforestation, and land conversion are forms of emissions.

Given the class of human beings as moral reference class, it follows that the environment is better, or its quality higher, the more it contributes to human survival and wellbeing, ceteris paribus. It also follows that while environ-mental quality is a good, pollution must be a "bad".

1.2 Patterns of Environmental Change

In 1979 Baumol and Oates wrote: "Because of growth in population and industrial activity we were convinced that virtually all forms of environmental damage were increasing, and that, in absence of powerful countermeasures, they would continue to accelerate more or less steadily. ... However, a more careful and extensive re-examination of the evidence has led us to revise this simplistic view of the course of environmental decay. We have found on closer study that trends in environmental quality run the gamut from steady deterioration to spectecular improvement." [p. 9]

Recent systematic research in this area has supplied further evidence in support of a more complex perspective of the economy-environment link. A short overview will now be given of the major data sources and the techniques that have been used to obtain the results encountered in the literature, some of which will be sketched in the subsequent sections. More extensive and detailed literature surveys can be found in Pearson (1994), Stern (1996), and Stern et al. (1996).

1.2.1 Data and Techniques

The first large-scale systematic study on the relationship between per capita income and environmental quality was Grossman and Krueger's (1991) working paper on the environmental impacts of the North Atlantic Free-Trade Agreement which was later published as Grossman and Krueger (1993). The authors use income data from the Summers and Heston (1991) tables, and air quality data from the Global Environmental Monitoring System (GEMS), a project jointly run by the World Health Organization and the United Nations Environment Program. Since 1977 the GEMS monitors indicators of air quality in urban areas and of water quality in selected rivers and lakes in developing and developed countries. The sample of locations where the measurements are taken has been chosen "to be fairly representative of the geographic conditions that exist in different regions of the world" [Grossman (1995), p. 23].

GEMS data are also used by Grossman (1995), Grossman and Krueger (1995), and Selden and Song (1994). Other authors base their studies on environmental data from the World Bank's (1992) World Development Report [Sengupta (1996); Shafik (1994a); Shafik and Bandyopadhyay (1992)], the Oak Ridge National Laboratory's (1992) CO_2 emission data

[Holtz-Eakin and Selden (1995), Roberts and Grimes (1997); Sengupta (1996)], the World Resouces Institute's (1991) tables [Selden and Song (1994)], and the Food and Agricultural Organization's various publications [Panayotou (1993), Shafik (1994b)]. All of these data cover several years and countries of all geographical regions and development stages.

With the increased availability of environmental data, research conditions improved in the 1990s and will continue doing so in the future. The previously rather anecdotal evidence on the relationship between economic activity and environmental quality has been complemented by larger, more detailed, and more standardised data sets. Nevertheless, data problems faced by researchers in this field still represent a serious obstacle to the completeness and the reliability of the results. Grossman and Krueger (1995), p. 354, for instance, write that they have attempted to consider "all of the dimensions of environmental quality for which actual measurements have been taken by comparable methods in a variety of countries", but still their study is limited to only fourteen such dimensions.

Moreover, due to the lack of sufficiently long time series of observations all studies had to fall back on panel data. The pooling of data from different countries can produce misleading results if the differences between the countries and monitoring sites are not appropriately taken care of through explanatory or dummy variables in addition to the income level, a time trend, and site characteristics. As an example, Stern et al. (1996) point out that countries may import or export environmental problems through trade. The effect of changing trade patterns, but also of changing sectoral structures on emissions or pollution should be captured separately from the possible income effect, for otherwise possible changes in pollution levels cannot be assigned correctly to the factors causing them.

Another data problem is associated with the changing sample compositions with respect to locations and numbers of monitoring stations over time, giving rise to a nonconstant variance of the error term in an ordinary least squares (OLS) estimation, that is, to heteroskedasticity [Stern et al. (1996), p. 1156]. Most of the studies mentioned above estimate single-equation models using the OLS method because of its simplicity. However, heteroskedasticity renders OLS estimators inefficient, and invalidates the tests of significance [Maddala (1992), p. 209] unless appropriate econometric techniques are employed to handle it; but no such measures are reported. Moreover, a simultaneity bias may be contained in the results if bidirectional causalities exist between the economy and the environment, i.e. if each influences the other. In such a case, a model of simultaneous equations has to be estimated because applying OLS to a single-equation model yields biased and inconsistent estimates [Maddala (1992), pp. 383-384; Stern et al. (1996), p. 1155].

Other technical and data problems of these studies may be identified which are, however, not a matter for discussion here. It is simply important to be aware that the results presented in the following sections must be treated with some caution. When curves will be drawn in a certain way, the focus will be on their qualitative, rather than the quantitative properties, and even the former may not be very robust. Once again it needs to be emphasised that the relationship between economic growth and environmental quality is neither simple, nor unambiguous, nor fully understood.

And, as Lovelock (1987) notes in his preface, p. xi: "Scientific argument and evidence about the environment is now presented as if in a court-room or at a public enquiry. It cannot be said too often that, although this may be good for the democratic process of public participation in matters of general concern, it is not the best way to discover scientific truth". The above careful formulation aims to avoid that such an impression is created.

1.2.2 Continued Environmental Deterioration

Contrary to what conventional wisdom on the economy-environment relationship would tell one to expect, the recent empirical literature provides only very few examples of continued anthropogenic deterioration of environmental conditions in the course of economic growth. This is certainly not to say that not more cases could be found, but it indicates that a pollutant-by-pollutant investigation is unavoidable to gain an insight into this nexus.

Probably the most prominent representative of those pollutants causing increasing damage to the environment as per capita income rises is CO_2. The emission of this global pollutant and greenhouse gas is, above all, related to the burning of fossil fuels for energy generation and transportation, but also to industrial processes, deforestation, and the conversion of grasslands into farmland. Roughly speaking, "both carbon emissions and energy consumption are closely correlated with the size of a country's economy. ... This relationship has been weakening somewhat since 1960 but carbon emissions are still essentially linearly related to national product per capita" [Roberts and Grimes (1997), p. 192]. Holtz-Eakin and Selden (1995), too, observe a continued rise in per capita CO_2 emissions as per capita income grows, but

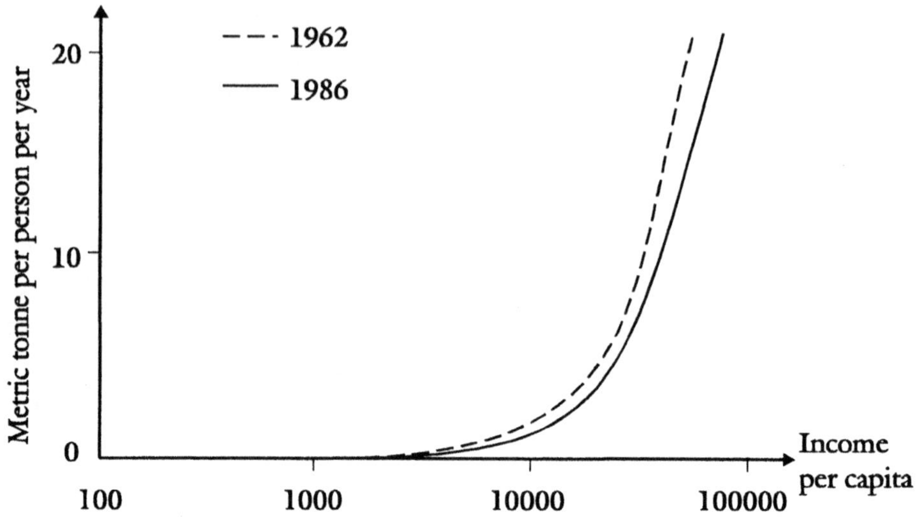

Figure 1.1: Carbon emissions per capita in relation to income per capita
Source: Shafik (1994a), p. 764; see also Shafik and Bandyopadhyay (1992), p. 25, and World Bank (1992), p. 11

they also find a diminishing marginal propensity to emit CO_2 per capita as economic activity increases.[5]

Figure 1.1 depicts a result obtained by Shafik (1994a). It shows that carbon emissions per capita rise with income per capita. Note that the income axis has a log scale, hence emissions per capita do not necessarily increase exponentially with per capita income, in any case not in higher income ranges where the curves tend to become linear. In these ranges the diminishing marginal propensity to emit CO_2 appears to play an increasing role. The two emission curves in figure 1.1 illustrate a significantly negative time trend in Shafik's regression: "carbon emissions per unit of capital stock have declined over time as countries have moved to cleaner burning fuels and technologies" [p. 768].

---

5 With their preferred specification of the model, where CO_2 is, inter alia, a function of squared per capita income, Holtz-Eakin and Selden obtain a maximum of CO_2 emissions per capita at an income level of about $35,000 (1986 US dollars) per capita. This income lies outside the sampled levels, and it is highly sensitive to the chosen funcional form, so the result should not be relied on. Still more doubtful appears Sengupta's (1996) finding that CO_2 emissions per capita peak at $8740 (1985 US dollars), and subsequently decline when emissions are a function of cubed income, per capita in both cases.

Since population growth rates are rarely negative, increasing emissions per capita in the vast majority of cases imply rising absolute emissions in the course of growth. Holtz-Eakin and Selden (1995), for example, forecast an annual growth of global CO_2 emissions of 1.8% until the year 2025 [p. 87]. But emissions are not a measure of the quality of the environment, given that the pollutant in question does not decay immediately. Environmental quality is expressed in terms of pollution levels or concentrations. As far as the atmospheric CO_2 concentration is concerned which has increased by 19% since the pre-industrial times [Schipper and Meyers (1992), p. 154], it is not clear whether or not anthropogenic emissions fully account for this rise. Nevertheless scientists seem to agree that the quantity of CO_2 emitted each year through economic activities exceeds the amount that is absorbed by plants and oceans. Hence humans contribute to the ongoing worsening of this dimension of environmental quality.

Besides CO_2, also municipal waste per capita has been found to be strictly increasing in income per capita [Shafik (1994a); Shafik and Bandyopadhyay (1992)]. Again, this is a measure of emissions, not of environmental quality. Depending on the way waste is treated (incineration, landfill, recycling) it will be associated with more or less environmental impact. Shafik (1994a) reports a strictly monotonic decline in the concentration of dissolved oxygen in rivers as per capita income rises. Dissolved oxygen is a precondition for aquatic animal life. Shafik conjectures that "Growing effluent pollution associated with industrialisation may play a role in reducing dissolved oxygen at higher incomes" [p. 765]. It is interesting to note that Grossman (1995) and Grossman and Krueger (1995) observe quite different relationships between dissolved oxygen concentrations and per capita income. Theirs will be addressed in section 1.2.4.

Environmental damage such as biodiversity loss, removed primary rainforest cover, or radioactive waste must be expected to keep aggravating in the future, too, since this is inherent in their practically irreversible nature. However, whether there exists a functional relationship between these forms of environmental impact and rising per capita income, or if these forms are better described by a time trend, does not seem to have been examined yet. It cannot be excluded, however, that a declining marginal propensity to cause such damages could be found.

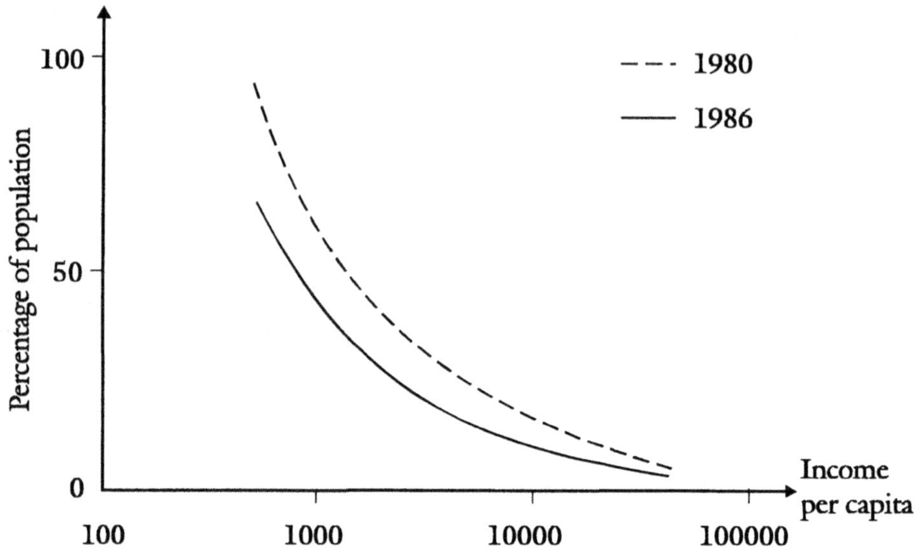

Figure 1.2: Lack of urban sanitation in relation to income per capita
Source: Shafik (1994a), p. 764; see also Shafik and Bandyopadhyay (1992), p. 25, and World Bank (1992), p. 11 and p. 41

1.2.3 Continued Environmental Improvements

The opposite end of the growth-environment spectrum is formed by local pollutants impinging much more directly on human wellbeing than those of the last section. Continued improvements of environmental conditions in the course of rising income per capita have been found with respect to access to drinking water and urban sanitation [Shafik (1994a); Shafik and Bandyopadhyay (1992); World Bank (1992)], the urban concentration of heavy or suspended particles [Grossman (1995); Grossman and Krueger (1995)], and the concentration of cadmium and lead in rivers [Grossman (1995)]. At least the latter two, however, must have increased rapidly at very low income levels that may even lie outside the data sample, to be able to improve at higher income. In this sense the reported strict monotonicity must be taken with a grain of salt.

Figure 1.2 is again taken from Shafik (1994a), and illustrates how urban sanitary conditions are related to per capita income. As before, the horizonal axis is in log scale, so the curves appear steeper than they would be with a linear income scale. Also as before, a time trend has been identified which works in favour of sanitation. "At any given income, a higher proportion of people in any country is likely to have access to sanitation today than in the past" [World Bank (1992), p. 41].

1.2.4 Environmental Kuznets Curves

In most of the reported cases pollution neither rises nor falls monotonically. Instead, a particular pattern has been identified that seems to be characteristic for a number of pollutants. At low per capita income levels, economic growth is associated with increasing pollution levels or concentrations. As income rises pollution gradually levels off and, after income has passed a certain threshold level, eventually falls again. The resulting graph has been dubbed *Environmental Kuznets Curve* [Dasgupta and Mäler (1994), p. 5], insinuating the similarity of this graph with the so-called Kuznets curve which relates a measure of distributional inequality to per capita income.

An Environmental Kuznets Curve has for instance been found to exist for the concentration of suspended particulate matter (SPM). SPM is a local air pollutant which has both natural and anthropogenic sources. While the former include dust, sea spray, forest fires, and volcanoes, the latter are mainly incomplete fuel combustion and industrial chemical processes.[6] Most of the naturally produced particulates are relatively large, having rather minor health effects but reducing visibility. Particulates originating from human activity are finer, can cause eye and lung damage, and have been found to aggravate respiratory illness (e.g. coughs, asthma, bronchitis). They also lead to increased mortality rates among children and the elderly, and can carry carcinogenic or poisonous heavy metals into the lungs. Anthropogenic emissions of SPM can be reduced through the use of control equipment, and by switching to fuels other than coal [Grossman (1995), p. 27; Grossman and Krueger (1993), p. 18].

While qualitatively similar, the results arrived at by the authors differ in the estimated per capita income level at which the "environmental turnaround" is supposed to take place. Using a cubic function of per capita GDP (i.e. per capita GDP enters in the form of a polynomial of third degree) Grossman and Krueger (1993) obtain a peak of urban SPM concentration at

---

6 There seems to exist some confusion in terminology. According to Grossman (1995) "dark matter" is the finer and more hazardous form of SPM [p. 27]. Grossman and Krueger (1993) regard dark matter and smoke as the same thing [p. 18]. Beckerman again (1992) treats SPM and smoke as identical [p. 10].

around \$5000 (1985 US dollar), with all three GDP variables being jointly highly significant [p. 32]. In their 1995 article they find the turning point at \$6151 [p. 367], again based on a cubic equation. The deviation is likely to reflect differences in sample size and composition. According to Shafik (1994a) who uses different data sources and chooses a quadratic model, urban SPM concentration reaches its maximum at around \$3280. Selden and Song (1994) base their study on aggregate SPM emissions rather than urban concentrations, locating a turning point at a per capita income level that exceeds \$8000.

Another air pollutant for which an Environmental Kuznets Curve has been reported by several authors is sulphur dioxide (SO_2). It is released during the burning of fossil fuels, especially those with a high sulphur content such as brown coal and high-sulphur oil, mainly in electricity generation, heating, and by road traffic. SO_2 emissions can be controlled by installing scrubbers, and by switching to fuels with a lower sulphur content. The health effects of sulphur dioxide are similar to those of SPM but not as grave. Today's main concern is about acid rain of which SO_2 is a major contributor. Acid rain which is not a local but a regional environmental problem, causes serious damage to trees, crops, buildings, and aquatic ecosystems [Grossman (1995), p. 32].

Figure 1.3 depicts the Environmental Kuznets Curve for urban SO_2 concentrations as obtained by Shafik (1994a) with a quadratic function. At low per capita levels the SO_2 concentration rises monotonically with per capita income, peaks at an income level of \$3670 [p. 365], and declines as income grows further. Technology which has once again been captured by a time trend in Shafik's model tends to reduce the SO_2 concentration by 5% annually [p. 367]. This is reflected in figure 1.3 by the downward movement of the SO_2 concentration curve between 1972 and 1986. According to Grossman and Krueger (1993) who estimate a cubic equation, the turn-around for urban SO_2 concentration lies at around \$5000 [p. 23] like that of SPM, whereas Grossman and Krueger (1995) report an income level per capita of \$4053 [p. 367]. Once more, with over \$8000 Selden and Song (1994) find a higher turn-around income level on the basis of emissions data rather than urban SO_2 concentrations.

Further Environmental Kuznets Curves appear to exist, inter alia, for the local air pollutant carbon monoxide (CO) and the regional air pollutant nitrous oxides (NO_x) [Grossman (1995) who restricts his analysis to the U.S.; Selden and Song (1994)], for the bacteria fecal coliform which indicate

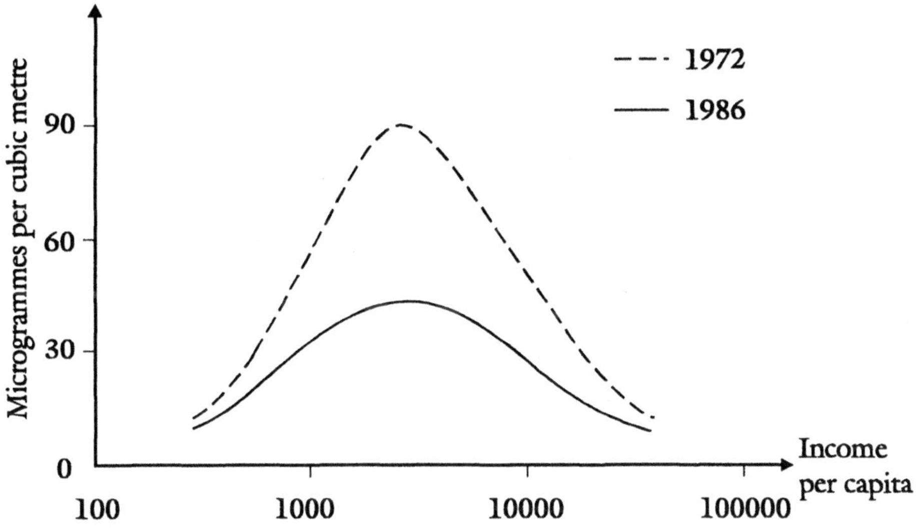

Figure 1.3: Urban sulphur dioxide (SO_2) concentration in relation to income per capita
Source: Shafik (1994a), p. 764. His labelling of the vertical axis as "Percentage of population" is erroneous and should read "Microgrammes per cubic metre". See also Shafik and Bandyopadhyay (1992), p. 25; World Bank (1992), p. 11 and p. 41

the presence of pathogenes in water resulting from untreated sewage discharge [Grossman (1995); Grossman and Krueger (1995); Shafik (1994a)], for the concentration of mercury and arsenic in rivers, for chemical and biological oxygen demand of rivers, for the concentration of nitrats and dissolved oxygen[7] in rivers [Grossman (1995); Grossman and Krueger (1995)]. Moreover, inverted U-shaped relationships have been identified for the rate of deforestation [Panayotou (1993); Shafik (1994a, 1994b)], and for the toxic intensity per unit of GDP [Hettige et al. (1992)]. These latter two relationships should not be referred to as Environmental Kuznets Curves because it makes a qualitative difference if rates and intensities are related to per capita income, or proper measures of environmental quality.

A problem sometimes faced by authors working with cubic functional specifications to model Environmental Kuznets Curves is that for very high income levels pollution is predicted to rise again. Graphically this curve resembles an "N". In most cases the cubic function is likely to be responsible

[7] Note the striking difference to Shafik's (1994a) result mentioned in section 1.2.2 according to which dissolved oxygen is monotonically decreasing in per capita income.

for this N-curve because the cubed-income term must ultimately dominate all others. Due to lacking observations in the respective high income range this second upward-sloping part of the pollution curve fails to pass significance tests.

In one case, however, this technical explanation does not seem to be sufficient. Shafik (1994a) chooses a cubic model to estimate the effect of income changes on fecal coliform concentrations. As mentioned above he finds an Environmental Kuznets Curve which peaks at $1375, and which almost reaches a zero concentration level at $10,000. The improvement is presumably the result of improved urban sanitation and sewage treatment. However, beyond a per capita income level of $11,400 his model indicates that the concentration of fecal coliform rises again steeply. "The cubic shape of the fecal content is not an artifact of the functional form. ... [It] is based on 38 observations from seven rivers in three countries (Australia, Japan, and United States)" [p. 765]. A possible explanation for this apparently real N-curve for pollution will be given in section 2.5.4 of the next chapter.

In the face of the different relationships they identify, Grossman and Krueger (1995), pp. 370-371, conclude that "we find no evidence that economic growth does unavoidable harm to the natural habitat. Instead we find that while increases in GDP may be associated with worsening environmental conditions in very poor countries, air and water quality appear to benefit from economic growth once some critical level of income has been reached. The turning points in these inverted U-shaped relationships vary for the different pollutants, but in almost every case they occur at an income of less than $8000 (1985 dollars). For a country with an income of $10,000, the hypothesis that further growth will be associated with deterioration of environmental conditions can be rejected at the 5 percent level of significance for many of our pollution measures."

1.3 Objectives and Methodology

The present study attempts to investigate the main economic, but also some political factors and causal relationships that seem to be responsible for the patterns of environmental quality change that have just been sketched. Its objective is to *contribute to a positive theory of economic-environmental interaction*. This enterprise is justified by the value of the theory itself to which it wants to add. On the one hand, such a theory may be said to have an existence value because it represents a form of knowledge. Deeper understanding and more thorough knowledge of the world have always been ends by themselves.[8] On the other hand, the theory has a use value which is rooted in its three more or less separate functions: explanation, prediction, and research-guidance.

First, a positive theory of economic-environmental interaction will allow to explain the occurrence and shape of Environmental Kuznets Curves, given a set of boundary conditions or "circumstances". Second, while short-run predictions of environmental quality changes can be made by extrapolating recent trends, longer-run forecasts need to take into account factors that tend to be taken as constant in regression analysis, but which may well alter over an extended period of time. To point out such factors, and to provide an indication at least of the sign of their change, if not of their magnitude, is the role of the theory. Third, a sound theoretical foundation will reduce, if not remove the ad hoc character of empirical research in this field. Theory should guide the researcher in the choice of explanatory variables and functional forms, and help embedding the results in a greater context which facilitates their interpretation. Theory-laden data selection, however, is to be avoided.

Certainly, the studies quoted in the last section do not report measurements without theory. Either their authors state hypotheses on the kind of relationship between the environmental data and per capita income that is expected to be observed, and these hypotheses have been derived through theoretical reasoning. Or the authors try to explain their empirical findings ex post by appealing to economic intuition and theory. In fact, many of the results that will be obtained in the present study have in some form or another already been stated elsewhere. An early example is Beckerman (1972, 1977) who anticipates much of what the empirical literature on Environmental Kuznets Curves has brought to light in the 1990s, based on theoretical economic considerations similar to those of the present study.

The contribution of the present analysis is twofold. It gathers the various theoretical fragments spread across the recent empirical literature on the economy-environment nexus, puts them together into a common context, and discusses their interrelations and implications. In doing this, the focus is on the forces that enable an environmental turn-around. In addition to that,

---

8 The striving for knowledge without any instrumental function was in fact characteristic of Aristotelian science ("episteme"). Knowledge as a means was referred to as "techne" [Höffe (1993), p. 40]. It was only in the 17th century that Francis Bacon gave science its strong functional orientation [p. 62].

this study borrows from other branches of economic theory, mainly endogenous policy theory, with the aim to investigate in greater detail some aspects of the political economy of environmental decision-making. This area of environmental economics seems to have been largely neglected.

All investigations will be carried out within the framework of formal economic models. This analytical approach ensures the logical consistency of the findings, but not their factual correctness. Results are derived through deduction from, what may be called, standard economic theory, and from a number of additional assumptions, rather than through induction from data. Nevertheless, empirical observations will be compared with the models' predictions as a sort of intuitive corroboration of the plausibility of the models. The assumptions underlying the models will, with very few exceptions, be in the tradition of ***neoclassical environmental economics*** which is thoroughly anthropocentric, and therefore fully compatible with the ethical position adopted earlier on.

1.4 Overview of this Study

Apart from the present introduction and the concluding *chapter 7* at the very end, this analysis comprises five core chapters which are loosely linked by cross references but do not depend on each other. Each of these core chapters develops its own model according to its specific needs, and closes with a "Concluding Remarks" section which summarises the main findings, placing them into the greater context of the whole study.

Chapter 2 is entitled "Economic Determinants of Environmental Quality Changes" which reflects its rather general character. Starting off with a decomposition exercise, it introduces three key factors to which any change in anthropogenic emission levels can be traced back: scale effect, composition effect, and technique effect. Under favourable circumstances the aggregate or net impact of these effects on the environment can be benign, and lead to improvements. Such environmental quality improvements may either be the unintentional by-product of some "exogenous" economic developments, or the result of measures deliberately taken to achieve them.

Intentional improvements usually involve an opportunity cost which reflects the decision-makers' marginal willingness to pay for them, and which can be used to value them in economic terms. This valuation issue is analysed in some detail by means of a model of socially optimal growth in which capital is associated with emissions which accumulate to a pollution stock ("stock model"). Pollution reduces environmental quality which is an input to production and utility, but emissions can be controlled. The model is specified in a way such that positive abatement is optimal at every moment. It yields a set of shadow prices which are interpreted to familiarise the reader with this concept which plays a central role throughout the whole study. The same steps are repeated for a model in which emissions do not accumulate ("flow model"). As an application of shadow price valuation, a "green" net national product is derived.

Next, both model versions are altered so as to admit corner solutions for pollution abatement. This modification splits the growth process into two phases. In the "development phase" it is optimal not to abate emissions because environmental quality is not valued highly enough. In the "environment phase", however, pollution control is carried out and may lead to a better environment, that is, an Environmental Kuznets Curve. The model demonstrates that one key factor determining the occurence and shape of an Environmental Kuznets Curve are so-called environmental preferences.

Chapter 3 is concerned with analysing the role of these preferences. Production effects of pollution are neglected. Using a version of the previous chapter's flow model, but with output proportional to the capital stock, it is shown that alone due to environmental preferences, socially optimal growth may tend to zero in the development phase. With pollution control measures being taken, however, diminishing growth rates may be overcome, and a sustainable growth path be reached asymptotically. If there are several types of pollution, each impinging differently on utility, and controllable at different cost, a hierarchic demand for abating the pollutants is shown to result. This finding corresponds quite closely to empirical observations. To prepare the ground for what follows, the flow model is functionally specified so as to generate an Environmental Kuznets Curve.

Next, the hypothesis is discussed that environmental quality is a luxury. It is demonstrated that the shape of the abatement expenditure curve on which this hypothesis rests, tends to be misinterpreted, and that some characteristics of environmental quality which distinguish it from normal goods are responsible for it. So environmental quality may, but need not, be a luxury.

In a static framework, *chapter 4* addresses the possible influence of the distribution of incomes on the demand for a better environmental quality or, alternatively, for a stricter environmental policy by the government, thus dropping the assumption of social optimality. On a rather general level it is shown how distributional inequality may be linked to the households' average desired environmental policy. Unfortunately, the sign of this relationship turns out to be ambiguous. Empirical evidence, however, seems to speak a clearer language: the share of "green" voters, activists, and supporters of environmental organisations in the (upper) middle class is higher than in any other group of the public. Based on the hypothesis of green middle-class elitism it is argued that if the distribution of income alters in a way such that the share of the middle class in the total population increases, the demand and support for a stricter environmental policy will grow. Provided that governmental policy in some way reflects public political demand it is likely that this will lead to environmental quality improvements. Moreover, if this distributional change occurs in the course of rising per capita income it will affect the shape of Environmental Kuznets Curves.

Two distinct economic explanations of green middle-class elitism are proposed. The first one exploits the fact that different compositions of income (profits, labour income, etc.) may be associated with different income sensitivities to changes in environmental policy. Households whose income is reduced significantly by a stricter policy will tend to oppose it, while households with a rather policy-independent income can support a tightening of policy almost without "paying" for it. The combination of income level and income composition may lead to a situation in which the middle-income households favour a stricter environmental policy than other household groups.

The second explanation of middle-class environmentalism holds that environmental quality is not a pure public good but can be supplemented by private measures or defensive expenditure. The optimal level of such expenditure is shown to rise with household income. If defensive expenditure is fixed, or at least rigid in the short run, the rich households gain a higher independence from public environmental quality than other household groups and may find it optimal to support a more lenient policy than, for instance, the middle class. If furthermore the middle-class households have not been able to afford private environmental-quality-improving measures, they will demand a stricter public policy than the poor households, again ending up as the "green" elite.

The political economy of public environmental policy is also the concern of *chapter 5*. First, the nature of concern about pollution is discussed. It is shown how this subjective element affects the households' demand for environmental policy. A democratic government will orientate its policy towards this demand, and the firms will adapt their pollution control efforts to the government's policy, so the level of public environmental concern influences the level of pollution across several stages of decision making. Next, the impact of environmental campaigns on the level of pollution is analysed. For this end it is assumed that a small group of highly concerned households, which is too small to influence governmental environmental policy directly, may spend part of their income on measures aimed at raising other households' environmental concern. Via the political market and the firms' cost-minimisation, this higher concern ultimately induces an improved environment. However, campaigning causes social inefficiency, and there is also an incentive for the "victims" of green campaigns to call for a prohibitive tax on green campaigning.

Firms, facing higher costs as a consequence of stricter environmental policy, can counteract green campaigns by lobbying. They may regard it optimal to offer the governing party financial or other contributions in return for a more lenient policy. Just like campaigning, lobbying is a source of social inefficiency, and it may tempt the victims to push for a ban. When both firms and campaigners know each others' reaction functions, and simultaneously decide about their respective use of resources, a Cournot equilibrium of campaigning and lobbying is reached.

Chapter 6 returns to the dynamic analysis. It demonstrates how scale effect, composition effect, and technique effect which have been introduced in chapter 2, arise from the combined, decentralised decision-making of households, firms, and the government. The model which involves two factors of production, two commodities, five sectors, and pollution control, allows to study a dynamic endogenous environmental policy. In the development phase this policy gives rise to substitution effects in consumption and production, to changes in the economy's sectoral structure, and to a declining emission intensity of production. In the environment phase these relationships remain constant as a balanced growth path is reached asymptotically. Like in the functionally specified model of chapter 3, an Environmental Kuznets Curve occurs.

Chapter 7, finally, sums up a number of results of this study, and relates them to a common context. Furthermore, it highlights the most serious obstacles to Environmental Kuznets Curves, and suggests that their removal should be a central concern of future research in this area.

Chapter 2 Economic Determinants of Environmental Quality Changes

It is no paradox to say that in our most theoretical moods we may be nearest to our most practical applications. A. N. Whitehead[9]

In the last chapter some evidence has been presented that seems to negate the existence of an unambiguous or even an unambiguously negative relationship between real per capita income and the level of physical environmental quality associated with it. The question immediately suggesting itself is: what are the economic determinants of the state of the environment? And in particular: why have environmental turn-arounds taken place?

There are basically two levels at which these questions can be answered. At a first level one would explain environmental quality improvements by the simple fact that economic agents have emitted less than before, given a sufficiently high natural assimilative capacity to allow for absolute improvements. How these lower emissions have been achieved is merely a technical matter. Section 2.1 will take a look at the effects to which any change in emissions can be traced back, and which must therefore - at least on the surface - be responsible for the occurrence of Environmental Kuznets Curves.

But to leave it at that, and to regard the phenomenon of Environmental Kuznets Curves as explained, would clearly be unsatisfactory because one still wonders *why* economic agents have emitted less than before. To give the deeper reasons is the concern of the second level. In other words, the first level deals with the behaviour of economic agents in response to some external economic or economically relevant conditions or circumstances, whereas the second level provides the background on how these circumstances have arisen; they explain the circumstances.

This study concentrates on the deeper or second-level economic reasons of environmental improvements. Since economic activity in markets is guided by incentives, a rising environmenal quality can be expected to be the result of a particular incentive structure. Hence the analysis of benefits and costs of different agents under varying institutional settings will be given considerable

9 Quoted by Motz and Weaver (1993), p. 247.

weight. The purpose of the present chapter is to introduce a few basic concepts on a rather general level. One of its focal points will be the economic valuation of environmental quality as an application of benefit-cost analysis. This will provide the insights necessary to understand and explain when and why it is efficient to control emissions which can ultimately lead to a better state of the environment

But before turning to these second-level issues, the more immediate or first-level causes of environmental quality changes will now briefly be addressed. They will make clear why the relationship between the level of economic activity and the state of the environment by no means needs to be negative. It must be assumed, though, that environmental damage is reversible, for otherwise even a zero-emission level would not permit a recovery of the environment.

2.1 Emission Accounting

A well-known technique to investigate the sources of economic growth is the so-called *growth accounting*. It aims at breaking down an economy's total growth rate into a number of separate rates such as the rate of capital accumulation, of population growth and of technical progress. A similar approach has been taken to analyse the environmental impact of economic activity. It may be called *emission accounting*.

Ehrlich and Holdren (1971) propose to summarise the environment-growth nexus by the equation

$$I = P \cdot A \cdot T.$$

"The impact (I) of any group or nation on the environment can be viewed as the product of its population size (P) multiplied by per capita affluence (A) as measured by consumption, in turn multiplied by a measure of the damage done by the technologies (T) employed in supplying each unit of consumption" [Ehrlich and Ehrlich (1991), p. 7]. As Commoner (1972) has emphasised, if this equation is expressed in appropriate dimensions it takes the form of an identity:

$$\text{emissions} = \text{population} \cdot \frac{\text{goods}}{\text{population}} \cdot \frac{\text{emissions}}{\text{goods}}. \tag{2.1}$$

It says that economic growth - in terms of population size, per capita consumption, or both - may but need not be associated with rising emission levels. If growth is accompanied by sufficient emission-reducing efficiency gains of technology, economic growth will be environmentally neutral or even benign. In other words, as long as the sum of the growth rates of population and consumption per head does not exceed the rate of emission-reducing technological progress, then according to (2.1) the economy-wide emission level will not rise.

In an early contribution to the emerging body of environmental economics literature, Leontief (1970) takes a different approach by presenting an input-output model involving emissions from production. He shows that "any reduction or increase in the output level of pollutants can be traced either to changes in the final demand for specific goods and services, changes in the technical structure of one or more sectors of the economy, or to some combination of the two" [p. 266]. Hence Leontief distinguishes technical and demand-related factors as determinants of emissions. He does not explicitly mention the role of changes in the population size; however, the effect of population growth on emissions is captured by the changes in final demand.

Grossman (1995), finally, proposes to decompose total emissions in the form of the identity

$$\text{emissions} = \text{total output} \cdot \sum_i \frac{\text{emissions sector } i}{\text{output sector } i} \cdot \frac{\text{output sector } i}{\text{total output}} \qquad (2.2)$$

where the first term of the sum may be called the i-th sector's *emission intensity*. Even more than Leontief, Grossman highlights the importance of taking into account the sectoral structure of the economy if the sectors differ in their emission intensity of production. A comparison of (2.2) and (2.1) reveals that the term "total output" in the former corresponds to the term "population · (goods/population)" in the latter. Moreover, the emission intensity in (2.2) would be the same as the ratio "emissions/goods" if the sectoral structure was neglected in Grossman's identity. If fact, all three decompositions are quite similar, differing mainly in the emphasis they place on population size and sectoral structure.

Throughout the entire study *the population size will be assumed constant*. Grossman's identity and the conclusions he draws from it will thus be a more suitable starting point for later chapters than Ehrlich and Holdren's identity.

Therefore the former will now be looked at more closely. For this end, (2.2) is restated in mathematical terms:

$$E = F\sum_i e_i s_i \tag{2.3}$$

where e_i are emissions emitted per unit of output in sector i (the sectoral emission intensity), and s_i is the share of the i-th sector's output in total output F, implying that $\Sigma_i s_i = 1$. By logarithmically differentiating (2.3), and defining the share of the i-th sector's emissions in total emissions released by the economy as

$$m_i \equiv \frac{e_i s_i}{\sum_j e_j s_j},$$

one obtains the growth rate of emissions in Grossman's identity:

$$\hat{E} = \hat{F} + \sum_i m_i \hat{s}_i + \sum_i m_i \hat{e}_i \tag{2.4}$$

where a "hat" over a variable denotes a rate of change, e.g. $\hat{E} = dE / E$.

Based on this result Grossman [see also Grossman and Krueger (1993), pp. 14-15] distinguishes three effects which together determine how emissions behave over time. First, if sectoral shares s_i and the emission intensities e_i remain constant, then emissions rise at the same rate as economic activity: $\hat{E} = \hat{F}$. This is the *scale effect* "feared by environmental pessimists: *all else equal*, an increase in output means an equiproportionate increase in pollution" [Grossman (1995), p. 20; italics in the original; see also Beckerman (1993), p. 6].[10]

The ambiguity of the relationship between economic activity, emissions, and ultimately pollution which was emphasised in chapter 1 enters through the two remaining components on the right-hand side of (2.4). They represent a composition effect and a technique effect. For emissions to fall in a growing economy these two effects must work against the scale effect and offset it. The *composition effect* occurs when sectoral shares s_i of total output change. Since sectoral emission intensities are likely to differ, an altered

---

10 Strictly speaking, "pollution" in this quotation should be replaced by "emission". While the level of pollution may depend on a number of environmental conditions and on the properties of the pollutants in question, emissions are the result of human activities alone. However, many authors use both terms interchangeably.

composition of output will usually be associated with more or less emissions even if total output itself, expressed in terms of a numeraire or accounting unit, remains the same.

The composition effect may - but need not - work in favour of a better environment. Schipper and Meyers (1992), for instance, note that "many developing countries have been at a stage of development in which the use of commercial energy tends to grow faster than GDP due to increase in the role of manufacturing and building of basic infrastructure" [p. 17]. Provided that the emission intensity of energy generation is constant, overall emissions from energy generation will grow at a higher rate than aggregate output due to the composition effect.

The *technique effect* concerns changes in the sectoral emission intensities. If a unit of output of sector i can be produced at a lower e_i then - ceteris paribus - *absolute* emissions decline. The technique effect is mostly environmentally benign and can have several sources which include technological progress, substitution of "dirty" by "clean" processes and inputs, or "end-of-pipe" environmental protection measures. The m_i in (2.4) weigh the growth rates according to the contribution of the respective sectors to total emissions.

Since in equilibrium the structure of output adapts to changes in demand, Leontief's demand-related factors clearly correspond to Grossman's combined composition effect and scale effect; and the counterpart to Leontief's technical factors is Grossman's technique effect. But since Grossman's decomposition is more detailed, and its formal version much easier to handle than Leontief's input-output model, Grossman's approach and terminology seem more useful for the purposes of the present study.

A natural question to ask is what the driving forces, or second-level causes, behind the three effects are that sum up to the rate of change of emissions. As to the scale effect, economic growth means that the level of production or output increases. Hence those factors that fuel economic growth are the same that are responsible for the scale effect. Since the literature abounds with analyses of the sources of economic growth, this point will not be investigated here in greater depth. Rather than dealing with the quantity of growth - the scale effect - it will be focused on the *quality of growth* which involves the composition effect and the technique effect.

For the occurence of these effects, various explanations can be given, some of which will be outlined in the course of this analysis. However, two fundamentally different types of explanations can be distinguished. The composition effect and the technique effect may either occur as ***unintentional*** side-effects which naturally or accidently accompany economic growth, possibly leading to lower emissions. Or they are the result of measures deliberately taken to achieve a better environmental quality. In that case lower emissions are the primary objective, and one may speak of ***intentional*** emission reductions.

2.2 Unintentional Emission Reductions

Various economic circumstances may favour unintentional emission reductions by offering incentives to firms and households to act in a way that happens to be environmentally friendlier. But to which extent do unintentional emission reductions account for Environmental Kuznets Curves? In other words, are Environmental Kuznets Curves unintentional? Provided that these environmental turn-arounds in the course of a rising per capita income are a real and robust phenomenon, they must involve a systematic component that is linked to typical characteristics of a developing and growing economy. By means of two examples this aspect will now be discussed.

2.2.1 Structural Change

According to the so-called 3-sector-hypothesis which was proposed by Fisher (1939) and developed further by Fourastié (1969), a strong agricultural orientation is typical for economies in their early stage of development. The comparatively moderate level of output per capita at that stage, combined with the low emission intensity of traditional agricultural production, do not put a significant strain on the natural environment. Pollution levels are still low. However, as economies develop and grow, they enter a second stage which is characterised by industrialisation. Income generated in the industrial sector grows at a higher rate than total income. In addition to that, industrial output is more emission-intensive than agricultural output on average. Hence scale effect, technique effect, and composition effect together lead to a significant decline in environmental quality.

This is felt especially in urban areas: "... cities in some countries get the worst of both worlds. On the one hand, their old-fashioned machinery, techniques and industrial structures make them highly pollution intensive and, on the other, economic growth brings with it newer forms of pollution

- particularly those associated with automobile, urban congestion and waste disposal - before they have adequately reduced their exposure to more traditional pollutants" [Beckerman (1992), p. 7]. Because both traditional and modern environmental and health risks come together in this phase, it has been called "risk overlap" [Smith (1990), p. 236].

The third stage of development is marked by a rise in the share of services in total income. Income earned in the service sector can be expected to be less emission-intensive than in the other two sectors. So the composition effect associated with an increasing share of the tertiary sector is environmentally benign. But continued economic growth implies two more aspects. First, the scale effect counteracts the composition effect. And second, in each sector a technique effect occurs which tends to lead to a declining sectoral emission intensity because, as Grossman (1993), p. 21, points out, economic growth allows low and middle income countries to replace old and inefficient capital goods by more modern ones.

Whether an inverted U-curve for emissions results from this structural transformation can be determined by means of equation (2.4). If $\hat{E} < 0$, and if in consequence also the pollution level declines, an Environmental Kuznets Curve results. This term is justified in that context because the pollution level is, roughly speaking, a function of the stage of economic development and, more indirectly, of per capita income. The environmental improvement involved is ***unintentional***. This follows from the assertion of the 3-sector-hypothesis that the process of sectoral transformation in the course of economic growth is a "natural" evolution of economic activity. In other words, structural transformation is a typical, systematic pattern of economic development. The pollution reduction which may accompany this transformation is only a side-effect.

The following counterexample will show, however, that by far not every initial rise and subsequent (unintentional) decline of pollution can justly be called an Environmental Kuznets Curve, even it takes place while per capita income keeps rising.

2.2.2 Price Shocks

Demand for ordinary goods and factors decreases when their price rises, and everything else remains the same. If the production or use of such goods and factors is associated with some form of emissions, ***a price increase induces lower*** *emissions*. While prices can be raised artificially through policy measures such as emission charges, scarce marketable emission permits, or environmental regulations and standards in combination with punishment in case of noncompliance, with the explicit objective to protect the environment, prices will largely rise for reasons that have nothing to do with environmental protection. Any resulting decreases in emissions are therefore unintentional.

Such emission reductions have, for instance, been caused by the two oil price crises of the 1970s.[11] From 1973 to 1974, the price of crude oil on the world market rose by the factor four over its level in 1972. The cause was the Arab-Israeli war in which OPEC used oil as a weapon, inter alia, by cutting back production and putting an embargo on oil exports to the United States and the Netherlands in order to harm the economies of those states which supported Israel. During the second price shock in 1979-1980, the oil price doubled over its 1978 level. This time it was the consequence of the war between Iran and Iraq, and again oil supplies were disrupted. Between 1970 and 1980 the real price of a barrel of imported oil rose from \$1.97 to \$18.99 (1972 US dollar) by 960% in the United States.

Figure 2.1 depicts how crude oil consumption in the United States has reacted to the oil price changes between 1973 and 1981. From 1979 to 1981 oil consumption in the United States dropped by almost 800 million barrels (15%) per year, and worldwide by 2,159 million barrels (nearly 10%). Regarding the fact that the conversion of oil into energy releases CO_2, SO_2, NO_2, and other emissions, the declining amounts of oil consumed after 1978 must have caused significant emission reductions. Low short-run price elasticities of demand for oil products (between -0.07 and -0.22 for fuel oil, and between -0.11 and -0.41 for gasoline) further indicate that the immediate possibilities for substituting oil by other energy sources were very limited. So the emission reductions due to the lower oil consumption have not been offset by an increased use of natural gas or coal in the short run.

However, *this kind of resource price shocks* - despite causing emission reductions, and in the longer run also creating incentives for technological adaptation - *cannot account for Environmental Kuznets Curves*. There is no reason why price shocks should be typical or symptomatic for certain stages of economic growth. Therefore, even if higher prices are associated with less pollution, price shocks cannot be responsible for the regular Environmental Kuznets Curve pattern.

---

[11] Details about the oil price crises are taken from Hartwick and Olewiler (1986), ch. 7.

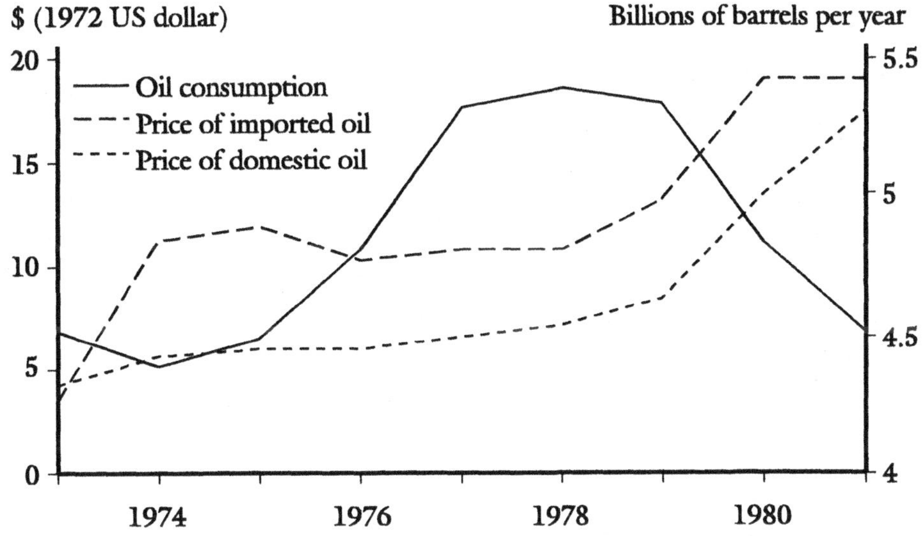

Figure 2.1: Oil consumption and the prices of imported and domestic oil in the United States 1973-1981
Source: Hartwick and Olewiler (1986), p. 185, table 7.1 (oil consumption data), and p. 188, table 7.2 (oil prices)

Moreover, the more open economies are, and the more intensive their trade relationships are, the more easily is a price shock transferred from one economy to another, and the more will its effects be felt in all countries, irrespective of their per capita income. In consequence, "price-sensitive" pollution levels in open economies can be expected to peak at about the same time (like in the oil price crises), rather than at the same per capita income, provided that the prices in question behave similarly everywhere, and are not overly distorted by taxes or tariffs. This open-economy argument is not restricted to price shocks, but extends also to continuous scarcity-induced market price increases.[12]

---

12 The Hotelling rule, for instance, states that a nonrenewable resource is extracted efficiently if its shadow price rises at a rate equal to the market rate of interest, provided that a number of conditions are met [e.g. Devarajan and Fisher (1981)]. The difference between the shadow price and the market price is often taken to be the (constant or rising) marginal cost of extracting the resource [e.g. Slade (1982), Hartwick (1990], so it can be inferred from the shadow price on the market price. Efficient depletion of a nonrenewable resource hence implies a rising resource market price which represents an incentive to economise on the resource, possibly even to do without it. If the resource use harms the environment, an inverted U-curve for pollution may result.

2.3 Intentional Emission Reductions

The remainder of the present study will deal with intentional emission reductions. To begin with, it should be noted that if pollution did not affect people in any way, directly or indirectly, there would be no reason to care about emissions and environmental protection. All observed emission reductions would be purely accidental side-effects of general economic or political developments. But pollution is something undesirable, almost by definition. This is the necessary condition for pollution reductions to become an objective on their own. Whether this objective is actually and successfully pursued is a different matter and depends, inter alia, on the competing uses of scarce resources.

2.3.1 Opportunity Cost

In general, economic activities take place if they yield a benefit that is valued higher than the effort or cost associated with them. A marketed consumer good, for instance, has a price. In equilibrium the price indicates how much of the numeraire good households are willing to give up for one unit of that commodity rather than for another. The price thus reflects the household's willingness to forego the opportunity of consuming an alternative good. In other words, the value attached by a consumer to an extra unit of a marketed good in equilibrium does not only equal its price, but also its marginal opportunity cost.

A similar concept can be applied when valuing non-marketed goods such as pollution reduction or environmental quality improvements. Although the quality of the environment has no market price it may still be valued positively. By giving up a certain amount of a private good with a positive price in order to enjoy a better environment, economic agents show that they prefer a combination of the private good and higher environmental quality to more of the private good and a poorer state of the environment.

Many aspects of environmental quality have the character of a public good, which means that there is an incentive for individuals to understate their true willingness to pay, and to free-ride at the contributors' expense. Nevertheless, evidence can be found that free-riding is far from complete. Examples include voluntary deeds such as money donations to environmental organisations, or the active support of green political parties or environmental legislation. There are also market prices which reflect differences in environmental quality variables such as housing sale prices [Johansson (1987), p. 104], or the cost people take upon themselves when travelling to recreation areas and sites of natural beauty [ib., pp. 115-125].

Summing over all households' (opportunity) costs accepted to achieve a better environment gives a lower bound of the marginal private value of environmental quality.[13] It follows that *observed pollution reductions are intentional if they are associated with some form of opportunity cost*. This does not exclude the (lucky but rare) case of intentional reductions with zero opportunity cost, but whenever an opportunity cost is involved, a pollution reduction cannot be purely accidental.

Environmental Kuznets Curves provoke the question why pollution levels are allowed to rise, only to be reduced again later on. If these reductions really are intentional, then how can it be explained that pollution is not kept at a moderate level right from the beginning? Or, considering what has just been said about opportunity cost: why is the people's willingness to pay for pollution avoidance not sufficient in lower per capita income regions to preserve a certain environmental quality? In the following two sections these questions will tentatively be answered.

2.3.2 Materialism Versus Post-Materialism

The anwers offered are based on two hypotheses about the emergence of environmentalism which seem to have found their way into the literature in the early 1970s. In the present context these hypotheses will be used more broadly to explain the emergence of any form of willingness to pay, or to accept an opportunity cost, for a better environment.

Advocates of the *materialist hypothesis* hold that economic growth is associated with an increasing input of matter and energy into production. By the laws of thermodynamics this leads to a growing output of waste and emissions. The resulting decline in environmental quality causes a rising scarcity, and hence appreciation, of natural services and unspoilt environments.

The materialist interpretation of environmentalism is given by Martínez-Alier (1995) without any particular reference to earlier sources, possibly because the materialist view has dominated the early environmental literature,

[13] Since the households' true marginal willingness to pay may still be higher than what they reveal, only a lower bound of the marginal private value of environmental quality can be determined empirically.

and is still popular today. Influential authors like Boulding (1966), Daly (1992), Georgescu-Roegen (1975) and Meadows et al. (1972, 1992) are clearly representatives of the materialist approach. Their call for zero economic growth is defended with arguments involving exclusively physical (i.e. material) scarcities.

Physical scarcities play a role also in the *post-materialist hypothesis*, but in a completely different way. It is argued that the rising supply or, equivalently, the decreasing scarcity of consumer goods in the course of economic per capita growth allows people to achieve a living standard that frees them from the most immediate material concerns. This decreased scarcity depreciates the traditional consumer goods relative to other goods such as intellectual, ethical or aesthetic satisfactions which are called post-material.

Inglehart, probably the best-known representative of this approach, starts his book "The Silent Revolution" (1977) with his conclusion: "The values of Western publics have been shifting from an overwhelming emphasis on material wellbeing and physical security toward greater emphasis on the quality of life. The causes and implications of this shift are complex, but the basic principle might be stated very simply: people tend to be more concerned with immediate needs or threats than with things that seem remote or non-threatening. Thus, a desire for beauty may be more or less universal, but hungry people are more likely to seek food than aesthetic satisfaction. Today, an unprecedentedly large portion of Western populations have been raised under conditions of exceptional economic security. Economic and physical security continue to be valued positively, but their relative priority is lower than in the past." [p. 3]

Both the materialist and the post-materialist hypothesis require an economy to grow and to reach a certain stage of maturity in before demand for a better environment arises. Everything else equal, economic growth per capita brings about more environmental damage and more material well-being. *Each of these processes on its own leads to an appreciation of environmental quality relative to consumption*. According to the materialist hypothesis this appreciation is rooted in the declining supply of the environmental quality, whereas the post-materialist hypothesis sees the increasing supply of consumption as the cause. Ultimately, however, both hypotheses arrive at the same conclusion, namely that *a stage of economic growth may be reached where environmental quality starts being demanded like a consumer good*. It remains to be discussed how this demand may be expressed, and how environmental improvements are achieved in the end.

The two hypotheses represent very extreme positions, mutually ignoring the respective other's point. Implicitly, the materialist hypothesis assumes a constant consumption level, while the post-materialist hypothesis supposes that the extent of environmental destruction in the course of growth does not change. If these assumptions were to be maintained, the two hypotheses would be mutually exclusive. However, experience tells one to expect truth to lie somewhere between extreme positions, and hence to presume the correctness of both the materialist and post-materialist arguments.

A synthesised single new hypothesis must therefore assert that in the course of economic growth, environmental quality appreciates relative to consumption due to an increasing scarcity of the former and an increasing abundance of the latter. Greater exposure to pollution and visibility of environmental damages, combined with a higher value placed on immaterial goods induces people sooner or later to develop a positive willingness to pay for, or to accept the opportunity cost of, environmental protection.

2.4 Valuing Environmental Quality Improvements

To illustrate the points just made, and to give it some more depth, a formal model will now be developed. Its basic structure will be used throughout the entire study, although various simplifying assumptions will be made in later chapters. The following sections will focus on the valuation of changes in environmental quality by deriving expressions for the marginal present net benefits of pollution abatement and the marginal opportunity costs associated with it. The concept of shadow prices will play a central role here, but quasi-monetary accounting prices of environmental quality can be obtained even if no shadow prices are available. To demonstrate the use of such prices, it will be shown in which way they enter pollution abatement decisions, and how they can be employed to derive an environmentally adjusted or "green" net national product.

2.4.1 Assumptions of the Model

The consumer side of a perfectly competitive economy is assumed to consist of a single representative household. The household's function of instantaneous utility is given by $U(X,Q)$ where $X \geq 0$ represents current consumption of a single homogeneous commodity, and $Q \geq 0$ is the quality of the environment. $U(X,Q)$ is real-valued (like all functions that occur in this study) and defined on R_+^2. It has the following properties:

$$\frac{\partial U}{\partial X} > 0, \frac{\partial^2 U}{\partial X^2} < 0, \frac{\partial U}{\partial Q} > 0, \frac{\partial^2 U}{\partial Q^2} < 0, \frac{\partial^2 U}{\partial X \partial Q} > 0 \text{ for } X>0 \text{ and } Q>0 \quad (2.5)$$

which means that utility is increasing and strictly concave in each argument. Hence the households regard environmental quality as a good. The last property says that an improved state of the environment raises the marginal utility of X, and vice versa. The marginal utilities of X and Q are defined on R_{++}^2, and taken to be unbounded at the boundary:

$$\lim_{X \to 0} \frac{\partial U}{\partial X} = \infty \text{ for } X>0 \quad \text{and} \quad \lim_{Q \to 0} \frac{\partial U}{\partial Q} = \infty \text{ for } Q>0. \qquad (2.6)$$

It will prove useful further to assume $U(X,Q)$ to be linearly homogeneous.

Environmental quality Q is a stock variable. In order to distinguish the present model from others where Q will be treated as a flow it will be referred to as *stock model*. Q behaves over time according to the differential equation

$$\dot{Q} = \delta(\overline{Q} - Q) - E(A, K) \qquad (2.7)$$

where $\overline{Q} - Q \geq 0$ and $\delta > 0$. $\overline{Q}$ is constant and represents the natural value of Q, its upper bound, and also its initial state. $\delta(\overline{Q} - Q)$ is a regeneration function which describes the process of "natural purification" or assimilation of Q. The difference

$$\overline{Q} - Q(t) = \int_0^t E[A(s), K(s)] \exp[\delta(s - t)] ds \equiv P(t) \qquad (2.8)$$

can be called "pollution". Hence in accordance with the definition of environmental quality in section 1.1, $Q = \overline{Q} - P$ is absent pollution, and because $\delta(\overline{Q} - Q) = \delta P$, the parameter δ is the rate of pollution "decay". The integral expression is obtained by solving (2.7) (see appendix A).

$E(A,K) \geq 0$ is defined on R_+^2 and represents aggregate net emissions which add to the pollution stock, reducing the quality of the environment. The net emissions function is further characterised by the properties

$$\frac{\partial E}{\partial K} > 0, \ \frac{\partial^2 E}{\partial K^2} \geq 0 \quad \text{for } A \geq 0 \text{ and } K > 0,$$
$$\frac{\partial E}{\partial A} < 0, \ \frac{\partial^2 E}{\partial A^2} \geq 0, \ \frac{\partial^2 E}{\partial A \partial K} \leq 0, \ \lim_{A \to 0} \frac{\partial E}{\partial A} = -\infty \quad \text{for } A > 0 \text{ and } K > 0. \tag{2.9}$$

Net emissions are thus increasing and convex in the total man-made capital stock K, but decreasing and convex in abatement A. At the boundary the marginal efficiency of abatement is infinite. In connection with the assumption about the unboundedness of marginal utility of environmental quality, this property guarantees that $A>0$. The last assumption of (2.9) says that a given unit of abatement may become more efficient the more "polluting" capital there is.

Abatement is an alternative use of output beside consumption and saving. This implies the following equation of motion of real capital:

$$\dot{K} = F(K, Q) - X - A. \tag{2.10}$$

Output $F(K,Q) \geq 0$, defined on R_+^2, is increasing and strictly concave in K and in Q. Furthermore, a low quality of the environment impinges on the marginal productivity of K:

$$\frac{\partial F}{\partial K} > 0, \ \frac{\partial^2 F}{\partial K^2} < 0, \ \frac{\partial F}{\partial Q} > 0, \ \frac{\partial^2 F}{\partial Q^2} < 0, \ \frac{\partial^2 F}{\partial K \partial Q} > 0 \qquad \text{for } K>0 \text{ and } Q>0.$$

2.4.2 Shadow Prices as Opportunity Costs

A hypothetical omniscient social planner steers the economy by choosing the time paths for X, A and $\dot{K}$ so as to maximise intertemporal utility or welfare, given by

$$\int_0^\infty U[X(t), Q(t)] \exp(-\rho t) dt,$$

subject to (2.7), (2.10), and the initial values of the capital stock and environmental quality, $K(0)$ and $Q(0)$.[14] The parameter $\rho>0$ is the constant

[14] It is assumed that $K(0)$ is small enough for optimal growth to be positive. The precise condition for this to apply will be derived in chapter 3.

rate of pure time preference. The current-value Hamiltonian for this problem reads

$$\mathscr{H} = U(X,Q) + \mu[F(K,Q) - X - A] + \chi[\delta(\overline{Q} - Q) - E(A,K)] \tag{2.11}$$

where μ and χ are the costate variables associated with the state variables K and Q. Maximisation yields the following first-order conditions which are assumed also to be sufficient for a global maximum[15]:

$$\frac{\partial \mathscr{H}}{\partial X} = 0 \Leftrightarrow \mu = \frac{\partial U}{\partial X}, \qquad \frac{\partial \mathscr{H}}{\partial A} = 0 \Leftrightarrow \chi = -\frac{\mu}{\partial E / \partial A} \tag{2.12}$$

$$\frac{\partial \mathscr{H}}{\partial K} = \mu\rho - \dot{\mu}, \qquad \frac{\partial \mathscr{H}}{\partial Q} = \chi\rho - \dot{\psi} \tag{2.13}$$

As pointed out by Dorfman (1969), the costate variables of a Hamiltonian function turn into *shadow prices* of the respective state variables when the Hamiltonian is maximised. Hence the conditions (2.12) say that the shadow price of man-made or real capital is the marginal utility of consumption, and that the shadow price of environmental quality equals marginal abatement cost, given by $-(\partial E/\partial A)^{-1}$, times the shadow price of man-made capital. In both cases the shadow prices do not express the *benefit* the households derive from the respective stock but rather the *opportunity cost* the households are willing to accept when adding something to the respective stock. Capital accumulation means giving up current consumption. Environmental improvements require additional abatement spending or disinvestment, or a combination of both. But there would be no willingness to accept such opportunity cost if the households did not get a benefit in return worth to them at least as much.

2.4.3 Shadow Prices as Net Present Benefits

An insight into the benefit of investment and improvements of environmental quality is gained from (2.13). Integration of the first condition gives

---

[15] The Mangasarian sufficiency theorem requires $\mathscr{H}$ to be jointly concave in all states and controls. A weaker condition is provided by Arrow's sufficiency theorem [e.g. Chiang (1992), pp. 214-221].

$$\mu(t)=\int_t^{\infty}\frac{\partial\mathcal{H}(\cdot)}{\partial K(s)}\exp[-\rho(s-t)]ds \tag{2.14}$$

where

$$\frac{\partial\mathcal{H}(\cdot)}{\partial K(s)}=\frac{\partial U(\cdot)}{\partial X(s)}\left[\frac{\partial F(\cdot)}{\partial K(s)}+\frac{\partial E(\cdot)/\partial K(s)}{\partial E(\cdot)/\partial A(s)}\right].$$

According to (2.14), an extra unit of man-made capital is worth the present value of the future stream of net benefits it will yield, discounted at the rate of time preference. The instantaneous gross benefit of investment is an increase in production, and the instantaneous cost associated with investment consists in higher emissions valued at the marginal abatement cost. The more efficient the available abatement technology, that is, the greater $-\partial E/\partial A$, the higher is the value of investment. Ceteris paribus, an improving environmental quality raises the value of man-made capital because its marginal product $\partial F/\partial K$ increases (recall that $\partial^2 F/\partial K\partial Q>0$).

The shadow price of environmental quality improvements in terms of benefit (as opposed to opportunity cost) is obtained by integrating the second condition of (2.13). This produces again a present-value expression:

$$\chi(t)=\int_t^{\infty}\frac{\partial\mathcal{H}(\cdot)}{\partial Q(s)}\exp[-\rho(s-t)]ds \tag{2.15}$$

where

$$\frac{\partial\mathcal{H}(\cdot)}{\partial Q(s)}=\frac{\partial U(\cdot)}{\partial Q(s)}+\frac{\partial U(\cdot)}{\partial X(s)}\left[\frac{\partial F(\cdot)}{\partial Q(s)}+\frac{\delta}{\partial E(\cdot)/\partial A(s)}\right]$$

is the marginal current net benefit of a better environment. The first component is the positive effect of Q on current utility. The expression in brackets comprises a positive production effect and a negative assimilation effect. The former should be clear, given the above assumption that a low environmental quality impinges negatively on production. The latter has to do with the ability of the environment to regenerate itself. The higher Q, the more slowly the environment recovers. Therefore the effect is negative.

According to the forward-looking concept of capital, the value of a capital good is given by the present value of the future return it will yield. Since χ is the present value of the stream of future benefit of (or return on) a marginal increase in environmental quality, Q can be regarded as an environmental capital stock. A falling quality of the environment ($\dot{Q}<0$) then represents a form of capital consumption. Similar to man-made capital, a more efficient abatement technology raises the environment's capital value.

By equating the current benefit of consumption $\mu = \partial U / \partial X$ with the present net benefit of investment (2.14), the trade-off between consumption and saving is highlighted. In optimum, the marginal benefit of output must be the same in these alternative uses. More specifically, foregoing the current benefit of consumption in order to accumulate real capital must be compensated by the benefit that this extra capital will yield in the future. Of course, the same equal-marginal-benefit rule applies to abatement, the third possible use of output. Reducing consumption to pay for abatement is only justified if the benefit that the households will get from a better environment now and in the future is at least as high as the benefit they would have gotten by consuming more. By equating χ as given in (2.12) with (2.15) one finds that the benefit of environmental quality improvements must at least equal abatement cost at the margin for A to be positive. If the marginal benefit of abatement was less than its marginal cost, it would be optimal for the households not to abate - the case of a corner solution which has been excluded here by assumption, but which will play a central role in later chapters. In that case abatement would lead to an *opportunity loss* equal to the difference between marginal benefit and marginal cost.

2.4.4 "Green" Net National Product

Net national product (NNP), the sum of the value of current consumption and net investment, has for long been regarded as a measure of economic welfare. As Weitzman (1976) has shown, traditional NNP is simply the appropriately normalised, optimised Hamiltonian of the standard neoclassical growth problem. Moreover, he gave a capital-theoretic interpretation of NNP. Solow (1986) was the first to apply these results in an environmental context. Building on those two papers, a whole body of literature on "green" national accounting emerged in recent years with the objective to come up with better economic welfare and performance measures which explicitly consider resource depletion and environmental destruction [e.g. Dasgupta (1993), ch. 10*, Hartwick (1990) and (1992), Mäler (1991)].

One key difficulty of the integration of natural resources and environmental quality in economic reasoning in general, and in national accounts in particular, is the valuation issue, i.e. giving money values to the non-marketed environment. But this is precisely what the last two sections have been dealing with, only that the shadow prices obtained were not given in monetary units but in units of utility. However, it will now be shown that applying Weitzman's method of calculating NNP to the present model produces quasi-monetary accounting prices as a by-product. Their appearance in a "green" NNP expression will facilitate their interpretation.

For this end substitute from conditions (2.12)-(2.13) into the current-value Hamiltonian (2.11) and apply Euler's theorem [see Chiang (1984), pp. 413-414] to the utility function[16]. The result is the optimised Hamiltonian

$$\mathcal{H}^* = \frac{\partial U}{\partial X}(X+\dot{K}) + \frac{\partial U}{\partial Q}Q - \frac{\partial U / \partial X}{\partial E / \partial A}\dot{Q}$$

This is a "green" net national product in units of utility. Taking consumption as numeraire, and dividing by $\mu = \partial U / \partial X$, the price of consumption, gives the "dollar-value" Hamiltonian (this term has been coined by Hartwick (1990)) or the "green" net national product

$$\frac{\mathcal{H}^*}{\partial U / \partial X} \equiv GNNP = NNP + q_1 Q + q_2 \dot{Q} \qquad (2.16)$$

where q_1 and q_2 are accounting prices which will be discussed below, and $NNP = X + \dot{K}$. This expression for *GNNP* suggests that $q_1 Q$ forms part of current income which is a *flow*, whereas in the last section Q was given the interpretation of a natural capital *stock*. This seeming contradiction can be resolved by interpreting $q_1 Q$ as the value of a flow of environmental amenities accruing from the stock Q, implying a proportionality between stock size and flow volume. Hence environmental quality enters *GNNP* both as a flow and as marginal changes in the stock. The accounting price of the flow is positive and equals

$$q_1 = \frac{\partial U / \partial Q}{\partial U / \partial X}. \qquad (2.17)$$

---

16 Instead of assuming the utility function to be linearly homogeneous, many authors approximate it by taking a first-order Taylor expansion around the optimum, essentially linearising the utility function.

So $q_1 Q$ is the household's normalised instantaneous utility or the "dollar value" of the flow of environmental amenities associated with the stock Q, just like X is the normalised instantaneous utility or the "dollar value" of consumption. But since no opportunity cost is associated with simply being exposed to a given environmental quality, q_1 is not immediately observable, and an alternative expression needs to be derived for practical environmental valuation. The accounting price of marginal increases in the stock of environmental quality is given by

$$q_2 = -\frac{1}{\partial E / \partial A} \tag{2.18}$$

which is the marginal cost of abatement and, in optimum, equals the normalised or real present value of the future net benefit of a better environment (see also (2.15)):

$$q_2(t) = \int_t^{\infty} v(s)\left[q_1(s) + \frac{\partial F(\cdot)}{\partial Q(s)} + \frac{\delta}{\partial E(\cdot) / \partial A(s)}\right] \exp[-\rho(s-t)] ds \tag{2.19}$$

where $v(s) \equiv [\partial U(\cdot) / \partial X(s)]/[\partial U(\cdot) / \partial X(t)]$. In order to obtain an expression for q_1 which is of some practical use, the time derivative of (2.19),

$$\dot{q}_2(t) = \rho q_2(t) - v(t)\left[q_1(t) + \frac{\partial F(\cdot)}{\partial Q(t)} + \frac{\delta}{\partial E(\cdot) / \partial A(t)}\right],$$

can be solved for q_1. After substituting from (2.18), and recalling that $v(t)=1$ one gets

$$q_1 = -\frac{\delta + \rho}{\partial E / \partial A} - \frac{\partial F}{\partial Q} - \dot{q}_2. \tag{2.20}$$

As can be seen, q_1 equals marginal abatement cost, multiplied by the sum of the rates of pollution decay and of time preference, less the marginal productivity of Q, and further corrected by changes in the price q_2. At least in theory, this is an observable magnitude which can be used to value the current flow of environmental amenities and services.

Adding $\partial F/\partial Q$ to both sides of (2.17) and (2.20) yields a version of the standard condition of optimal resources allocation:

$$q_1 + \frac{\partial F}{\partial Q} = \frac{\partial U / \partial Q}{\partial U / \partial X} + \frac{\partial F}{\partial Q} = -\frac{\delta + \rho}{\partial E / \partial A} - \dot{q}_2$$

which says that, in optimum, the normalised current marginal benefit of (the flow of) environmental quality must equal the normalised marginal opportunity cost associated with its provision.

2.4.5 Environmental Quality as a Flow

An assumption often encountered in the literature is that pollution does not accumulate, but coincides with net emissions. This assumption is appropriate for certain pollutants for which the receiving medium has a very high absorptive capacity, leading to an almost immediate assimilation of pollution; but it is also made to simplify a formal analysis because it reduces the number of optimum conditions. Environmental quality in the sense of absent pollution then reads

$$Q(A,K) = \overline{Q} - E(A,K).$$

Note that Q is now a flow of environmental services and amenities accruing from the existing stock of environmental capital. Hence this model can be called *flow model* as opposed to the stock model of the last sections. If there were no emissions, the flow of environmental services would amount to $\overline{Q}$ which is again taken to be constant. Hence $\overline{Q}$ is a flow in this model, too. The environmental capital stock which yields the flow does not appear explicitly in the flow model.

The welfare function $\int_0^\infty U[X, Q(A,K)]\exp(-\rho t)dt$ is maximised with respect to X, A and $\dot{K}$, subject to $\dot{K} = F[K, Q(A,K)] - X - A$ and $K(0)>0$. The current-value Hamiltonian reads

$$\mathcal{H} = U[X, Q(A,K)] + \mu[F(K, Q(A,K) - X - A], \tag{2.21}$$

so there are one state and one costate variable less than in the stock model. Maximisation yields the condition for optimal static allocation of income:

$$\frac{\partial \mathcal{H}}{\partial X} = \frac{\partial \mathcal{H}}{\partial A} = 0 \Leftrightarrow \mu = \frac{\partial U}{\partial X} = \frac{\partial U}{\partial Q}\frac{\partial Q}{\partial A}\left(1 - \frac{\partial F}{\partial Q}\frac{\partial Q}{\partial A}\right)^{-1}. \tag{2.22}$$

According to (2.22), the marginal benefits of consumption and of abatement must be equal in optimum. Applying Euler's theorem to the utility function in (2.21), and substituting from (2.22) gives the maximised Hamiltonian

$$\mathcal{H}^* = \frac{\partial U}{\partial X}(X + \dot{K}) + \frac{\partial U}{\partial Q} Q$$

which turns into the "dollar-value" Hamiltonian or green net national product upon normalisation:

$$\frac{\mathcal{H}^*}{\partial U / \partial X} \equiv GNNP = NNP + q_3 Q. \tag{2.23}$$

This says that the value of the flow of amenities and services accruing from environmental quality should be added to conventional NNP in order to obtain an appropriate measure of welfare. The accounting price of environmental quality q_3 is found by rearranging (2.22) and considering that $\partial Q/\partial A = (\partial Q/\partial E)/(\partial E/\partial A) = -\partial E/\partial A$:

$$q_3 \equiv \frac{\partial U / \partial Q}{\partial U / \partial X} = -\frac{1}{\partial E / \partial A} - \frac{\partial F}{\partial Q}. \tag{2.24}$$

A comparison of (2.17) and (2.20) with (2.24) reveals that q_3 is closely related to q_1. The only differences consist in elements that are introduced by the dynamic character of the environmental capital stock that underlies q_1, namely the rates of time preference and pollution decay, and the changes in q_2. By adding $\partial F / \partial Q$ to both sides of (2.24) one arrives at the usual optimum condition that, in equilibrium and with $A > 0$, the marginal benefit of environmental quality - which is the sum of normalised marginal utility and marginal productivity of Q - must equal marginal abatement cost. At least in principle, the latter can again be used in practical environmental valuation as a proxy for the missing market price.

2.5 The Emergence of Demand for Pollution Reductions

Under the assumption of an omniscient social planner, external effects pose no problem to the model economy because all agents are effectively merged to a single entity, so that nothing is left that may be "external" to this entity. Public goods are provided in the socially optimal amounts since all agents' true marginal willingness to pay or to accept opportunity cost is known by the planner. Although this framework is normative in the sense that it describes an unrealistically perfect economy, it can still be employed to study and explain certain real phenomena as long as these phenomena do not *depend* on the existence of market or government failures. This argument can also be reversed: if the modelling of Environmental Kuznets Curves turns out to be possible in a theoretical first-best framework, one may conjecture that the occurence of inverted-U curves for pollution in the real world does not depend on the existence of market or government failures either.

2.5.1 Corner Solutions of Abatement

Demand for a private good depends, inter alia, on the market price: if the price exceeds the marginal willingness to pay, or to accept an opportunity cost for the good, then demand is zero, even though preferences for this good exist. The same holds for environmental quality. When agents are faced with high opportunity costs of "purchasing" or achieving a better environment they may choose to opt out and not demand that pollution control efforts be increased. Opting out in a first-best world does *not* mean hoping to free-ride. It means consciously accepting a smaller supply of the public good. That this supply may still increase due to others' higher willingness to contribute does not influence the individual's decision. So despite the existence of environmental preferences and possible production-enhancing effects of a higher quality of the environment, there need not be a positive demand for pollution reductions.

In the social optimum, demand for a better environment is met by a supply in the form of abatement being carried out. On the other hand, if demand for environmental improvements is zero, so will be pollution abatement. Technically speaking, abatement will then have a corner solution. Such solutions may occur if the efficiency of abatement is bounded, i.e. if

$$\left.\frac{\partial E}{\partial A}\right|_{A=0} > -\infty . \tag{2.25}$$

This modification seems to have been proposed first by Selden and Song (1995). (2.25) replaces the limit condition in (2.9). Since A will no longer be strictly positive, the restriction $A \geq 0$ needs to be added to the optimisation problem of section 2.4.2. The resulting current-value Lagrangean or generalised Hamiltonian reads

$$\mathcal{H} = U(X,Q) + \mu[F(K,Q) - X - A] + \chi[\delta(\overline{Q} - Q) - E(A,K)] + \lambda A \tag{2.26}$$

where λ is the Lagrangean multiplier of the nonnegativity restriction on A. In a maximum the complementary slackness conditions $\lambda \geq 0$, $A \geq 0$ and $\lambda A = 0$, and the optimum conditions (2.12) and (2.13) must hold, with the only difference that the second condition of (2.12) now contains λ:

$$\frac{\partial \mathcal{H}}{\partial A} = 0 \Leftrightarrow \chi = \frac{\lambda - \mu}{\partial E / \partial A}$$

Equating this with (2.15), substituting from the first condition of (2.12) for μ, and rearranging slightly gives

$$\lambda(t) = \frac{\partial U(\cdot)}{\partial X(t)} + \frac{\partial E(\cdot)}{\partial A(t)} \int_t^\infty \frac{\partial \mathcal{H}(\cdot)}{\partial Q(s)} \exp[-\rho(s-t)] ds \tag{2.27}$$

where the integral is the same as in (2.15). The first term on the right-hand side of (2.27) is the marginal utility of consumption. Abating pollution means foregoing consumption, hence the marginal utility of consumption is the opportunity cost of a better environment. The higher the level of consumption already is, the lower is its marginal utility, and the lower the opportunity cost of, and loss due to, abatement.

Already in 1972, Beckerman uses this relationship as an argumant in his defence of economic growth: "In fact, the irony of the increasing hostility to economic growth among some sections of the community is that it is precisely this economic growth that has enabled the richer countries to make great progress in the eradication of mass poverty, squalor, and disease, and hence to give more priority to environmental considerations" [p. 194].

The second term of (2.27) represents the negative of the marginal net present benefit of abatement. λ will be positive if the opportunity cost of pollution reductions exceeds the benefit at the margin, so λ can be interpreted as the ***marginal opportunity loss*** associated with abatement. A marginal opportunity loss of zero is the necessary condition for a positive demand for pollution reduction. From (2.27) it can be seen that λ declines if consumption increases, if the first unit of abatement gets more efficient, and if improvements in environmental quality are valued higher, for instance due to a higher pollution level or a lower rate of time preference ρ.

The simpler flow model of section 2.4.5 can be modified in the same way. Again it only needs to be assumed that the efficiency of the first unit of abatement is bounded (see (2.25)). When the current-value Hamiltonian (2.21) of that section is extended by the nonnegativity restriction on A, the resulting generalised Hamiltonian reads

$$\mathcal{GH} = U[X, Q(A,K)] + \mu[F(K,Q) - X - A] + \lambda A.$$

Maximisation with respect to the controls X and A requires the same complementary slackness conditions to hold as above, in addition to

$$\frac{\partial \mathcal{GH}}{\partial X} = \frac{\partial \mathcal{GH}}{\partial A} = 0 \Leftrightarrow \mu = \frac{\partial U}{\partial X} = \left(\frac{\partial U}{\partial Q}\frac{\partial Q}{\partial A} + \lambda\right)\left(1 - \frac{\partial F}{\partial Q}\frac{\partial Q}{\partial A}\right)^{-1}$$

which is a slightly modified version of condition (2.22). Solving it for λ, and making again use of the fact that $\partial Q / \partial A = -\partial E / \partial A$ gives

$$\lambda = \frac{\partial U}{\partial X} + \frac{\partial E}{\partial A}\left(\frac{\partial U}{\partial Q} + \frac{\partial U}{\partial X}\frac{\partial F}{\partial Q}\right) \tag{2.28}$$

which looks very similar to (2.27), and has the same meaning. The right-hand side represents the difference between marginal opportunity cost and marginal benefit of abatement. So λ is again the marginal opportunity loss of abatement which needs to vanish before a positive demand for a better environment arises.

2.5.2 Abatement Spending in the Course of Growth

The results just obtained can now be used to investigate how the optimal level of abatement spending correlates with other variables of the model. For this end λ is set equal to zero, the resulting optimum condition is differentiated with respect to time, and solved for changes in A. These operations produce quite messy expressions and have therefore been relegated to the appendices B and C.

Independent of whether environmental quality is modelled as a stock or as a flow, both a growing capital stock and rising consumption make increased abatement spending optimal: $dA/dK>0$ and $dA/dX>0$.[17] More capital is associated with higher emissions, all else equal, so that abatement becomes a more attractive use of resources. The link between consumption and abatement is similar to the link between consumption and λ: the higher the consumption level, the lower the marginal utility of consumption which is the opportunity cost of a better environment. In addition to that, a rising X drives up the marginal utility of Q because $\partial^2 U / \partial X \partial Q > 0$, which means that a better environmental quality is valued even higher, representing an additional incentive to abate. Finally, if the *stock* of environmental quality declines (i.e. if the environment is depleted in the stock model), ceteris paribus, optimal abatement spending increases: $dA/dQ<0$.

Economic growth is marked by rising output. With a constant population size this means rising per capita income and, given a positive savings ratio, a growing per capita capital stock. In the real world one can also expect current consumption per head to increase when income per capita does. In combination with what has just been said about the relationship between A, X and K, and with last section's results, this leads to the following interpretation of the results.

At early stages of economic growth people are poor, their consumption possibilities are modest. Emissions associated with the limited production and the small real capital stock do not yet put a significant strain on the environment, so the level of pollution is low. In this situation additional consumption is worth more to the people than environmental improvement. Abatement would lead to a positive marginal opportunity loss ($\lambda>0$), so it is not carried out ($A=0$). Since economic development is the priority in this phase of growth, it will be called *development phase*.

If over time, the material wellbeing increases at the cost of a deteriorating environmental quality up to a point where the pollution level is so high and

---

17 Partial derivatives of *explicit* functions are written using the symbol "∂", e.g. $\partial E/\partial A$. To distinguish them from derivatives of *implicit* functions, "∂" is replaced by "d" in the latter, e.g. dA/dK. A confusion with total differentials such as $dE=(\partial E/\partial A)dA+(\partial E/\partial K)dK$ should not arise.

the marginal utility of consumption so low that a demand for a better environment arises ($\lambda=0$), then abatement efforts will be started ($A\geq 0$). Further economic development and the associated expansion of consumption possibilities is now only one of two objectives of equal importance, and it has to be balanced against environmental protection. This phase will be referred to as *environment phase*.

Interestingly, the model confirms the conjecture stated in section 2.3.2 that neither the materialist nor the post-materialist hypothesis alone sufficiently explain the emergence of a positive demand for a better environment, but that a combination of both applies. The relationship $dA/dK>0$ reflects the materialist argument, namely that rising pollution levels due to the operation of an ever-growing capital stock decrease the availability of good environmental quality, leading to its increased appreciation. Through more "effluents of affluence" the incentive to abate emissions rises. At the same time the marginal value of consumption declines because consumption per capita becomes more abundent in the course of economic growth. As a result, post-materialist, that is, non-consumption related uses of income such as pollution abatement become more attractive the higher the material living standard gets. This is reflected by $dA/dX>0$.

2.5.3 Emissions and Pollution in the Course of Growth

In the development phase, with positive growth rates and no abatement being undertaken, environmental quality declines strictly. However, nothing has yet been said about how it behaves in the environment phase. Before addressing this question it will prove useful to take a closer look at the relationship between emissions and the resulting stock of pollution.

According to (2.7) and (2.8), $\dot{P}=E-\delta P$ in the stock model. Now assume that emissions remain constant ($\dot{E}=0$) for all times. If $E=\delta P$ then pollution will be constant forever at the level $P=E/\delta$. If $E>\delta P$ or $E<\delta P$ then P asymptotically converges towards E/δ strictly monotonically.[18] This is an important property because the fact that the pollution level "tries" to reach this particular level implies that if E rises or falls monotonically over some period, P will adopt the same qualitative behaviour, though with a time lag that depends inversely on δ. Figures 2.2 and 2.3 illustrate this relationship. In

[18] That there are no oscillations around that level follows from $\ddot{P}=\dot{E}-\delta\dot{P}=-\delta\dot{P}$ which says that the curvature does not change in the course of convergence.

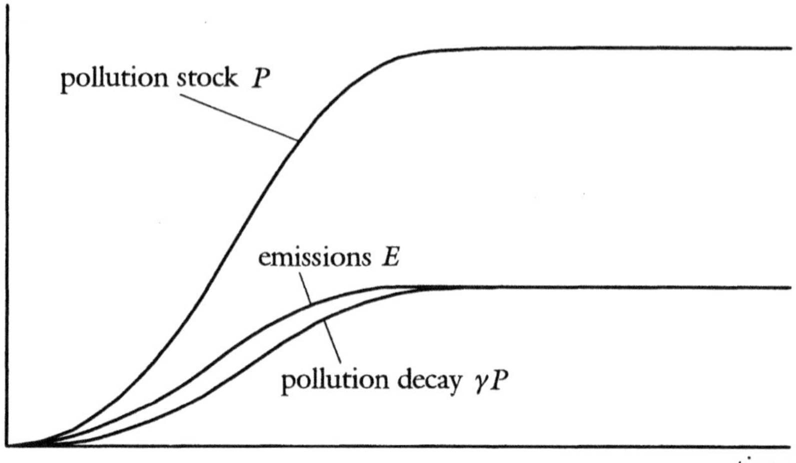

Figure 2.2: The behaviour of a pollution stock when emissions reach a constant level

both cases, emissions start at a low level and rise over some time. The pollution stock follows this movement. As long as the "emissions" curve lies above the "pollution decay" curve, i.e. $E > \delta P$, pollution increases. In figure 2.2 emissions reach a constant level. It can be seen that the "pollution decay" curve gradually catches up with the "emissions" curve which means that δP approaches E ($\delta = 0.4$ in both figures).

Figure 2.3 highlights the sluggishness of the pollution stock. Emissions reach a maximum and decline thereafter. The pollution level keeps increasing beyond the emission maximum and peaks at the moment when the "emissions" curve intersects with the "pollution decay" curve.

However, as before the qualitative long-run behaviour of the pollution stock is the same as of the emission level. The inverted U-curve for emissions is followed by one for the pollution stock. Hence provided that δ is not equal to zero which would mean irreversible environmental damage, *approximating the behaviour of the stock variable "pollution" by the flow variable "emissions" seems a justifiable simplification if short-run deviations do not matter.*

Returning to the original problem of determining the sign of changes in environmental quality during the environment phase of growth, it follows from the this discussion that in the long run, $\operatorname{sgn}\dot{Q} = -\operatorname{sgn}\dot{P} = -\operatorname{sgn}\dot{E}$ if Q is a stock, and $\dot{Q} = -\dot{P} = -\dot{E}$ if pollution does not accumulate.

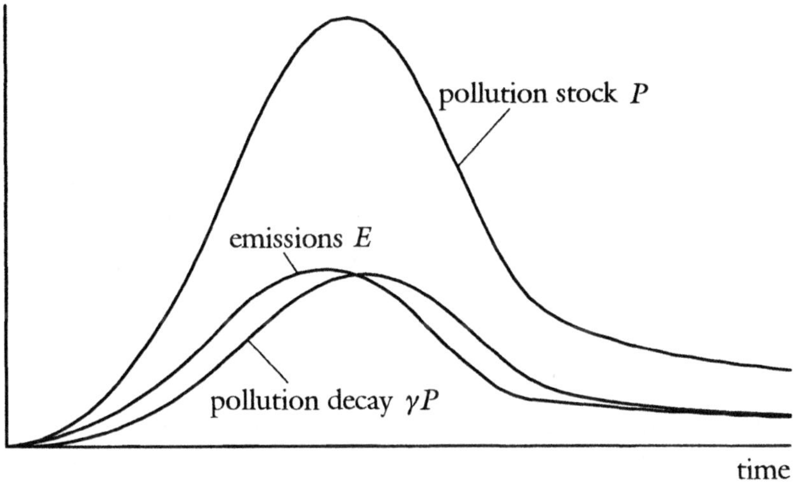

Figure 2.3: The behaviour of a pollution stock when emissions reach a maximum and decline subsequently

Now the analysis of the behaviour of pollution over time can be reduced to the behaviour of emissions. Appendix D shows that the emissions E are negatively related to the consumption level X, that is, $dE/dX<0$. The impact of investment on emissions is two-fold:

$$\frac{dE}{dK}=\frac{\partial E}{\partial K}+\frac{\partial E}{\partial A}\frac{dA}{dK}$$

Investment is directly associated with additional emissions but also correlates positively with abatement ($dA/dK>0$ according to section 2.5.2) which reduces emissions. The concrete expressions for the total effect of changes in K on E which are derived in appendix D for both models reveal that the sign remains ambiguous unless further assumptions are made. The role of $\partial^2 E / \partial A \partial K$ needs to be emphasised in this context: the more the marginal efficiency of abatement rises with investment, the more likely it is that capital accumulation has an environmentally benign net effect. Only in a special case the sign is uniquely determined. If the efficiency of abatement is completely independent of the capital stock ($\partial^2 E / \partial A \partial K = 0$), emissions unambiguously increase with K.

According to the last section's discussion, pollution in the stock model will tend to follow the same movements as emissions, but with a time lag. So the results obtained for the dependence of emissions on the level of consumption and the capital stock size can generally be transferred to the pollution stock in a long-run analysis. However, one difference between the stock model and the flow model needs to be taken into account. If pollution accumulates, then the optimal emission level depends positively on the environmental quality stock: $dE/dQ>0$ (see appendix D). This relationship has a dampening effect on optimal pollution. If the environment is already highly polluted lower additional emissions are optimal than if the pollution level was low.

2.5.4 Explaining the N-Curve of Fecal Coliform

With the insights gained so far, not only the occurrence of Environmental Kuznets Curves may be explained, but also the N-curve of fecal coliform concentrations reported by Shafik (1994a), and described in section 1.2.4. Fecal coliform bacteria do not affect human health, but their concentration in rivers and lakes is an indicator of untreated sewage discharge which seriously impinges on local water quality and the corresponding aquatic ecosystems. From the first rise and the subsequent decline in fecal coliform concentrations of the N-curve, it can thus be inferred on an Environmental Kuznets Curve for organic water pollution.

Provided that the water quality improvements are the result of deliberate pollution control efforts, such as the installation of sewage treatment facilities, there must have been a positive demand for cleaner water in rivers and lakes, probably related to drinking and fishing, rather than leisure activities, for the improvements have occured between per capita income levels of \$1375 and \$10,000. What might have caused this demand to decline again at a higher income level? Since people need drinking water, the demand for it cannot have dropped to zero. However, a substitute may have become available to them, making them increasingly independent of the prevailing water quality of nearby lakes and rivers. Better water supply systems and imported low-cost fish can be thought to have cut the formerly close link between the people's wellbeing and local water quality.

In terms of the flow model this means that the marginal utility $\partial U/\partial Q$ and the marginal productivity $\partial F/\partial Q$ of local water quality Q have declined rapidly. Given a certain marginal cost $(\partial Q/\partial A)^{-1}$ of water quality improvements, this has lead to a significant imbalance of the marginal benefit of clean water in lakes and rivers, and the marginal opportunity cost of achieving it. Formally, the opportunity loss λ of "abatement" in (2.28) has become positive, rendering it inefficient to devote resources to water treatment. In consequence, water pollution has started rising again.

Shafik (1994a), p. 765, utters the same conjecture: "The increased fecal coliform may reflect improvements in water supply systems where people no longer depend directly on rivers for water and therefore may be less concerned about river water quality." On a more general level, Beckerman (1972), p. 196, notes that "If any meaning at all is to be given to the value to society of the environment it must, surely, be related to the degree to which the population is in contact with that part of the environment."

2.6 Concluding Remarks

This chapter has been concerned with identifying some fundamental macro-economic forces which are at work in a hypothetical first-best world when the quality of the environment changes. The focus was on intentional pollution reductions taking place in the course of economic growth, that is, in presence of a positive scale effect. The intention to reduce pollution requires a motivation which can have two main sources: environmental preferences and a possible productivity-enhancing effect of a better environment.

At the same time pollution reductions can usually not be achieved for free. If the marginal opportunity cost of avoiding or reducing pollution exceeds the marginal benefit of a better environment, nothing will be done to stop or even reverse environmental degradation. Any unit of income spent on abating emissions would lead to a positive opportunity loss. This is most likely to be the case in low per capita income ranges, and it represents one possible reason why it may be optimal to let the environment deteriorate. Therefore, in the early phase of an economy's growth, the pollution level tends to rise with per capita income.

Trends in environmental quality may be reversed once it becomes efficient to control emissions, i.e. when the marginal benefit of avoided emissions justifies the marginal opportunity cost associated with it. In this second phase of economic growth, technology and preferences jointly determine whether or not pollution actually declines and Environmental Kuznets Curves occur.

To conclude this chapter, it can be stated that the turn-arounds in environmental quality which have been observed empirically may well reflect an at least near-optimal behaviour, and hence need not be the result of some particular, randomly or accidentally arising circumstances.

Appendix

Appendix A: The Pollution Stock

The solution of $\dot{Q} = \delta(\overline{Q} - Q) - E(A,K)$ is

$$Q(t) = \exp(-\delta t)\left\{ Q(0) + \delta\overline{Q}\int_0^t \exp[\delta(s-t)]ds - \int_0^t E(\cdot)\exp[\delta(s-t)]ds \right\}$$

$$= Q(0)\exp(-\delta t) + \overline{Q}[1-\exp(-\delta t)] - \int_0^t E(\cdot)\exp[\delta(s-t)]ds$$

Since $Q(0) = \overline{Q}$ this reduces to

$$Q(t) = \overline{Q} - \int_0^t E(\cdot)\exp[\delta(s-t)]ds$$

where the integral represents the stock of pollution $P(t)$.

Appendix B: The Implicit Abatement Function (Stock Model)

For simplicity let the partial derivative $\partial U / \partial X$ be denoted by U_X etc. Then condition (2.27) with $\lambda = 0$ reads

$$U_X + E_A \int_t^\infty \left[U_Q + U_X\left(F_Q + \frac{\delta}{E_A} \right) \right] \exp[-\rho(s-t)]ds = 0 \qquad \text{(B1)}$$

Define the current marginal net benefit of Q as

$$B \equiv U_Q + U_X\left(F_Q + \frac{\delta}{E_A} \right),$$

then the time derivative of (B1) equals

$$U_{XX}\dot{X} + U_{XQ}\dot{Q} + (E_{AA}\dot{A} + E_{AK}\dot{K})\int_t^\infty B(s)\exp[-\rho(s-t)]ds$$

$$+\rho E_A \int_t^\infty B(s)\exp[-\rho(s-t)]ds - E_A B(t) = 0$$

or, solved for changes is A,

$$\dot{A} = -\frac{1}{E_{AA}}\left\{E_{AK}\dot{K} + \frac{U_{XX}\dot{X} + U_{XQ}\dot{Q} - E_A B(t)}{\int_t^{\infty} B(s)\exp[-\rho(s-t)]ds} + \rho E_A\right\} \tag{B2}$$

Since $B>0$ for $\lambda=0$ it follows that $dA/dX>0$, $dA/dK>0$ and $dA/dQ<0$.

Appendix C: The Implicit Abatement Function (Flow Model)

In the simplified notation introduced in appendix B, condition (2.28) reads

$$U_X + E_A(U_Q + U_X F_Q) = 0 \tag{C1}$$

Differentiation with respect to time yields

$$\begin{aligned}
&U_{XX}\dot{X} + U_{XQ}(Q_K\dot{K} + Q_A\dot{A}) + (E_{AA}\dot{A} + E_{AK}\dot{K})(U_Q + U_X F_Q) \\
&+E_A U_{QQ}(Q_K\dot{K} + Q_A\dot{A}) + E_A U_{QX}\dot{X} + E_A U_{XX} F_Q \dot{X} \\
&+E_A U_{XQ}(Q_K\dot{K} + Q_A\dot{A})F_Q + E_A U_X F_{QQ}(Q_K\dot{K} + Q_A\dot{A}) \\
&+E_A U_X F_{QK}\dot{K} = 0
\end{aligned}$$

Taking into account that $Q_A = -E_A$ and $Q_K = -E_K$, and sorting leads to

$$\begin{aligned}
&\left[-U_{XQ}E_A(1+F_Q E_A) + U_Q E_{AA} + U_X F_Q E_{AA} - U_{QQ}E_A^2 - U_X F_{QQ} E_A^2\right]\dot{A} \\
&= \left[U_{XQ}E_K(1+F_Q E_A) - U_Q E_{AK} - U_X F_Q E_{AK} + U_{QQ}E_A E_K\right. \\
&\left.+U_X F_{QQ} E_A E_K - U_X F_{QK} E_A\right]\dot{K} + \left[-U_{XX}(1+F_Q E_A) - U_{QX}E_A\right]\dot{X}
\end{aligned}$$

which can be solved for

$$\dot{A} = \frac{\left[U_{XQ}E_K(1+F_Q E_A) - U_Q E_{AK} - U_X F_Q E_{AK} + U_{QQ}E_A E_K \ldots\right.}{-U_{XQ}E_A(1+F_Q E_A) + U_Q E_{AA} + U_X F_Q E_{AA} - U_{QQ}E_A^2 - U_X F_{QQ}E_A^2}$$

$$\frac{\left.\ldots + U_X F_{QQ}E_A E_K - U_X F_{QK}E_A\right]\dot{K} + \left[-U_{XX}(1+F_Q E_A) - U_{QX}E_A\right]\dot{X}}{\ldots}$$

To determine the sign of the term $1+F_Q E_A$ which appears in both brackets and the denominator rewrite (C1) so as to get $1+F_Q E_A = -U_Q E_A / U_X$ which is positive. It follows that both brackets as well as the denominator have positive values which means that $dA/dK>0$ and $dA/dX>0$.

Appendix D: The Implicit Emission Function

The time derivative of emissions is given by $\dot{E} = E_K \dot{K} + E_A \dot{A}$. Upon substitution from (B2) one obtains for the *stock model*

$$\dot{E}(\cdot) = \frac{E_{AA}E_K - E_{AK}E_A}{E_{AA}}\dot{K} - \frac{E_A}{E_{AA}}\left\{\frac{U_{XX}\dot{X} + U_{XQ}\dot{Q} - E_A B(t)}{\int_t^{\infty} B(s)\exp[-\rho(s-t)]ds} + \rho E_A\right\}$$

from which it follows that $dE/dX<0$ and $dE/dQ<0$. The sign of dE/dK is ambiguous unless $E_{AK}=0$ (in this case $\partial E/\partial K>0$) or assumptions are made about the sign of $E_{AA}E_K - E_{AK}E_A$.

The time derivative of emissions in the *flow model* reads

$$\dot{E} = \frac{\left[(U_Q + U_X F_Q)(E_{AA}E_K - E_{AK}E_A) - U_X F_{QK} E_A^2\right]\dot{K} \ldots}{-U_{XQ}E_A(1+F_Q E_A) + U_Q E_{AA} + U_X F_Q E_{AA} - U_{QQ}E_A^2 - U_X F_{QQ} E_A^2}$$

$$\frac{+E_A\left[-U_{XX}(1+F_Q E_A) - U_{QX}E_A\right]\dot{X}}{\ldots}$$

so $dE/dX<0$ whereas dE/dK is again ambiguous just like in the stock model.

Chapter 3 Environmental Preferences, Socially Optimal Growth, and Pollution

Los Angeles is the city in which one is wakened by the sound of birds coughing. W. J. Baumol[19]

In the model economy of chapter 2, environmental quality matters for two reasons. First, it appears as an argument in the production function, playing the role of a factor input, thereby positively influencing the marginal productivity of capital, and the level of output. Output can be consumed, used for abatement, or invested to earn returns in the future. Hence via production, Q contributes to welfare in an *indirect* way.

Second, the quality of the environment has an immediate or *direct* impact on the representative household's welfare because its utility rises, ceteris paribus, if pollution declines. The appearence of Q in the utility function means that the household values the quality of the environment for its own sake, and not only as an instrument for pursuing other valuable objectives such as consumption. A household with this kind of utility function has been said to have "environmental preferences".

This chapter focuses on this direct welfare effect of the environment. It studies the impact of environmental preferences on the socially optimal growth path of an economy, first on a more general level, and then by means of a functionally specified and fully solved example. The conditions of sustainable optimal growth, properties of the abatement function, and the emergence of Environmental Kuznets Curves will be of special interest.

Abatement curves that result from these growth models bear a strong resemblance to typical Engel curves for luxury goods. Based on this observation, the widely held view that environmental quality is a luxury will be assessed critically.

---

[19] Baumol (1967), p.423.

3.1 The General Model and its Dynamics

The model presented in this section will provide a formal framework and serve as a point of departure for most later sections and chapters. It is a simplified version of the flow model introduced in chapter 2. The advantage of the flow model over the stock model consists in a smaller number of unknowns, and in the reduction of the initial conditions to one. This means that the economy, which is again assumed to be steered by the omniscient, hence perfectly forward-looking social planner, immediately "jumps" onto its optimal path and remains there. Transitional dynamics and the related complex stability analyses are avoided.

3.1.1 Assumptions of the General Model

Like in the model of chapter 2, the consumer side of the economy consists of a single representative household. All assumptions about its instantaneous utility function $U(X,Q)$ as stated in (2.5) carry over except one: the marginal utilities of X and Q are now taken as independent, that is,

$$\frac{\partial^2 U}{\partial X \partial Q} = 0. \tag{3.1}$$

This assumption of linear separability goes back to Forster (1973). It simplifies many calculations greatly and eliminates a number of ambiguous results. Furthermore, and again for reasons of simplicity, the elasticity of marginal utility of consumption is assumed constant. On the other hand, linear homogeneity of $U(X,Q)$ which was assumed in chapter 2 in order to facilitate the derivation of the NNP expression is not required anymore.

Environmental quality is once more to be understood as a measure of the absence of pollution: $Q \equiv \overline{Q} - P$ where $Q \geq 0$, $P \geq 0$, and $\overline{Q}$ is constant. In the flow model pollution coincides with current emissions since it does not accumulate. Pollution increases with the stock of capital K employed in production, but pollution can again be countered by spending part of output on pollution abatement A. Therefore the environmental quality function $Q(A,K)$ has the following properties:

$$\frac{\partial Q}{\partial A} > 0, \; \frac{\partial^2 Q}{\partial A^2} \leq 0, \; , \; \left.\frac{\partial Q}{\partial A}\right|_{A=0} < \infty \qquad \text{for } A \geq 0 \text{ and } K > 0. \tag{3.2}$$
$$\frac{\partial Q}{\partial K} < 0, \; \frac{\partial^2 Q}{\partial K^2} \leq 0, \; \frac{\partial^2 Q}{\partial A \partial K} = 0$$

Their interpretation should be clear since they correspond to (2.9), but refer to environmental quality Q instead of emissions E. Note, however, that the cross partial derivative in (3.2) differs from that in (2.9), saying that the marginal efficiency of abatement is independent of "polluting" capital. Note further that the limit term in (2.9) has been replaced by an expression that corresponds to (2.25), and means that the marginal efficiency of abatement is bounded, allowing for corner solutions of A (see section 2.5.1).

The third set of assumptions concerns production. In the line with Forster (1973), the production function does not include environmental quality as input anymore since the model will focus on the role of environmental preferences. Neglecting a possible productivity effect of pollution means that the imputed values of environmental quality improvements in this model will be *lower* than in the flow model of chapter 2. Output is given by

$$F(K) = \alpha K \tag{3.3}$$

where $\alpha > \rho > 0$.[20] This production function, known as "AK"-model, has been widely used in endogenous growth theory as a proxy for technologies with more than a single capital input, the marginal productivities of which remain constant in a steady state as well [Rebelo (1991); Barro and Sala-i-Martin (1995), pp. 140-144]. Capital here is to be understood as a composite input comprising all factors that can be (re)produced and accumulated, such as human capital and physical capital

---

[20] This parametric restriction is necessary, but not sufficient, to ensure positive economic growth. In addition to that, the initial capital stock $K(0)$ must be small enough. What this means will become clear in section 3.1.6 where the model will be functionally specified. Furthermore, the linear technology does not exclude infinite output. In order to avoid intertemporal utility or welfare to be unbounded (so that maximisation would make no sense) certain restrictions have to be imposed on parameters of the welfare function as will be shown for the specific model. However, in absence of specific functional forms it can only be postulated that welfare has a finite upper bound.

3.1.2 The Social Optimum

Welfare $\int_0^{\infty} U(X,Q)\exp(-\rho t)dt$ is maximised by the social planner with respect to X, A and $\dot{K}$, subject to the equation of motion of capital, $\dot{K} = \alpha K - X - A$, the nonnegativity restriction on A, and $K(0)>0$ which is the first of two boundary conditions required to fully determine the optimal solution. A separate nonnegativity restriction on Q is not needed since the assumption (2.6) ensures that any optimal Q will be positive. The restriction $P\geq 0$, on the other hand, should be considered in the maximisation. However, for now assume it to be fulfilled in optimum. That this needs not be the case, and what that means for the solution, will be shown in section 3.2. From the generalised Hamiltonian

$$\mathcal{H} = U[X, Q(A,K)] + \mu(\alpha K - X - A) + \lambda A$$

(where μ is again the costate variable associated with the state K, and λ is the Lagrangean multiplier on the restriction that $A \geq 0$) one obtains the optimum conditions[21]

$$\frac{\partial \mathcal{H}}{\partial X} = 0 \Leftrightarrow \mu = \frac{\partial U}{\partial X} \tag{3.4}$$

$$\frac{\partial \mathcal{H}}{\partial A} = 0 \Leftrightarrow \mu = \frac{\partial U}{\partial Q}\frac{\partial Q}{\partial A} + \lambda \tag{3.5}$$

$$\frac{\partial \mathcal{H}}{\partial K} = \mu\alpha + \frac{\partial U}{\partial Q}\frac{\partial Q}{\partial K} = \mu\rho - \dot{\mu} \tag{3.6}$$

and the complementary slackness conditions $\lambda\geq 0$, $A\geq 0$ and $\lambda A=0$. Furthermore, the transversality condition

$$\lim_{t\to\infty} \mu K \exp(-\rho t) = 0 \tag{3.7}$$

provides the second boundary condition. First, a few fundamental relationships need to be derived which will be put to work in later sections. Logarithmic differentiation of (3.4) gives

[21] Appendix A proves that $\mathcal{H}$ is concave in X, A and K. Since by (3.4) $\mu>0$, the two requirements of the Mangasarian sufficiency theorem [Chiang (1992), pp. 214-217] are fulfilled, and the first-order conditions are sufficient for a global maximum.

$$-\hat{\mu} = \sigma\hat{X} \tag{3.8}$$

where $\sigma \equiv -\frac{\partial^2 U / \partial X^2}{\partial U / \partial X} X$ is the elasticity of marginal utility with respect to consumption which has been assumed constant. Dividing (3.6) by μ and rearranging yields $-\hat{\mu} = r - \rho$. Equating this with (3.8) leads to the optimal consumption growth rate

$$\hat{X} = \frac{r - \rho}{\sigma} \tag{3.9}$$

where

$$r \equiv \alpha + \frac{(\partial U / \partial Q)(\partial Q / \partial K)}{\partial U / \partial X} \tag{3.10}$$

is the real social benefit of investment or the *social return on capital*. The normalisation consists in the division by $\mu = \partial U / \partial X$, so consumption serves as numeraire just like in the NNP expressions in chapter 2. The positive effect of investment $\dot{K}$ on the economy, given by the constant marginal productivity of capital, is reduced by a negative side-effect of the use of K in production. This negative effect consists in marginal utility reductions due to rising pollution and, in consequence, a declining environmental quality.

Conditions (3.4) and (3.5) can be equated and solved for

$$\lambda = \frac{\partial U}{\partial X} - \frac{\partial U}{\partial Q}\frac{\partial Q}{\partial A}. \tag{3.11}$$

This condition corresponds to (2.28) of the flow model in chapter 2. The marginal utility of consumption is again the opportunity cost of abatement spending, and needs to be compared with the marginal benefit of abatement.

3.1.3 Environmental Quality and Growth in the Development Phase

As long as $\lambda > 0$ in (3.11), the opportunity cost of abatement exceeds its benefit at the margin. The economy passes through the *development phase* (see section 2.5.2), no abatement is carried out, and Q declines strictly while capital is accumulated: $\dot{Q} = (\partial Q / \partial K)\dot{K} < 0$. In order to analyse the growth pattern a phase diagram in the (X, K)-plane can be drawn. First the zero-motion loci need to be determined. From $\dot{K} = \alpha K - X$ it follows that the $\dot{K} = 0$ locus is a straight line through the origin with slope α. According to (3.9), $\dot{X} = X(r-\rho)/\sigma$, so the $\dot{X} = 0$ locus is characterised by $r=\rho$.[22] Hence the $\dot{X} = 0$ locus has the slope

$$\left.\frac{dX}{dK}\right|_{\dot{X}=0} = -\frac{\partial r / \partial K}{\partial r / \partial X}$$

which is negative because

$$\frac{\partial r}{\partial K} = \frac{\frac{\partial^2 U}{\partial Q^2}\left(\frac{\partial Q}{\partial K}\right)^2 + \frac{\partial U}{\partial Q}\frac{\partial^2 Q}{\partial K^2}}{\frac{\partial U}{\partial X}} < 0 \quad \text{and} \quad \frac{\partial r}{\partial X} = -\frac{\frac{\partial U}{\partial Q}\frac{\partial Q}{\partial K}\frac{\partial^2 U}{\partial X^2}}{\left(\frac{\partial U}{\partial X}\right)^2} < 0 \quad (3.12)$$

The intersection of the two zero-motion lines indicates a stationary-state equilibrium for this model. $\tilde{X}$ and $\tilde{K}$ are the respective stationary-state values which are only approached but never reached in finite time. Since $dX / dK = \dot{X} / \dot{K}$, trajectories passing the $\dot{X} = 0$ locus have a slope of zero, and trajectories crossing the $\dot{K} = 0$ locus have an infinite slope at the respective point.

The zero-motion lines divide the phase plane into four isosectors in each of which the direction of motion is uniquely determined. In figure 3.1 the respective directions are indicated by pairs of arrows. For any combination (X, K) lying above the $\dot{K} = 0$ locus $X>\alpha K$, so that $\dot{K} < 0$, and the horizontal arrows point towards a lower K. Below the $\dot{K} = 0$ locus the opposite relationship holds. Combinations (X, K) above the $\dot{X} = 0$ locus are characterised by $r<\rho$ which leads to $\dot{X} < 0$, and the corresponding vertical arrows point towards a lower X. Again, below the $\dot{X} = 0$ locus the opposite applies.

From the directions of motion in the four isosectors one can infer that *the equilibrium is a saddle-point*. The trajectories leading into the equilibrium (as indicated by arrows) are its stable arms; the trajectories leading out of the equilibrium are the unstable arms. According to appendix B which proves the *global saddle-point stability* of the model, the unique optimal growth path of the economy is one of the stable arms, depending on the initial endowment with capital $K(0)$. Since by assumption $K(0)$ is small enough for optimal

---

[22] The trivial solution $X=0$ can be ruled out because it would violate the transversality condition (3.7).

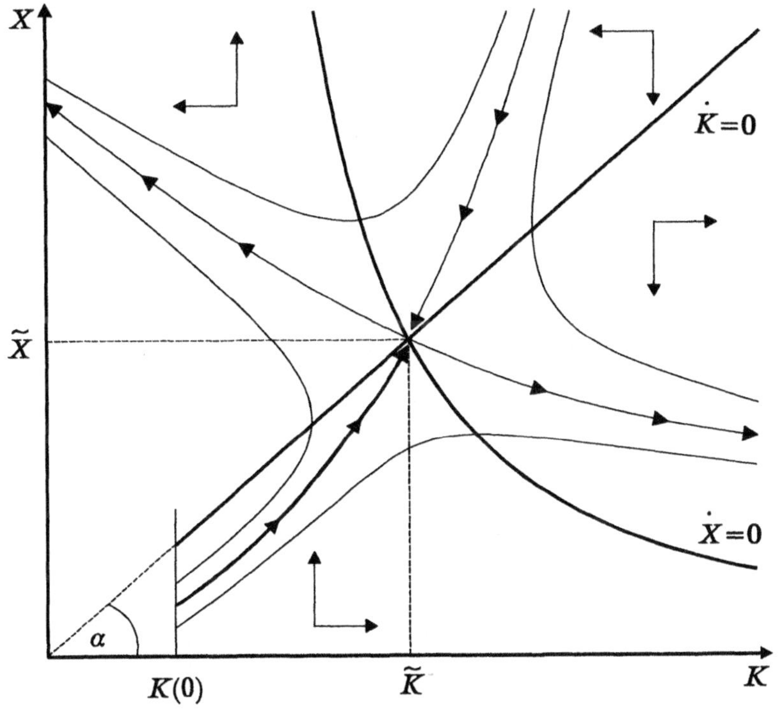

Figure 3.1: Saddle-point equilibrium in the (X, K) phase plane

growth to be positive (i.e. $r>\rho$), the optimally steered economy grows along the *rising* stable arm (the bold arrow), heading for the stationary state.

It is worth pointing out that if in this model people had no environmental preferences, $(\partial U / \partial Q = 0)$ consumption would rise at the constant rate $(\alpha - \rho) / \sigma$, implying that the capital stock would have to grow at the same rate. Economic growth would be sustainable. This is of course the consequence of the particular linear production function and the immunity of production to pollution. With a neoclassical function and no exogenous technological progress, sustainable growth would not be feasible in the first place, even in absence of environmental preferences or pollution. The "AK"-model has been chosen to ensure that any non-constant social returns on capital necessarily originate from the influence of pollution on utility.

In the present model the economy *could* grow indefinitely; no physical barriers have been erected to prevent it from doing so. But it is (socially) optimal not to use the technical growth potential to its full extent. *The optimum scale of the economy is not its maximum scale*. Up to this point the recommendation of "The Limits to Growth" [Meadows et al. (1972)] to slow down and ultimately abandon economic growth is supported by the model.

However, setting $A=0$ and differentiating (3.11) shows that

$$\frac{\partial \lambda}{\partial X} = \frac{\partial^2 U}{\partial X^2} < 0 \text{ and } \frac{\partial \lambda}{\partial K} = -\frac{\partial^2 U}{\partial Q^2}\frac{\partial Q}{\partial A}\frac{\partial Q}{\partial K} < 0.$$

So the opportunity loss of abatement declines while the economy grows. Unless $\tilde{X}$ and $\tilde{K}$ are so low that $\tilde{\lambda} > 0$, and hence the economy "gets stuck" in the development phase, λ will vanish, opening up new possibilities for further socially optimal economic expansion.

3.1.4 The Environment Phase

In the *environment phase*, marked by $\lambda=0$, (3.11) turns into the standard condition that the marginal utilities of income must be equated in all alternative uses, namely consumption and pollution abatement. Differentiating (3.11) with respect to time, setting $\lambda=0$, and solving for changes in abatement yields

$$\dot{A} = \frac{\frac{\partial^2 U}{\partial X^2}\dot{X} - \frac{\partial^2 U}{\partial Q^2}\frac{\partial Q}{\partial A}\frac{\partial Q}{\partial K}\dot{K}}{\frac{\partial^2 U}{\partial Q^2}\left(\frac{\partial Q}{\partial A}\right)^2 + \frac{\partial U}{\partial Q}\frac{\partial^2 Q}{\partial A^2}} \quad \text{if } \lambda=0, \tag{3.13}$$

hence $dA/dX>0$ and $dA/dK>0$. The same result has already been obtained in section 2.5.2 for the more general models of chapter 2.

Figure 3.2 illustrates the economy's optimal budget allocation as a function of nonsaved income or total expenditure $I \equiv \alpha K - \dot{K} = X + A$. The dashed 45°-line represents total expenditure. The curves labelled X and A depict the expenditure categories consumption and abatement which add up to total expenditure. Their curvature is arbitrary since no functional forms have been specified; however, their slopes must always be positive which follows from $dA/dX>0$.

During the development phase the abatement curve coincides with the horizontal axis. Once the environment phase is reached it "takes off" while the slope of the consumption curve decreases. Expenditure shares are shifted

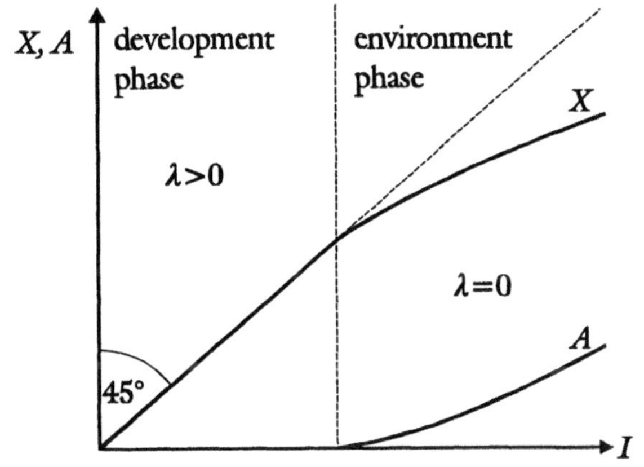

Figure 3.2: The allocation of non-saved income

from consumption to abatement which illustrates the opportunity cost of abatement, namely a utility loss due to foregone consumption.

Substitution from (3.13) into the time derivative of the environmental quality function, given by $\dot{Q} = (\partial Q / \partial K)\dot{K} + (\partial Q / \partial A)\dot{A}$, leads to

$$\dot{Q} = \frac{\frac{\partial^2 U}{\partial X^2}\frac{\partial Q}{\partial A}\dot{X} + \frac{\partial U}{\partial Q}\frac{\partial Q}{\partial K}\frac{\partial^2 Q}{\partial A^2}\dot{K}}{\frac{\partial^2 U}{\partial Q^2}\left(\frac{\partial Q}{\partial A}\right)^2 + \frac{\partial U}{\partial Q}\frac{\partial^2 Q}{\partial A^2}} \quad \text{if } \lambda = 0 \tag{3.14}$$

which means that $dQ/dX > 0$ and $dQ/dK < 0$. The ambiguous sign of the latter relationship that was found in the chapter 2 models has disappeared due to the assumption that $\partial^2 Q/\partial A \partial K = 0$. Whether pollution keeps rising, remains constant, or declines in the environment phase depends on the model's functional forms of $U(X,Q)$ and $Q(A,K)$ [e.g. Pezzey (1989), p. 27], rather than on its parametric configuration.

To give an example for the importance of the choice of functional forms, and for the relative insignificance of parameter values in this context, suppose the marginal efficiency of abatement to be constant at the level $\partial Q/\partial A \equiv a^{-1}$. Therefore, the second-order derivative $\partial^2 Q/\partial A^2$ equals zero. In consequence (3.14) simplifies to

$$\dot{Q} = a\frac{\partial^2 U}{\partial X^2}\left(\frac{\partial^2 U}{\partial Q^2}\right)^{-1}\dot{X}$$

which says that Q is strictly increasing in X and independent from changes in K. It can be concluded that *environmental preferences, combined with a constant efficiency of abatement, are sufficient to ensure that environmental quality improves with rising per capita income once abatement is carried out.* This holds not only for linearly separable environmental quality functions but for general ones because a constant $\partial Q/\partial A$ implies that $\partial^2 Q/\partial A\,\partial K=0$, no matter which assumptions have been made regarding $\partial^2 Q/\partial A\,\partial K$. Moreover, this result puts the blame on technology, should the pollution level rise rather than decline in the environment phase.

Upon substitution from (3.11), the social return on capital reduces to

$$r = \alpha + \frac{\partial Q / \partial K}{\partial Q / \partial A}. \tag{3.15}$$

Through differentiation of (3.15) one obtains

$$\frac{\partial r}{\partial K} = \frac{\partial^2 Q / \partial K^2}{\partial Q / \partial A} - \frac{\partial Q / \partial K}{(\partial Q / \partial A)^2}\frac{\partial^2 Q}{\partial A^2}\frac{dA}{dK} \leq 0 \text{ and}$$

$$\frac{\partial r}{\partial X} = -\frac{\partial Q / \partial K}{(\partial Q / \partial A)^2}\frac{\partial^2 Q}{\partial A^2}\frac{dA}{dX} \leq 0,$$

which says that, by the assumptions made earlier, and with K and X increasing, the social return on capital may keep declining despite abatement being carried out, driving the economy towards a stationary-state equilibrium similar to that in the development phase. However, if both second-order derivatives of Q equal zero, r will remain on a constant level. In that case consumption will grow forever at a constant rate (see (3.9)), implying that capital has to be accumulated at an even higher rate, at least temporarily, in order to sustain both consumption and abatement.

But a constant r does not depend on constant second-order derivatives of Q. The necessary and sufficient condition is weaker than that; it only requires $(\partial Q/\partial K)/(\partial Q/\partial A)$ to be constant for all times. Transversality conditions such as (3.7) are commonly taken as equivalent to requiring that the state and control variables approach their steady-state growth rates in the long run

[Mulligan and Sala-i-Martin (1991), p. 5]. In a steady state, X and K will therefore grow at the same rate, and since according to (3.13) A is increasing in both magnitudes one can expect also abatement to grow at that constant rate. Provided that Q is homogeneous of degree zero, a constant steady-state ratio A/K ensures that $(\partial Q/\partial K)/(\partial Q/\partial A)$, and therefore also r and the growth rate of consumption will be constant in the environment phase.[23] Moreover, homogeneity of degree zero implies that environmental quality will remain on a constant level while the economy keeps growing in the steady state.

3.2 Extension to *n* Dimensions of Environmental Quality

So far the model has only been taking a single type of pollution into account. However, the environmental crisis extends to several different environmental problems. Hence available resources have to be divided not only between consumption and environmental care, but also among various uses within the broad category of environmental care. To gain an insight into the principles, on the basis of which such allocation decisions should be made, is the objective of this section.

The general model of section 3.1 can be extended to $n>1$ pollutants in a straight-forward manner. Let $Q \equiv [Q_i]$ be an n-vector of levels of different dimensions or aspects i of environmental quality, each of which represents a measure of the absence of a particular type of pollution: $Q_i = \overline{Q}_i - P_i \geq 0$. The utility function now reads $U(X,Q)$, and with respect to each Q_i it has the same properties as assumed in section 3.1.1. Additionally,

$$\frac{\partial^2 U}{\partial Q_i \partial Q_j} = 0 \quad \text{where } i \neq j. \tag{3.16}$$

This linear separability assumption is made to simplify the analysis and means that the marginal utility derived from any individual dimension of environmental quality is independent from other aspects of the state of the environment. Just like assumption (3.1), it says that there is no "joint

---

23 Proof: According to Euler's theorem for homogeneous functions [Takayama (1994), pp. 48-49] a function homogeneous of degree zero is characterised by
$$\frac{\partial Q}{\partial K}K + \frac{\partial Q}{\partial A}A = 0 \Leftrightarrow -\frac{\partial Q/\partial K}{\partial Q/\partial A} = \frac{A}{K}.$$

production" of utility, but it also implies that there is no physical interaction between different pollutants.

For each dimension of environmental quality there is a function $Q_i(A_i, K)$. In addition to the properties stated in (3.2), it will be assumed that abatement is pollutant-specific:

$$\frac{\partial Q_i}{\partial A_j} = 0 \quad (i \neq j) \tag{3.17}$$

where A_j denotes efforts to abate pollutant j. Hence efforts made to reduce one type of pollution, and thus to raise the respective environmental quality, do not affect the level of other pollutants.
Capital now accumulates according to

$$\dot{K} = \alpha K - X - \sum_{i=1}^{n} A_i .$$

Given that A_i may again be zero or positive, n nonnegativity restrictions must be included in the generalised Hamiltonian, each one with its own multiplier λ_i:

$$\mathcal{H} = U(X, Q) + \mu\left(\alpha K - X - \sum_{i=1}^{n} A_i\right) + \sum_{i=1}^{n} \lambda_i A_i$$

Condition (3.4) according to which the shadow price of capital is the marginal utility of consumption remains the same. The following two optimum conditions correspond directly to (3.5)-(3.6):

$$\frac{\partial \mathcal{H}}{\partial A_i} = 0 \Leftrightarrow \mu = \frac{\partial U}{\partial Q_i}\frac{\partial Q_i}{\partial A_i} + \lambda_i \tag{3.18}$$

$$\frac{\partial \mathcal{H}}{\partial K} = \mu\alpha - \sum_{i=1}^{n} \frac{\partial U}{\partial Q_i}\frac{\partial Q_i}{\partial K} = \mu\rho - \dot{\mu} \tag{3.19}$$

In addition to that, the usual complementary slackness conditions $\lambda_i \geq 0$, $A_i \geq 0$ and $\lambda_i A_i = 0$ apply. For the opportunity loss associated with abating pollutant i one obtains

$$\lambda_i = \frac{\partial U}{\partial X} - \frac{\partial U}{\partial Q_i}\frac{\partial Q_i}{\partial A_i}. \tag{3.20}$$

This condition allows a ranking of all pollutants according to their abatement priority. The lower λ_i, the greater is the priority of reducing pollutant i. As can be seen, the ranking is based on three factors: preferences $(\partial U / \partial Q_i)$, the efficiency of the available abatement technology or, alternatively, the inverse of marginal abatement cost $(\partial Q_i / \partial A_i)$, and finally the level of pollution $P_i = \overline{Q}_i - Q_i$ itself which affects both of these partial derivatives. The *hierarchic demand for abatement* implied by (3.20) suggests that *those types of pollution will be abated first which have directly harmful effects, but also those which can be abated at relatively low cost* [see Grossman (1995), p. 22, who comes to the same conclusion].

Examples for the former are the introduction of soot filters to prevent respiratory illnesses, and the building of sewage systems to avoid epidemics. A famous example for the latter are the Montreal Protocol and the subsequent London Agreement in which the signatory nations committed themselves to a complete phase-out of halons and chlorofluorocarbons (CFCs) [see Tietenberg (1992), pp. 435-437]. A decisive precondition for these agreements were comparatively low switching costs.

Obviously being aware of this kind of hierarchy, Lovelock (1979) sees the true danger in those environmental problems which have the least direct harmful effect: "It seems therefore that the principal dangers to our planet arising from man's activities may not be the special and singular evils of his urbanised industrial existence. When urban industrial man does something ecologically bad he notices it and tends to put things right again. The really critical areas which need careful watching are more likely to be the tropics and the seas close to the continental shores. It is in these regions, where few do watch, that harmful practices may be pursued up to the point of no-return before their dangers are recognised; and so it is from these regions that unpleasent surprises are most likely to emerge." [p. 121]

Coming back to the model, the social return on capital equals

$$r = \alpha + \sum_{i=1}^{n} \frac{(\partial U / \partial Q_i)(\partial Q_i / \partial K)}{\partial U / \partial X}. \tag{3.21}$$

Only after *all* λ_i in (3.20) have vanished, so that the economy has reached the environment phase with respect to all dimensions of environmental quality, this reduces to

$$r = \alpha + \sum_{i=1}^{n} \frac{\partial Q_i / \partial K}{\partial Q_i / \partial A_i}, \tag{3.22}$$

and only if for *every* pollution function the ratio $(\partial Q_i / \partial K) / (\partial Q_i / \partial A_i)$ is constant, a steady state with positive growth rates will ultimately be reached

3.3 Functional Forms for Utility and Environmental Quality

Now the results of the last sections will briefly be illustrated by functionally specifying utility and environmental quality of the general model of section 3.1. The specification of the model also prepares the ground for later sections where particular properties of environmental preferences will be studied; specific functional forms will facilitate this analysis significantly.

The particularly simple functions chosen will be both the strength and the weakness of the model. The strength lies in the possibility to fully determine the optimal trajectories analytically, and to solve explicitly for all variables in the environment phase. The insights gained here will be useful in later sections. The model's weakness is a certain rigidity which results from the linearity of the environmental quality function (linearity in abatement is needed here to ensure explicit solvability) since different parameter constellations do not lead to qualitatively different optimal growth paths.

3.3.1 Assumptions and Optimum Conditions

All assumptions of the general model of section 3.1.1 carry over. A utility function that meets all the criteria demanded reads

$$U(X, Q) \equiv \frac{\beta X^{1-\sigma} + (1-\beta) Q^{1-\sigma} - 1}{1-\sigma} \tag{3.23}$$

where $0<\beta<1$, and $0<\sigma$ is the constant elasticity of marginal utility of consumption and of environmental quality.[24] Due to the linear production function (3.3) which in principle allows for infinite output, an additional assumption is required to limit welfare or intertemporal utility to finite values (see appendix C):

$$\frac{(\alpha-\rho)(1-\sigma)}{\sigma}<\rho \tag{3.24}$$

The following, admittedly simple, linear specification of the environmental quality function will be considered:

$$Q(A,K)=\overline{Q}-\xi K+\zeta A \tag{3.25}$$

where $\overline{Q}\geq\xi K-\zeta A\equiv P\geq 0$. $\xi>0$ and $\zeta>0$ are parameters. If $\partial Q/\partial K=\xi=0$ there would be no pollution. With $\partial Q/\partial A=\zeta=0$ no abatement would be possible. The generalised Hamiltonian reads

$$\mathcal{H}=\frac{\beta X^{1-\sigma}+(1-\beta)Q^{1-\sigma}-1}{1-\sigma}+\mu(\alpha K-X-A)+\psi P+\lambda A. \tag{3.26}$$

ψ and λ are the Lagrangean multipliesr of the nonnegativity restrictions on $P=\overline{Q}-Q$ and A. Maximisation of $\mathcal{H}$ leads to the optimum conditions[25]

$$\frac{\partial\mathcal{H}}{\partial X}=0\Leftrightarrow\mu=\beta X^{-\sigma} \tag{3.27}$$

$$\frac{\partial\mathcal{H}}{\partial A}=0\Leftrightarrow\mu=(1-\beta)\zeta Q^{-\sigma}-\psi\zeta+\lambda \tag{3.28}$$

$$\frac{\partial\mathcal{H}}{\partial K}=\mu\alpha-(1-\beta)\xi Q^{-\sigma}+\psi\xi=\mu\rho-\dot{\mu} \tag{3.29}$$

---

[24] If $\sigma=1$ then this utility function reduces to $U=\beta\ln X+(1-\beta)\ln Q$. Since numerator and denominator of (3.23) both tend to zero as $\sigma\to 1$, the proof requires the application of l'Hôpital's rule [see Chiang (1984), pp. 429-430]:

$$\lim_{\sigma\to 1}\frac{\beta X^{1-\sigma}+(1-\beta)Q^{1-\sigma}-1}{1-\sigma}=\lim_{\sigma\to 1}\frac{-\beta X^{1-\sigma}\ln X-(1-\beta)Q^{1-\sigma}\ln Q}{-1}=\beta\ln X+(1-\beta)\ln Q.$$

[25] Since $U(\cdot)$ and $Q(\cdot)$ fulfill all assumptions of the general model of section 3.1, the Hamiltonian of which has been proved to be concave (see footnote 20), it follows that the first-order conditions are again sufficient for a global maximum.

and the complementary slackness conditions $\lambda \geq 0$, $A \geq 0$, $\lambda A = 0$, $\psi \geq 0$, $P \geq 0$ and $\psi P = 0$. The transversality condition is again given by (3.7).

First of all, the values of the multipliers merit a brief comment. If $A=0$ then $\lambda \geq 0$, $P>0$ and $\psi=0$. On the other hand, $A>0$ means that $\lambda=0$ and may lead to a situation where $P=0$ and thus $\psi \geq 0$. As can be seen, *at least one of the two multipliers is always zero.*

Combining (3.27) and (3.28) yields the opportunity loss of abatement

$$\lambda = \beta X^{-\sigma} - (1-\beta)\zeta Q^{-\sigma} + \psi\zeta. \tag{3.30}$$

The marginal utility of consumption $\beta X^{-\sigma}$ is the opportunity cost of improving environmental quality. The lower the level of consumption X, and the greater the weight β attached to consumption in the utility function, the higher will this cost be. The marginal benefit of abatement $(1-\beta)\zeta Q^{-\sigma}$ is the higher the lower β, the greater the efficiency ζ of abatement, and the lower environmental quality Q. Finally, as mentioned above, the multiplier ψ will only be positive if $P=0$, but a necessary condition for this is that $\lambda=0$.

By reworking the steps of section 3.1.2 one finds that the social return on capital equals

$$r = \alpha - \frac{1-\beta}{\beta}\xi\left(\frac{X}{Q}\right)^{\sigma} + \frac{\psi\xi}{\mu}. \tag{3.31}$$

3.3.2 The Development Phase

In the development phase $\lambda>0$, so $\psi=0$. But although the last element of the sum in (3.31) drops out, the model cannot be solved explicitly for capital because r is not constant. However, it has already been shown in section 3.1.3 that in the development phase the social return on capital is strictly decreasing in X and K, and that Q declines while K is accumulated. Hence there is no need to take a closer look at the model in that phase.

3.3.3 The Environment Phase

Suppose for now that $P>0$ which implies that $\psi=0$. When the opportunity loss of abatement λ vanishes as the economy enters the environment phase[26], condition (3.30) can be solved for abatement

$$A = \left(\frac{1-\beta}{\beta}\zeta\right)^{1/\sigma}\frac{X}{\zeta} + \frac{\xi}{\zeta}K - \frac{\overline{Q}}{\zeta} \tag{3.32}$$

which is a linearly increasing function of X and K. Moreover, optimal abatement efforts rise with the pollution coefficient ξ and, provided that $\sigma \leq 1$, with the efficiency of abatement ζ. A higher weight β given to consumption in the utility function, and a higher initial or naturally provided environmental quality $\overline{Q}$, all else equal, are associated with a lower A. The meaning of each term of (3.32) will be discussed in greater detail in section 3.4.

The inverse of the marginal efficiency of abatement $\partial Q/\partial A=\zeta$ is the marginal abatement cost. The term $\overline{Q}/\zeta$ in (3.32) is simply the initial endowment of Q, valued in terms of marginal abatement cost. So $\overline{Q}/\zeta$ is the cost that *would* have to be paid to provide this amount of Q entirely through abatement. But since $\overline{Q}$ is free initial environmental quality, this suggests to interpret $\overline{Q}/\zeta$ as *income in the form of abatement expenditure saved.*

Substitution from (3.32) into (3.31) yields the social return on capital

$$r = \alpha - \frac{\xi}{\zeta}. \tag{3.33}$$

which is constant. By (3.9), the consumption growth rate then equals

$$\hat{X} = \frac{1}{\sigma}\left(\alpha - \frac{\xi}{\zeta} - \rho\right).$$

Hence a necessary and sufficient condition for the economy to reach the environment phase is that $\zeta>\xi/(\alpha-\rho)$. This condition is most likely to hold if abatement is highly efficient, capital is only little polluting, and the productivity of capital is significantly greater than the rate of time preference.

The growth rate of capital exceeds that of consumption:

---

[26] If ζ is "too" small (see next page for a more precise statement) it may occur that $r=\rho$ before $\lambda=0$, and the environment phase is never reached. Note, for instance, that if abatement was completely inefficient ($\zeta=0$), λ would never vanish in finite time.

$$\hat{K} = \frac{r-\rho}{\sigma}\left(1+\frac{\overline{Q}}{r\xi K}\right) > \hat{X} \tag{3.34}$$

(see appendix D). This divergence can be explained by the fact that in the environment phase the capital stock does not only have to ensure a production level sufficiently high to sustain consumption and continued investment but, in addition to that, to allow for abatement activities. The new expenditure category drives a wedge between the rates of consumption growth and capital accumulation. This wedge becomes smaller the more $\hat{A}$ approaches $\hat{X}$. In the long run, $\hat{K}$ and $\hat{A}$ converge to $\hat{X}$ (see appendices D and E).

Finally, substitution from (3.32) into (3.25) reveals that, in optimum, environmental quality is proportional to consumption:[27]

$$Q = \left(\frac{1-\beta}{\beta}\zeta\right)^{1/\sigma} X, \tag{3.35}$$

from which it follows that $\hat{Q} = \hat{X} > 0$. So with a declining Q in the development phase and a rising Q in the environment phase ***this model produces an Environmental Kuznets Curve***. This inverted U-curve for pollution, together with the corresponding abatement curve, is depicted in figure 3.3.

The bold lines represent the pollution and abatement curves, drawn against consumption.[28] This implies that pollution and abatement can be reduced to functions of the consumption. In fact, the phase diagram of figure 3.1 shows that along the optimal trajectory in the development phase there exists a one-to-one relationship between consumption and capital, and since $P=\xi K$ in this phase, pollution can be transformed into a function of consumption. It is increasing in X but strictly concave from below due to the rising consumption-capital-ratio.[29] If abatement is too inefficient, the

---

[27] This result can also be obtained directly from (3.30) by setting $\lambda=\psi=0$.

[28] The dotted extensions of the straight pollution and abatement curves to the vertical axis indicate the respective *hypothetical* vertical intercepts.

[29] As can be seen from the phase diagram in fig. 3.1, capital increases with consumption along the optimal trajectory if $K(0)$ is smaller than the stationary-state capital stock $\tilde{K}$. Therefore the pollution curve in fig. 3.3 rises with X. The curvature of P in the development phase is a result of the fact that X/K declines as the economy approaches the stationary state. Positive growth requires $\dot{K} = \alpha K - X > 0$ or $\alpha > X/K$. In the stationary state, however, $\dot{K} = \alpha K - X = 0$ or $\alpha = X/K$, implying that X/K rises in the course of growth. This means that K and therefore also P increases underproportionally with consumption, hence the concavity of the pollution curve.

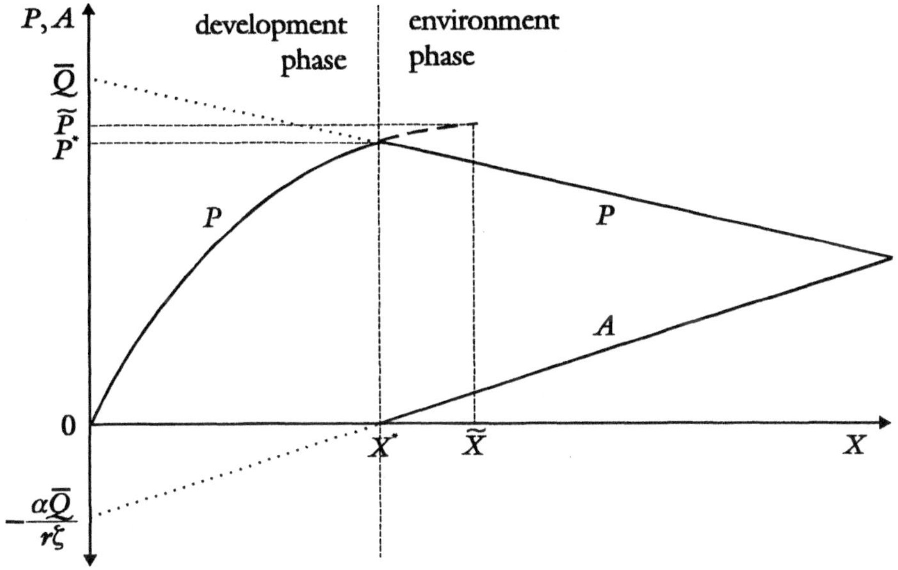

Figure 3.3: Inverted U-curve for pollution and abatement curve

economy converges to a stationary state (see section 3.1.3) associated with the finite levels $\tilde{X}$ and $\tilde{P}$ of consumption and pollution, respectively.

However, if $\lambda=0$ before $X=\tilde{X}$ (recall that this requires $\zeta>\xi/(\alpha-\rho)$), the economy escapes the fate of the asymptotic zero-growth equilibrium by entering the environment phase. $X^*<\tilde{X}$ is the threshold consumption level at which $\lambda=A=0$, and P^* is the corresponding level of pollution. In this case P peaks at $X=X^*$. As consumption continues to grow beyond X^* pollution decreases linearly in X. This linearity follows from (3.35) and $P=\overline{Q}-Q$.

Abatement in the development phase is zero. Based on appendix D where capital is shown to be a linear function of consumption in the environment phase (see (D5)), appendix E derives the following abatement function:

$$A=\Delta X-\frac{\alpha\overline{Q}}{r\zeta} \tag{3.36}$$

where

$$\Delta\equiv\left[1+\left(\frac{1-\beta}{\beta}\zeta\right)^{1/\sigma}\frac{1}{\zeta}\right]\left(1+\frac{\xi}{\zeta}\frac{\sigma}{\rho+r\sigma-r}\right)-1$$

is the strictly positive, constant slope (see (E1)). Thus also abatement is a linear function of consumption. The curve A "takes off" from the horizontal axis at $X=X^*$; this horizontal intercept is found by setting $A=0$ in (3.36) and solving for

$$X^* = \frac{\alpha\overline{Q}}{r\zeta\Delta} > 0. \tag{3.37}$$

(3.36) and (3.37) shed some light on the effect of parameter changes on the abatement curve. For instance, the value of $\overline{Q}$ has no impact on the slope of this curve, only on the consumption level X^* at which abatement is first carried out. A rising $\overline{Q}$ thus leads to a parallel downward shift of the abatement curve, thereby increasing X^*, prolonging the development phase and raising P^*. More relationships can be found through differentiation, however, they are of no importance here.

3.3.4 The Post-Environment Phase

The proportionality of Q and X in (3.35) implies that if Q had no upper bound $\overline{Q}$, environmental quality would get infinitely high in infinite time. But since $Q = \overline{Q} - P$, pollution would become negative. In order to handle this problem, the nonnegativity restriction on P has been included into the Hamiltonian (3.26). Since $\lambda=0$ once abatement is positive, (3.30) can be solved for

$$\psi = \frac{(1-\beta)\zeta Q^{-\sigma} - \beta X^{-\sigma}}{\zeta} \geq 0. \tag{3.38}$$

A positive ψ indicates that the nonnegativity restriction on P has taken effect and that, as a result, the marginal utilities of consumption and abatement are no longer equal. Consumption continues to rise, whereas environmental quality cannot be increased any further through additional abatement efforts. While $\lambda>0$ and $\psi=0$ mark an economy's development phase, and $\lambda=0$ and $\psi=0$ characterise its environment phase, the combination of $\lambda=0$ and $\psi>0$ defines a third phase of economic growth. It may be titled *post-environment* phase. Since in this third phase $P=\xi K-\zeta A=0$, the new abatement function must read

$$A = \frac{\xi}{\zeta} K. \tag{3.39}$$

Abatement of this amount keeps the quality of the environment at its highest possible level $\overline{Q}$ while the economy continues growing. To obtain the rate at which consumption grows in the post-environment phase, the return on capital is needed. Substituting from (3.38) and (3.27) into (3.31) yields

$$r = \alpha - \frac{1-\beta}{\beta}\xi\left(\frac{X}{\overline{Q}}\right)^{\sigma} + \frac{\xi}{\zeta}\frac{(1-\beta)\zeta\overline{Q}^{-\sigma} - \beta X^{-\sigma}}{\beta X^{-\sigma}} = \alpha - \frac{\xi}{\zeta}$$

which is constant and identical with (3.33). Hence neither the return on capital nor the growth rate of consumption are affected by the economy's entrance into the new phase of growth.

Upon substitution from (3.39), the equation of motion of capital reads $\dot{K} = (\alpha - \xi / \zeta)K - X = rK - X$. With X growing at the rate $\hat{X} = (r - \rho) / \sigma$ it is not hard to show that K grows at the same rate[30]. Finally, it follows from (3.39) that $\hat{A} = \hat{K}$. So in the post-environment phase, growth is balanced.

Whether the post-environment phase has a real-world counterpart is not easy to say. It may be a purely theoretical construct, resulting from the assumptions of environmental preferences, constant pollution coefficient, constant marginal efficiencies of abatement, and an upper bound to environmental quality. The post-environment phase hinges in particular on the available abatement technology. As already noted earlier, in many cases pollution abatement will be insufficient to reduce emissions to levels close to zero, and a post-environment phase will not be reachable unless the inputs and processes giving rise to pollution can be replaced entirely.

On the other hand, there are pollutants which are considered so harmful that the products which contain them have been banned completely in richer countries, and substituted by others. Examples include various pesticides such as DDT [Tietenberg (1992), p. 527], or aerosol propellants, industrial foams, air conditioning systems and refrigerators containing CFCs. In other words, the optimal levels of these pollutants are corner solutions which are rendered possible through non-prohibitively high marginal avoidance costs at the boundary.

---

[30] This result can be proved by adapting the equations (C1) and (C2) of appendix C, and reworking the same steps.

3.4 Is Environmental Quality a Luxury?

The popularity that environmental protection issues have gained among the broader public primarily in rich countries is of rather recent date. This has given rise to a particular view: "environmental commodities are often thought to be luxury goods" [Dasgupta and Mäler (1994), p. 5] that only the rich can or want to afford [see also Grossman, Krueger and Laity (1994), p. 2]. The purpose of this section is to critically assess this view, and to reflect on its implications for Environmental Kuznets Curves.

3.4.1 Essential and Necessary Goods

Before entering the discussion, two terms that are important in this context need to be defined properly in order to avoid later misunderstandings. An input is called *essential* if it is indispensable for the production of a positive output, or if its marginal productivity is unbounded when the input is reduced to zero, or both. Correspondingly, a good is called *essential* if it is required for any positive utility level, or if its marginal utility is unbounded when its consumption tends to zero, or both.

On the other hand, a good is *necessary* by definition if its income elasticity of demand is less than one at a given income level. This means that if, with increasing income, the budget share of a good declines, prices being held constant, it is called necessary. The opposite of a necessary good is a *luxury* good. As will be shown later, an essential good can be a necessity, or a luxury, or neither of them. An inessential good will - at least over a certain income range - be a luxury. The following example should suffice to illustrate this distinction.

It seems quite plausible to expect people to spend their first units of income on food in order not to starve, rather than dividing it between food and cleaning up a polluted lake, even if that means the death of the lake. In such a case one would call food *essential* because without it no positive utility level could be attained, and if the people can do without the lake, the latter is *inessential*. Cleaning up the lake can wait until more income is available, and when it is ultimately done it is a *luxury* at least initially because the budget share of cleanup expenditure rises from zero to a positive value.

Not saving the lake becomes a questionable strategy if the lake is the only source of food. Here, also some minimum quality of the environment is *essential*, namely for the production of food. In that case, people may be caught in a poverty trap: not eating means starving today, not cleaning up the lake means starving tomorrow. Many natural-resource-based subsistence economies in developing countries face this dilemma, and most models of this study are certainly inappropriate to analyse their environmental problems because it has been abstracted from the impact of pollution on production. Only the chapter 2 model in which environmental quality enters the production function may be suitable for this purpose. But even if production is independent of Q it is not difficult to identify environmental goods that are clearly essential: the absence of lethal radioactivity is a precondition for survival, and for a positive utility level.

Note that nothing has yet been said or implied as regards the necessity of a cleaner lake. Perhaps a minimum of water quality is sufficient for food production, but after an initial cleanup phase people discover how much they enjoy a clean lake for swimming, so they spend an ever increasing share of their rising income on improving the water quality. The quality of the environment would then be both essential and a luxury. This is to emphasise that a good which is essential for survival or production is not automatically a necessary good in the economic sense.

3.4.2 Engel Curves

The evolution of demand in response to changing per capita income has been investigated in depth by many authors. The most prominent study was published by Engel (1857) in which he put forward an empirical law, today referred to as Engel's law, which states that the proportion of income spent on food declines as income rises, qualifying food as a necessity. Similar laws have also been formulated for other categories of expenditure [e.g. Houthakker (1957)]. The resulting Engel curves are thus mostly nonlinear. An Engel curve is a graph of the demand for one good as a function of income, with all prices being held constant [Varian (1993), p. 97]. Figure 3.4 depicts typical Engel curves for (a) an (essential) necessary good N and (b) for an (inessential) luxury good L.[31] The Engel curve for a good with an

[31] Engel curves with a *negative* slope over some income range are also possible. However, the underlying class of inferior goods is of no interest here, so their graphical representation has been omitted.

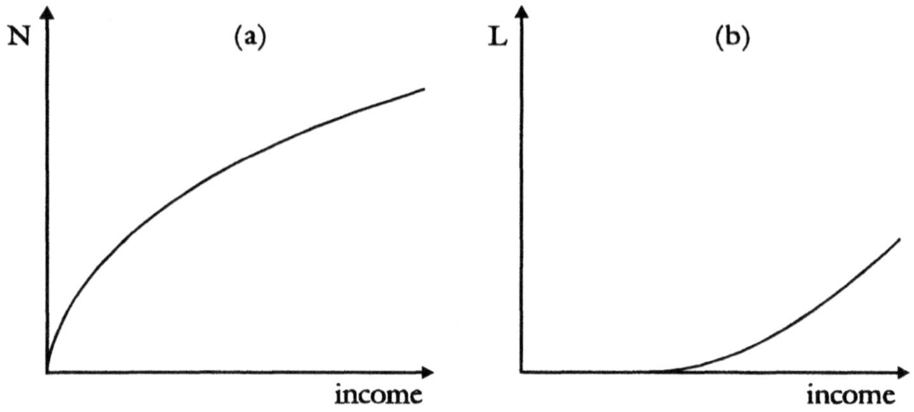

Figure 3.4: Engel curves for (a) a necessary good and (b) a luxury good

income elasticity of demand of unity would be a straight line through the origin: income and expenditure for that good are strictly proportional.

A comparison of the Engel curve (b) for the luxury good with the abatement curve in figure 3.2 reveals a striking similarity. In both cases the curves take off from the horizontal axes only after some threshold income level has been passed, and the new expenditure categories reduce the budget shares of the respective other good. One may be tempted to conjecture that environmental quality which is provided through abatement is inessential and a typical luxury good indeed.

3.4.3 Preferences, Prices and Technology

Whether a good belongs to the class of luxury goods, or to the necessities, or to none of both, is a matter of preferences and the income level, but not of the good itself or its properties. Provided that the utility function and the income level are known, each of its arguments can be assigned to a category. When drawing an Engel curve the influence of changing prices on demand is eliminated by holding all prices fixed, so that the curve only reflects preferences, and not technological factors which would otherwise enter through the prices.

Having said this, it is immediately obvious that figure 3.2 does not depict an Engel curve for abatement. If particular preferences are conditional for environmental quality to be a luxury, but no such preferences have previously been specified, why should the abatement curve, of all the values the income elasticity of demand for a better environment may take, reflect an elasticity greater than one? Clearly this would be a mere coincidence. Therefore, the particular shape and position of the abatement curve are determined by factors other than preferences, and to identify those will be the objective of this and the following section.

A first step in investigating what the abatement curve in figure 3.2 actually distinguishes from an Engel curve is to check whether prices have really been held constant, and if not, what that would change. The numeraire good is consumption, so the price of X equals unity. The price of an extra unit of environmental quality equals the marginal cost of its provision, given that there are no profits involved. The provision of environmental quality requires abatement. Marginal abatement cost is the inverse of the marginal efficiency of abatement, so the "price" of an extra unit of Q equals $(\partial Q / \partial A)^{-1}$. For arbitrary functions of Q this will not be constant. In the chapter 2 flow model, for instance, $\partial^2 Q / \partial A^2 < 0$ and $\partial^2 Q / \partial A \partial K > 0$. In such cases one has to fix $\partial Q / \partial A$ artificially at a positive, finite level, say $\partial Q / \partial A \equiv a^{-1}$, to eliminate the effect of changing prices on the shape of the abatement curve.

The two central conditions of the model which describe the position and shape of the abatement curve are (3.11) and (3.13). The former determines the horizontal intercept of the curve, the latter its slope. With the fixed price of environmental quality introduced above, these conditions read

$$\lambda = \frac{\partial U}{\partial X} - \frac{1}{a}\frac{\partial U}{\partial Q} \tag{3.40}$$

$$\dot{A} = a^2 \frac{\partial^2 U}{\partial X^2}\left(\frac{\partial^2 U}{\partial Q^2}\right)^{-1} \dot{X} - a\frac{\partial Q}{\partial K}\dot{K} \tag{3.41}$$

Not much has changed. If the abatement curve was drawn again, it would still have a positive horizonal intercept, and the positive dependence of A on K has also "survived" the elimination of price effects. The new abatement curve would not differ significantly from the previous one. Holding prices constant is obviously not the only adjustment to be made to obtain an Engel curve for abatement. The question about the cause of the particular position and shape of the abatement curve in figure 3.2 remains. If it is produced neither by preferences nor by technology, the cause must be related to a particularity of environmental quality itself.

3.4.4 Why Environmental Quality Is Not An Ordinary Good

Ordinary consumer goods have to be produced to come into existence, whereas certain a amount of environmental quality is supplied for free by nature. This free initial endowment has been denoted by $\overline{Q}$. As long as there is still enough left of it there is no need for pollution abatement, and all income that is not saved can be spent on consumption. This explains why abatement is not essential in early stages of economic development, even though environmental quality itself is essential according to the limit expression (2.6).

The effect of $\overline{Q}$ on the model can perhaps be compared with a free distribution of some food to every household. The graph of expenditure for food, drawn against income, would have a positive horizontal intercept because buying food would not be essential anymore. Yet this would not turn food into a luxury, nor would one call the expenditure curve an Engel curve.

Therefore, as a second adjustment necessary to turn the abatement curve into an Engel curve for abatement, the distortion created by $\overline{Q}$ needs to be eliminated by setting $\overline{Q} \equiv 0$. As a consequence, an optimally chosen A will be positive at every moment to ensure that $Q>0$ because Q is essential; λ in (3.11) vanishes, and with it the entire development phase.

Apart from $\overline{Q}$ there is yet another particularity through which environmental quality differs from ordinary goods. A marginal unit of capital in production reduces Q by $-\partial Q / \partial K$, and a marginal unit of abatment restores $\partial Q / \partial A = a^{-1}$ of it. For Q to remain exactly constant it must hold that

$$\dot{A} = -a\frac{\partial Q}{\partial K}\dot{K}.$$

So the second term on the right-hand side of (3.41) is the amount of abatement necessary to ***maintain*** a given level of environmental quality, hence to offset the environmental impact of current economic activity. This has no equivalent among ordinary goods, and it inflates abatement spending, thereby distorting the budget proportions. To correct this second distortion, the link between K and Q needs to be removed by setting $\partial Q/\partial K \equiv 0$. In consequence, (3.41) reduces to

$$\dot{A} = a^2\frac{\partial^2 U}{\partial X^2}\left(\frac{\partial^2 U}{\partial Q^2}\right)^{-1}\dot{X} \tag{3.42}$$

with $\overline{Q} \equiv \partial Q / \partial K \equiv 0$. Now abatement is now only a function of consumption, and the influence of functions other than the utility function is suppressed. With nonsaved income or total expenditure given by $I = X + A$, changes in abatement can be expressed as a function of changes in I:

$$\dot{A} = \frac{a^2 \frac{\partial^2 U}{\partial X^2}\left(\frac{\partial^2 U}{\partial Q^2}\right)^{-1}}{1 + a^2 \frac{\partial^2 U}{\partial X^2}\left(\frac{\partial^2 U}{\partial Q^2}\right)^{-1}} \dot{I}.$$

Together with (3.40) this equation fully determines A. Its graph is the Engel curve for abatement. If $\dot{A} / \dot{I} = dA / dI$ increases with I, implying that $(\partial^2 U / \partial X^2)/(\partial^2 U / \partial Q^2)$ rises, then environmental quality is a luxury. On the other hand, if dA/dI declines, Q is a necessity, and finally, if dA/dI remains constant, preferences are homothetic[32], leading to a linear Engel curve through the origin. In this special case environmental quality is neither a luxury nor a necessity.

3.5 Concluding Remarks

This chapter has dealt with the effect of environmental preferences on the socially optimal growth behaviour of an economy, and on the changes in environmental quality that accompany it. A potential limit to growth has been identified. It is neither rooted in natural resource scarcity, nor in negative production effects of pollution, but solely in the household preference structure which restricts the possibilities of trading off increases in consumption against environmental deterioration. One might speak of a social limit to growth [Hirsch (1976)].

---

32 A function $\Psi(x,y)$ is said to be homothetic if $(\partial\Psi/\partial x)/(\partial\Psi/\partial y)$ is constant for any constant x/y. This is the case if $\Psi = \psi[\Phi(x,y)]$ where $\psi'(\Phi) \neq 0$, and Φ is homogeneous of any degree. Since homogeneity implies that $(\partial\Phi/\partial x)/(\partial\Phi/\partial y)$ is constant for any given x/y, the same holds for

$$\frac{\partial\Psi / \partial x}{\partial\Psi / \partial y} = \frac{\psi'(\Phi)\partial\Phi / \partial x}{\psi'(\Phi)\partial\Phi / \partial y} = \frac{\partial\Phi / \partial x}{\partial\Phi / \partial y}.$$

Therefore, all homogeneous functions are homothetic, but not vice versa. Relevant in the above context is that homothetic functions produce linear expansion paths.

Even if pollution abatement is possible, there is no guarantee that it will keep the economy from ending up in a zero-growth equilibrium. As long as the marginal efficiency of abatement declines relative to the marginal pollution intensity of capital in the course of growth, there is no way to overcome the economy's tendency to converge to a stationary state. This narrows down the class of environmental quality functions, or abatement technologies, compatible with optimal steady-state growth at a positive rate.

For environmental quality to recover in optimum as a result of abatement efforts, no particular condition needs to be fulfilled by the marginal pollution intensity of capital, provided that the households have environmental preferences, and that the efficiency of abatement is constant. After an initial phase of rising pollution levels, this is sufficient to produce an Environmental Kuznets Curve.

The models suggest the existence of a hierarchic demand for abatement, according to which those types of pollution will be abated first which have directly harmful effects, but also those which can be abated at relatively low cost. So a real problem seems to be posed by pollutants which are neither cheap to avoid, nor cause visible or perceptible damage. This may be the case with pollution that builds up over very long periods of time, or that enters the food chain or other biological cycles only with significant time lags.

Not only preferences and technology determine when, or at which income level, resources are first allocated to the control of a certain kind of pollution. Another important determinant is the initial amount of environmental quality provided for free by nature. The greater this "endowment of absent pollution" is, ceteris paribus, the later will it become efficient to abate the respective pollutant. The resulting abatement expenditure function does not start in the origin, but has a positive horizontal intercept which seems to have given rise to the widespread belief that environmental quality is a luxury good.

However, the present chapter has shown that the abatement expenditure curve is no Engel curve for abatement, and that it cannot be inferred in a straight-forward manner from a positive horizontal intercept of the former on the preferences for environmental quality. On a more general level this means that the rather recent emergence of environmental issues in political and research agendas need not be the result of the people's preferences, but rather of the depletion of free environmental quality up to a point which is increasingly considered unacceptable and alarming by the broader public, raising a positive demand for pollution abatement efforts.

Appendix

Appendix A: Concavity of the Generalised Hamiltonian

The generalised Hamiltonian $\mathcal{H} = U[X, Q(A,K)] + \mu(\alpha K - X - A) + \lambda A$ consists of the objective function $U(\cdot)$ and two linear constraints with their respective multipliers. Due to the linearity of the constraints it suffices to prove the concavity of the objective function with respect to the controls X and A, and the state variable K. The proof is further simplified by the linear separability of utility which implies that all cross partial derivatives of $U(\cdot)$ involving X equal zero (see (3.1)). The Hessian determinant reads

$$|\mathrm{H}| = \begin{vmatrix} \partial^2 U / \partial X^2 & 0 & 0 \\ 0 & \partial^2 U / \partial A^2 & \partial^2 U / \partial A \partial K \\ 0 & \partial^2 U / \partial A \partial K & \partial^2 U / \partial K^2 \end{vmatrix}$$

the principal minors of which are

$$|\mathrm{H}_1| = \partial^2 U / \partial X^2 < 0$$

$$|\mathrm{H}_2| = \begin{vmatrix} \partial^2 U / \partial X^2 & 0 \\ 0 & \partial^2 U / \partial A^2 \end{vmatrix} = \frac{\partial^2 U}{\partial X^2}\frac{\partial^2 U}{\partial A^2} = \frac{\partial^2 U}{\partial X^2}\left[\frac{\partial^2 U}{\partial Q^2}\left(\frac{\partial Q}{\partial A}\right)^2 + \frac{\partial U}{\partial Q}\frac{\partial^2 Q}{\partial A^2}\right] \geq 0$$

$$|\mathrm{H}_3| = |\mathrm{H}| = \frac{\partial^2 U}{\partial X^2}\left[\frac{\partial^2 U}{\partial A^2}\frac{\partial^2 U}{\partial K^2} - \left(\frac{\partial^2 U}{\partial A \partial K}\right)^2\right]$$

$$= \frac{\partial^2 U}{\partial X^2}\left\{\left[\frac{\partial^2 U}{\partial Q^2}\left(\frac{\partial Q}{\partial A}\right)^2 + \frac{\partial U}{\partial Q}\frac{\partial^2 Q}{\partial A^2}\right]\left[\frac{\partial^2 U}{\partial Q^2}\left(\frac{\partial Q}{\partial K}\right)^2 + \frac{\partial U}{\partial Q}\frac{\partial^2 Q}{\partial K^2}\right] - \left(\frac{\partial^2 U}{\partial Q^2}\frac{\partial Q}{\partial A}\frac{\partial Q}{\partial K}\right)^2\right\}$$

$$= \frac{\partial^2 U}{\partial X^2}\left[\frac{\partial^2 U}{\partial Q^2}\left(\frac{\partial Q}{\partial A}\right)^2 \frac{\partial U}{\partial Q}\frac{\partial^2 Q}{\partial K^2} + \frac{\partial^2 U}{\partial Q^2}\left(\frac{\partial Q}{\partial K}\right)^2 \frac{\partial U}{\partial Q}\frac{\partial^2 Q}{\partial A^2} + \left(\frac{\partial U}{\partial Q}\right)^2 \frac{\partial^2 Q}{\partial A^2}\frac{\partial^2 Q}{\partial K^2}\right] \leq 0$$

The signs of the partial derivatives are stated in (2.5) and (3.2). The alternating signs of the successive principal minors, starting with a negative value, prove that $\mathcal{H}$ is at least concave. If all inequalities are strict, $\mathcal{H}$ is strictly concave.

Appendix B: Global Saddle-Point Stability in the Development Phase

The system of differential equations describing the dynamics of the economy in the development phase is given by $\dot{K} = \alpha K - X$ and $\dot{X} = X(r-\rho)/\sigma$. Since nonlinearity can enter the system through r (see (3.10)) it needs to be linearised around its equilibrium. The linear approximation system reads

$$\begin{bmatrix} \dot{K} \\ \dot{X} \end{bmatrix} = \Lambda \begin{bmatrix} K - \tilde{K} \\ X - \tilde{X} \end{bmatrix}$$

(a tilde marks an equilibrium value) with the coefficient matrix

$$\Lambda = \begin{bmatrix} \partial \dot{K} / \partial K & \partial \dot{K} / \partial X \\ \partial \dot{X} / \partial K & \partial \dot{X} / \partial X \end{bmatrix} = \begin{bmatrix} \alpha & -1 \\ \dfrac{X}{\sigma} \dfrac{\partial r}{\partial K} & \dfrac{r-\rho}{\sigma} + \dfrac{X}{\sigma} \dfrac{\partial r}{\partial X} \end{bmatrix}$$

In a stationary state $\dot{K} = \dot{X} = 0$. The trivial solution $X=K=0$ can be excluded since $X=0$ it would violate the transversality condition (3.7), and $K=0$ implies $X=0$ as can be seen by setting $\dot{K} = 0$. The nontrivial solution is given by $\alpha K=X$ and $r=\rho$ with $X>0$ and $K>0$. The Jacobian determinant $|\Lambda|$ evaluated at this nontrivial equilibrium equals

$$|\Lambda| = \begin{vmatrix} \alpha & -1 \\ \dfrac{X}{\sigma} \dfrac{\partial r}{\partial K} & \dfrac{X}{\sigma} \dfrac{\partial r}{\partial X} \end{vmatrix} = \frac{X}{\sigma} \left(\alpha \frac{\partial r}{\partial X} + \frac{\partial r}{\partial K} \right) < 0$$

The sign follows from (3.12) which states that $\partial r/\partial X<0$ and $\partial r/\partial K<0$. It implies that the two roots are nonzero and have opposite signs, so that the linear approximation system is globally saddle-point stable. According to the Liapunov theorem [Takayama (1994), p. 414] the original system must therefore be *locally* saddle-point stable.

The system has two equilibria both of which are feasible, but only the saddle-point equilibrium meets the transversality condition (3.7). Therefore, it is the unique optimum. Since the generalised Hamiltonian is concave (see appendix A), any optimum, provided it exists, must be global. It follows that the optimally steered economy must converge to this unique global optimum. In other words, the system is *globally* saddle-point stable.

Appendix C: Boundedness of Intertemporal Utility

Given the assumptions made, the growth rate of consumption *in absence of pollution* equals $\hat{X} = (\alpha - \rho)/\sigma$ which is constant. Since a pollution level of zero cannot a priori be excluded, a parametric restriction must be imposed that ensures that welfare

$$\int_0^\infty \frac{X^{1-\sigma} - 1}{1-\sigma} \exp(-\rho t) dt$$

is bounded. Since $X(t) = X(0)\exp\left(\frac{\alpha - \rho}{\sigma} t\right)$, welfare can be written as

$$\int_0^\infty \frac{X(0)^{1-\sigma}}{1-\sigma} \exp\left[\frac{(\alpha-\rho)(1-\sigma)}{\sigma} t - \rho t\right] dt - \int_0^\infty \frac{\exp(-\rho t)}{1-\sigma} dt$$

$$= \frac{X(0)^{1-\sigma}}{1-\sigma} \int_0^\infty \exp\left[\frac{(\alpha-\rho)(1-\sigma)}{\sigma} t - \rho t\right] dt + \frac{1}{\rho(1-\sigma)}$$

which may be unbounded unless the assumption $\frac{(\alpha-\rho)(1-\sigma)}{\sigma} < \rho$ is made.

Appendix D: Capital Growth in the Environment Phase

To simplify the notation let

$$u \equiv 1 + [(1-\beta)/\beta]^{1/\sigma} \zeta^{1/\sigma - 1} \quad \text{and} \quad v \equiv \overline{Q}/\zeta.$$

The abatement function (3.32) then reads

$$A = (u-1)X + \frac{\xi}{\zeta} K - v. \tag{D1}$$

Substituting from this into $\dot{K} = \alpha K - X - A$ and recalling that $r = \alpha - \xi/\zeta$ (see (3.33)) gives

$$\dot{K} = \alpha K - X - (u-1)X - \frac{\xi}{\zeta} K + v = rK - uX + v, \tag{D2}$$

the solution of which is

$$K = \exp(rt)\left\{K(0) - \int_0^t [uX(s) - v]\exp(-rs)ds\right\}. \tag{D3}$$

Two replacements can be made. First, since r is constant in the environment phase and $X = X(0)\exp[(r-\rho)t/\sigma]$ one can write

$$\int_0^t uX(s)\exp(-rs)ds = uX(0)\int_0^t \exp\left(\frac{r-\rho-r\sigma}{\sigma}s\right)ds$$
$$= \frac{\sigma uX(0)}{r-\rho-r\sigma}\left[\exp\left(\frac{r-\rho-r\sigma}{\sigma}t\right)-1\right]$$

Second, $\int_0^t v\exp(-rs)ds = -\frac{v}{r}[\exp(-rt)-1]$. Hence (D3) is equivalent to

$$K = \exp(rt)\left\{K(0) - \frac{\sigma uX(0)}{r-\rho-r\sigma}\left[\exp\left(\frac{r-\rho-r\sigma}{\sigma}t\right)-1\right] - \frac{v}{r}[\exp(-rt)-1]\right\} \tag{D4}$$

Upon substitution from (3.27), the transversality condition (3.7) reads

$$\lim_{t\to\infty} \beta X^{-\sigma}K\exp(-\rho t) = \lim_{t\to\infty} \beta X(0)^{-\sigma}\exp[-\sigma(r-\rho)t/\sigma]K\exp(-\rho t)$$
$$= \beta X(0)^{-\sigma}\lim_{t\to\infty} K\exp(-rt) = 0$$

where K can be replaced by (D4):

$$\beta X(0)^{-\sigma}\lim_{t\to\infty}\left\{K(0) - \frac{\sigma uX(0)}{r-\rho-r\sigma}\left[\exp\left(\frac{r-\rho-r\sigma}{\sigma}t\right)-1\right] - \frac{v}{r}[\exp(-rt)-1]\right\}$$
$$= \beta X(0)^{-\sigma}\left[K(0) + \frac{\sigma uX(0)}{r-\rho-r\sigma} + \frac{v}{r}\right]$$
$$-\beta X(0)^{-\sigma}\lim_{t\to\infty}\left[\frac{\sigma uX(0)}{r-\rho-r\sigma}\exp\left(\frac{r-\rho-r\sigma}{\sigma}t\right) + \frac{v}{r}\exp(-rt)\right]$$
$$= 0$$

The limit term converges to zero because both exponents are negative. This is obvious for the second. The negativity of the first exponent follows from the bounded utility assumption (3.24) and the fact that $r=\alpha-\xi/\zeta<\alpha$:

$$\frac{r(1-\sigma)-\rho}{\sigma}=\frac{(r-\rho)(1-\sigma)-\sigma\rho}{\sigma}=\frac{(r-\rho)(1-\sigma)}{\sigma}-\rho<0$$

The vanishing of the limit term means that

$$\beta X(0)^{-\sigma}\left[K(0)+\frac{\sigma u X(0)}{r-\rho-r\sigma}+\frac{v}{r}\right]=0$$

which implies that $K(0)=-\dfrac{\sigma u X(0)}{r-\rho-r\sigma}-\dfrac{v}{r}$. Substitution into (D4) gives

$$\begin{aligned}K&=\exp(rt)\left[-\frac{\sigma u X(0)}{r-\rho-r\sigma}\exp\left(\frac{r-\rho-r\sigma}{\sigma}t\right)-\frac{v}{r}\exp(-rt)\right]\\&=-\frac{\sigma u X(0)}{r-\rho-r\sigma}\exp\left(\frac{r-\rho}{\sigma}t\right)-\frac{v}{r}\\&=\frac{\sigma u X}{\rho+r\sigma-r}-\frac{v}{r}\end{aligned}\qquad\text{(D5)}$$

which can be solved for consumption:

$$X=\left(K+\frac{v}{r}\right)\left(\frac{\rho+r\sigma-r}{\sigma u}\right)$$

Using this expression, (D2) becomes

$$\begin{aligned}\dot{K}&=rK-uX+v=rK-u\left(K+\frac{v}{r}\right)\left(\frac{\rho+r\sigma-r}{\sigma u}\right)+v\\&=r\left(K+\frac{v}{r}\right)+\left(\frac{r-\rho}{\sigma}-r\right)\left(K+\frac{v}{r}\right)=\frac{r-\rho}{\sigma}\left(K+\frac{v}{r}\right)\end{aligned}$$

Division by K finally yields the capital growth rate

$$\hat{K}=\frac{r-\rho}{\sigma}\left(1+\frac{v}{rK}\right)=\frac{r-\rho}{\sigma}\left(1+\frac{\overline{Q}}{r\zeta K}\right)$$

which is strictly positive and asymptotically converges to

$$\lim_{t\to\infty}\hat{K}=\lim_{t\to\infty}\left[\frac{r-\rho}{\sigma}\left(1+\frac{v}{rK}\right)\right]=\frac{r-\rho}{\sigma}+\lim_{t\to\infty}\frac{r-\rho}{\sigma}\frac{v}{rK}=\frac{r-\rho}{\sigma}=\hat{X}\,.$$

Appendix E: Abatement in the Environment Phase

Define again

$$u \equiv 1 + [(1-\beta)/\beta]^{1/\sigma} \zeta^{1/\sigma - 1} \quad \text{and} \quad v \equiv \overline{Q}/\zeta.$$

According to (D1) and (D5)

$$A = (u-1)X + \frac{\xi}{\zeta}K - v \quad \text{and} \quad K = \frac{\sigma u X}{\rho + r\sigma - r} - \frac{v}{r}.$$

Substitution of the latter into the former gives

$$A = \left(u - 1 + \frac{\xi}{\zeta}\frac{\sigma u}{\rho + r\sigma - r}\right)X - v\left(1 + \frac{\xi}{r\zeta}\right) \tag{E1}$$

where $u - 1 + \frac{\xi}{\zeta}\frac{\sigma u}{\rho + r\sigma - r} = \left[1 + \left(\frac{1-\beta}{\beta}\zeta\right)^{1/\sigma}\frac{1}{\zeta}\right]\left(1 + \frac{\xi}{\zeta}\frac{\sigma}{\rho + r\sigma - r}\right) - 1$

and $1 + \frac{\xi}{r\zeta} = 1 + \frac{\xi}{\alpha\zeta - \xi} = \frac{\alpha\zeta}{\alpha\zeta - \xi} = \frac{\alpha}{\alpha - \xi/\zeta} = \frac{\alpha}{r}.$

Dividing both sides of (E1) by X, and letting time go to infinity shows that

$$\lim_{t\to\infty}\frac{A}{X} = \left(u - 1 + \frac{\xi}{\zeta}\frac{\sigma u}{\rho + r\sigma - r}\right) - \lim_{t\to\infty}\frac{v}{X}\left(1 + \frac{\xi}{r\zeta}\right) = u - 1 + \frac{\xi}{\zeta}\frac{\sigma u}{\rho + r\sigma - r}$$

which is constant. Therefore $\hat{A}$ asymptotically converges to $\hat{X}$.

Chapter 4 Income Distribution, Desired Environmental Policy, and Green Middle-Class Elitism

... the ordinary man - particularly among the middle classes - is attracted by the antigrowth school, which enables him to demonstrate his moral fiber and aesthetic sensibility at no cost. W. Beckerman[33]

The last two chapters have focused on the relationship between per capita income and the *socially optimal* abatement and pollution levels in particularly simplified, stylised model economies. Many factors that may play an important role in the determination of the *actual* pollution level have so far been neglected, such as household characteristics, the structure of the economy, the political and institutional framework, the existence and power of interest groups, or psychological aspects. To discuss the role of these factors will be the concern of the present and the following two chapters. For this purpose, the models that have been used in chapter 2 and 3 are not detailed and realistic enough, and will therefore be modified step by step.

The overriding objective of this chapter will be the analysis of the relationship between income distribution and public support of environmental policy. Distributional inequality implies a differentiation of households in terms of their individual disposable income or budget. This means that the concept of the representative household is not applicable anymore.

Second, the concept of the social planner will also be given up. Instead, the different economic agents will maximise their own objective functions in a decentralised manner. This reflects reality much better than the idealised approach taken up to now because self-interest becomes the driving force of economic activity rather than a striving for social optimality.

The third major modification of the model will consist in the introduction of a government. Its necessity and role will briefly be explained in the following section before turning to the possible impact of distributional aspects on the particular environmental policy that the households want their government to pursue.

---

33 Beckerman (1977), p. 240.

4.1 Environmental Policy and Environmental Quality

4.1.1 Public Goods and their Provision by the Government

Public goods are characterised by a lack of rivalry in use and the impossibility or inefficiency to exclude individuals from using them. Air quality can be seen as a public good since many people can enjoy it at the same time, and no wall or fence could keep them from doing so. Some amount of clean air is initially supplied for free by nature ($\overline{Q}>0$), but pollution emissions by the firms lower the air quality and hence the amount of this public good. Avoiding further deterioration or even reversing this trend is not costless: at least opportunity costs are involved.

But who should be interested in providing a good at positive costs that could be enjoyed for free if somebody else provided it? This is the key problem of the prisoner's dilemma: nobody. Noncooperative free-rider behaviour is the reason why the private provision of a public good normally fails, and the incentive to free-ride increases with the number of agents involved, e.g. because social control mechanisms become increasingly ineffective. So if there is (a) an incentive for firms to externalise the cost associated with their pollution, (b) no sufficient incentive for individual households to take private action, and (c) no central planner to steer the firms in a way such that pollution emissions are kept at a tolerable level, only the intervention of a superior or generally acknowledged power can remedy things.

The government is such a body. It can legislate, enforce laws and regulations, and this way exert influence of the economic agents' behaviour. If it decides, based on whatever rationale, to make environmental protection one of its primary objectives, its policy will aim at punishing environmentally harmful activities in order to raise the firms' and households' (opportunity) costs of such activities. On the other hand, if the government puts a higher value, say, on establishing its domestic chemical industry as a low-cost supplier to the world market it will avoid policies that would drive up the costs of chemical production, such as setting high standards for pollution control and environmental risk prevention.

Due to their incentive to free-ride, and because they are caught in an environmental prisoner's dilemma, the households cannot be expected to contribute voluntarily, and in significant amounts, to the reduction of pollution. Therefore, abatement expenditure should not be treated as one of the households' control variables. But in which other way can households exert influence on the quality of the environment?

Grossman (1995), p. 43, asserts that "the strongest link between income and pollution is in fact via an induced policy response; as nations or regions experience economic prosperity, their citizens demand of their leaders that greater attention be paid to the natural habitat." This suggests that the households have a control variable by which they are able to give public policy a certain direction. The most obvious control with this property in political systems with democratic elements is the vote .

In chapters 5 and 6, specific assumptions will be made concerning the political framework in place, and the government's rationale for pursuing a particular environmental policy. The present chapter, however, will be based on much weaker assumptions. No particular link will be postulated to exist between the households' political demand for a certain environmental policy, and the government's supply of such policy. This framework is compatible with any kind of political system, but it excludes the vote as the households' control variable. Instead, the households' control will be taken to be their answer in opinion polls about how strict they want public environmental policy to be.

The government's policy instrument is a *unit tax on pollution*. This tax is not to be understood literally, but rather as a proxy for the totality of all measures taken by the government to influence the economic agents' environmentally relevant decisions. In order to be able to come to reasonable conclusions about the level at which they want the tax rate to be set, the households need to understand how this tax rate influences the firms' environment-related decisions and actions, and hence the pollution level. This relationship will be established in the following section.

4.1.2 Abatement and the Pollution Tax

The model to be developed in this chapter (and in chapter 5) serves to analyse the economic agents' optimal behaviour *in the short run* only. The reason is that a number of magnitudes will be taken as given which may change over a longer period of time. Moreover, the firms will be assumed to make positive profits in a possibly perfectly competitive market. In long-run competitive equilibria profits are driven to zero by new competitors entering the market.

So suppose that identical profit-maximising firms, possibly acting under perfect competition, produce a single homogeneous good. Gross output $F>0$ is associated with pollution emissions P which are released into the environment where they do not accumulate. Like in the previous chapters, emissions can be reduced by using part of the output on pollution abatement. The net pollution function $P(A,F)$ is characterised by

$$\begin{aligned}&\frac{\partial P}{\partial F}>0,\ \frac{\partial^2 P}{\partial F^2}>0 \quad \text{for } A\geq 0 \text{ and } F>0\\ &\frac{\partial P}{\partial A}<0,\ \frac{\partial^2 P}{\partial A^2}>0,\ \frac{\partial^2 P}{\partial A\,\partial F}<0,\ \lim_{A\to 0}\frac{\partial P}{\partial A}=-\infty \quad \text{for } A>0 \text{ and } F>0\end{aligned} \tag{4.1}$$

The limit condition says that the marginal efficiency of abatement at the boundary is infinite. Just like in section 2.4 (see (2.9)), it rules out corner solutions for A. In the present chapter such corner solutions will not be needed for what is to be shown.

As mentioned above, the firms face the tax rate $\tau\geq 0$ which the government levies on each unit of pollution emitted. Moreover, they have to reward the factor labour $N>0$ which is needed for production $F(N)$. The wage rate equals $w>0$. Apart from the pollution tax and wages there are no other costs of production. If output is chosen as numeraire, and the price of output set equal to unity, the profit function reads

$$\Pi=F-\tau P-A-wN \tag{4.2}$$

where Π is assumed to be positive, τP is the pollution tax bill, and wN is the total cost of labour.

Suppose further that, in the short run, the levels of w and N are fixed, for instance be due to inflexible existing wage agreements and employment contracts. Hence both w and N, and therefore also the output level $F(N)$, are taken as given by the firms when adapting their behaviour to changes in the tax rate τ, so that the tax bill τP can only be influenced through the amount of abatement carried out. With abatement being the firms' only control variable, profit maximisation leads to the optimum condition

$$\frac{\partial \Pi}{\partial A}=0 \Leftrightarrow \tau=-\frac{1}{\partial P/\partial A} \tag{4.3}$$

which means that in optimum the tax rate is equated with the marginal abatement cost (which is the inverse of the marginal efficiency of abatement). Totally differentiating (4.3) while holding F constant, and rearranging yields

$$\frac{dA}{d\tau} = -\frac{\partial P / \partial A}{\tau \partial^2 P / \partial A^2} = \frac{(\partial P / \partial A)^2}{\partial^2 P / \partial A^2} > 0, \tag{4.4}$$

saying that ***optimal abatement rises with the pollution tax rate***. In other words, there exists an implicit abatement function $A(\tau)$ with a positive first-order derivative.[34] This link between public policy and abatement is central to most sections of this chapter, and it depends directly on the existence of interior solutions of A.

So given a particular output level F, the environmental quality function $Q = \overline{Q} - P$, and the implicit abatement function, pollution will be lower, and the quality of the environment higher, the stricter the government's policy is.

4.2 Distributional Inequality and Pollution

The implicit abatement function will now be exploited in an attempt to establish a general relationship between the inequality of income distribution and the environmental policy that is desired by the households.

4.2.1 Assumptions about the Consumer Side

Suppose that there are N households with identical utility functions $U(\cdot)$. The i-th household's utility is given by $U_i = U(X_i, Q)$. Environmental quality Q is a public good which is enjoyed by all households in the same amount, and therefore does not carry a household index. The utility function has the properties

$$\frac{\partial U_i}{\partial X_i} > 0, \frac{\partial^2 U_i}{\partial X_i^2} < 0, \lim_{X_i \to 0} \frac{\partial U_i}{\partial X_i} = \infty, \frac{\partial U_i}{\partial Q} > 0, \frac{\partial^2 U_i}{\partial Q^2} < 0, \frac{\partial^2 U_i}{\partial X_i \partial Q} = 0$$

[34] In order to ensure the sufficiency of the first-order conditions for a number of maximisation problems in this and the next chapter, assume that $d^2A/d\tau^2 < 0$.

for $X_i>0$, $Q>0$, and $i=1, ..., N$. National income I is composed of profits Π, wages wN and transfers Γ:

$$I=\Pi+wN+\Gamma. \tag{4.5}$$

Through Γ the public pollution tax revenues are redistributed to the households in order to keep the public budget balanced, hence $\Gamma\equiv\tau P$. Substitution from (4.2) into (4.5) shows that national income can also be written as

$$I=F-A. \tag{4.6}$$

Since abatement involves no factors of production it creates no income that could reappear elsewhere in the economy, so I represents a net income or disposable income.

The income of household i is a share $0<a_i<1$ of national income. The sum of all a_i equals unity or, put differently, the sum of household incomes equals national income. In order to keep the model static, suppose that the households do not save. This assumption is compatible with the present short-run analysis. With consumption remaining as the households' only use of disposable income it follows that

$$I_i=a_i(F-A)=X_i \tag{4.7}$$

where it is assumed that no income is wasted. Indirect utility thus reads

$$U_i=U[a_i(F-A),Q(F,A)]. \tag{4.8}$$

Suppose now that all households are asked in an poll for their opinion on the level at which the government should fix the pollution tax rate τ. To come up with an answer to this question, the i-th household treats τ like a control variable of its own, henceforth denoted by τ_i. Given that the households do not act strategically, they maximise their own utility with respect to τ_i, explicitly considering the firms' reaction function $A(\tau)$. Since the limit expression in (4.1) rules out corner solutions for A, and A will only be positive if τ is positive, it follows that τ_i can only have interior solutions.

4.2.2 The Households' Environmental Policy Choice

Maximisation of (4.8) with respect to τ_i yields the first-order condition

$$\frac{\partial U_i}{\partial \tau_i} = -a_i \frac{\partial U_i}{\partial X_i}\frac{dA}{d\tau_i} + \frac{\partial U_i}{\partial Q}\frac{\partial Q}{\partial A}\frac{dA}{d\tau_i} = 0. \tag{4.9}$$

which is also sufficient for a unique global maximum (for the proof see appendix A). The second term of the sum is the marginal benefit a household would derive from a higher pollution tax rate. It indicates that a higher τ_i leads to more abatement by the firms which ultimately improves environmental quality. The first term of the sum is the marginal opportunity cost of a higher τ_i. Dividing (4.9) by $dA/d\tau_i>0$, and rearranging leads to

$$a_i \frac{\partial U_i}{\partial X_i} = \frac{\partial U_i}{\partial Q}\frac{\partial Q}{\partial A(\tau_i)} \tag{4.10}$$

where $A(\tau_i)$ is the level of abatement that *would* be achieved if the government set the pollution tax at τ_i. Note that (4.10) does not determine the allocation of disposable income $I_i=a_iI$ (which is only used for consumption) but the allocation of gross output F. Through τ_i, each household hypothetically fixes a particular $A(\tau_i)$. The remainder $F-A(\tau_i)=I(\tau_i)$ is then distributed according to the given total income shares a_i.

Since $\partial Q/\partial A=-\partial P/\partial A$, and by (4.3) $-\partial P/\partial A=1/\tau$, condition (4.10) can be solved for the i-th household's desired tax rate

$$\tau_i = \frac{1}{a_i}\frac{\partial U_i / \partial Q}{\partial U_i / \partial X_i} \tag{4.11}$$

which bears a strong similarity with the accounting prices of environmental quality in (2.17) and (2.24).

Distributional inequality in this model means that the households differ in their consumption level X_i or, equivalently, in their national income shares a_i, since $I=F-A$ is the same for all households. On the other hand, when deciding about their desired pollution tax rate, the households anticipate the impact of a certain τ_i on $A(\tau_i)$, $I(\tau_i)$, and ultimately in their own X_i. Therefore, in a household's own cost-benefit analysis, dX_i need not be proportional to da_i, but is given by $dX_i=dI_i=(F-A)da_i-a_i(dA/d\tau_i)d\tau_i$. This suggests that, in order to investigate the effect of a higher income on household i's desired tax rate, (4.11) is to be differentiated with respect to a_i

rather than with respect to X_i. Based on these considerations, appendix B shows that

$$\frac{d\tau_i}{da_i} = \frac{\tau_i}{a_i\Delta_i}(\sigma_i - 1) \tag{4.12}$$

where $\Delta_i \equiv 1 - \frac{\partial^2 U_i}{\partial Q^2}\frac{\partial Q}{\partial A}\frac{dA}{d\tau_i}\left(a_i \frac{\partial U_i}{\partial X_i}\right)^{-1} - \frac{\partial U_i}{\partial Q}\frac{\partial^2 U_i}{\partial X_i^2}\frac{dA}{d\tau_i}\left(\frac{\partial U_i}{\partial X_i}\right)^{-1} > 0$, and

$$\sigma_i \equiv -\frac{\partial^2 U_i / \partial X_i^2}{\partial U_i / \partial X_i} X_i \tag{4.13}$$

is the elasticity of marginal utility with respect to consumption reflecting the curvature of the utility function and may take any positive value. Logarithmic utility, for instance, is characterised by $\sigma_i = 1$. If utility is is almost linear in X_i, the elasticity σ_i will be close to zero. Blanchard and Fischer (1989), p. 44, point out that the empirical estimates of σ_i reported in the literature are largely greater than unity.[35] For (4.12) this means that *the greater the share of national disposable income earned by a household, the stricter will be the environmental policy it desires*. In other words, the rich tend to support the strictest environmental policy.

Condition (4.12) implies a *desired-pollution-tax function* $\tau_i = \mathrm{T}(a_i)$. The sign of its second-order derivative, however, is not determined because Δ_i and σ_i may well be nonlinear in a_i. To remove this ambiguity, additional specifications of $U(\cdot)$ and $Q(\cdot)$ would be needed.

4.2.3 Does Distributional Inequality Matter for Desired Policy?

How does income distribution come into play? Assume for the moment that all a_i are equal to their mean value $1/N$, i.e. complete distributional equality prevails. In consequence, all households desire the same pollution tax rate $\tau_i = \mathrm{T}(a_i) = \mathrm{T}(1/N) = \bar{\tau}$ where

[35] Blanchard and Fischer (1989) denote the *intertemporal elasticity of substitution* (and not its inverse, the elasticity of marginal utility) with respect to consumption by σ. They write that "Estimates of σ ... usually lie around or below unity: the bulk of empirical evidence suggests a relatively low value of the elasticity of substitution." [p. 44] Since their σ corresponds to $1/\sigma_i$ in the present study, it follows that σ_i can be taken to exceed unity.

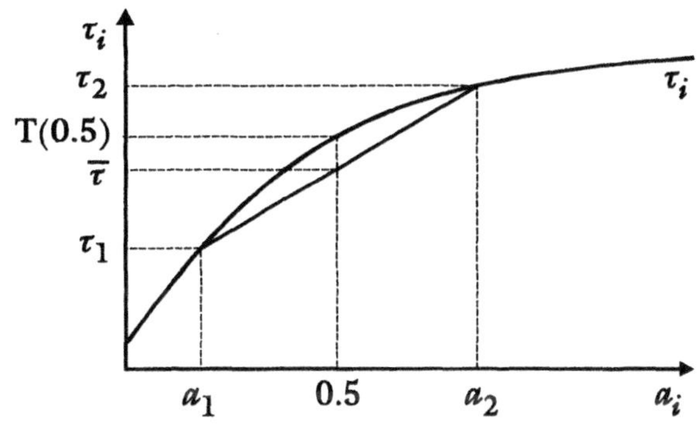

Figure 4.1: The effect of distributional inequality on $\overline{\tau}$ when τ_i=T(a_i) is strictly concave in a_i

$$\overline{\tau} \equiv \frac{1}{N}\sum_{i=1}^{N} \mathrm{T}(a_i)$$

is the arithmetic mean of households' desired tax rate.

Next, suppose that a_1 and a_2 deviate from their mean $1/N$ in a way such that $a_1<1/N<a_2$, while the remaining $a_i=1/N$ ($i\neq 1,2$). Although $(a_1+a_2)/2 = 1/N$, $\overline{\tau}$ need not equal τ_i=T(1/N) anymore. Whether or not it still does, depends on the curvature, or the second-order derivative, of the "desired-pollution-tax" function.

Figure 4.1 illustrates the case of a "desired-pollution-tax" function T(a_i) which is *strictly concave* in a_i. The number of households is $N=2$. The horizonal distance between a_1 and a_2 is halved by $1/N=0.5$, and the vertical distance between τ_1 and τ_2 is halved by $\overline{\tau}=(\tau_1+\tau_2)/2$. As can be seen, $\mathrm{T}(0.5)>\overline{\tau}$ which means that the tax rate which would be desired by a hypothetical average household exceeds the average tax rate desired by the actual households. More generally, it can be concluded from figure 4.1 that, on average, the households desire the stricter an environmental policy, the more equally income is distributed.

The opposite case is depicted by figure 4.2: T(a_i) is *strictly convex* in a_i, with the consequence that $\mathrm{T}(0.5)<\overline{\tau}$. Here, a more unequally distributed income will lead to a higher level of desired pollution tax rate on average. The borderline case where T(a_i) is a *linear* function of a_i has not been illustrated graphically because its implication that $\mathrm{T}(0.5)=\overline{\tau}$ is obvious. Only in this special case, distributional inequality does not matter for the average desired pollution tax rate.

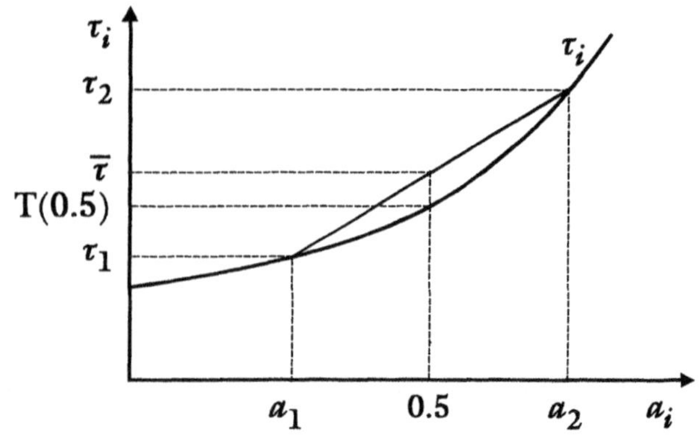

Figure 4.2: The effect of distributional inequality on $\bar{\tau}$ when τ_i=T(a_i) is strictly convex in a_i

The example of $N=2$ households can be generalised in a straight-forward manner to $N>2$ households with varying a_i. Their τ_i will all be located along the T(a_i)-curve, the curvature of which remains decisive for the sign of $\mathrm{T}(1/N)-\bar{\tau}$, that is, for the relevance of distributional inequality for the average desired pollution tax rate, given a certain per capita income level.

It must be emphasised that, within the present model framework, no conclusions can be drawn as to whether $\bar{\tau}$ is of any relevance for the government's decision at which level to set τ. The reason is that no assumption have been made regarding the political system, in particular about the government's objective function, and about political competition. These issues will not be addressed until chapter 5. However, provided that the households' support of an environmental policy does influence the government's decision in a way such that τ and $\bar{\tau}$ correlate positively, it can be concluded that the level of pollution control induced by public policy, and the resulting quality of the environment, are not only functions of income per capita, as the Environmental Kuznets Curve seems to suggest, but also of how income is distributed.

4.3 The Middle Class and Environmental Protection Issues

The ambiguity of the results obtained above is clearly not satisfying, but the assumptions necessary to remove the ambiguous curvature of the "desired-pollution-tax" function would be hard to justify, and involve an element of arbitrariness. So if theory does not provide a clue on how distributional aspects influence the public opinion about how strict environmental policy should be, perhaps empirical evidence does, on which further theorising can be based.

Indeed there seems to exist an empirical phenomenon which may shed some light on the qualitative link between distribution and environmental policy support. To describe this phenomenon, and to highlight its implications is the concern of the present section 4.3; to explain it will be attempted in sections 4.4 and 4.5.

4.3.1 The Middle Class as Environmental Elite

According to chapters 2 and 3, the rich can be expected to spend higher amounts of resources on environmental improvements than the poor, even if both groups are exposed to the same levels of pollution. The argument was that the rich with their higher consumption level have lower marginal opportunity costs of environmental protection. This result has been interpreted as to refer to countries or whole economies rather than to the micro level, but there seems to be at least no technical reason why this should not hold at the level of the individual household as well. In the face of this result, the rich should be expected to be the group of society which is most keen on a stricter environmental policy, which elects green politicians, and from which green organisations recruit their membership.

But this conjecture is not supported by empirical evidence. Poguntke (1989), in figure 15.3, p. 188, for instance, analyses electoral profiles of European green voters and finds that in Austria, Belgium, France, Germany and Sweden the "new" middle class is over-represented in the electorate of green parties, and not the rich or the upper class. According to Frankland (1989), p. 72, German "green ... candidates have run more strongly in urban residential areas of the 'new' middle classes ... and more weakly where workers or the self-employed are concentrated. 1987 national survey data indicate that low or middle level employees and officials were the occupational category ... most supportive to the Greens ... while unskilled workers were the least supportive ..."

Diani (1989), p. 117, writes about Italy: "In terms of socio-demographic variables, the green voters seem rather similar to the green activists: they are over-represented among young and middle-class people ...". Mohai (1985), p. 821, reviews a number of U.S. studies on the link between socio-economic status and involvement in environmental conservation issues, and concludes that "environmental activists tend to be drawn disproportionally from the upper-middle class". Eder (1996), p. 112, finally, reports that the South Korean environmental NGO movement "has become largely dominated by middle-class activists and leaders".

Hence there seems to be a - though not undisputed - case for *environmental elitism of the middle class*. Explanations given in the literature for this phenomenon are vague. Socio-cultural and educational aspects of the middle class seem to play a role, but both have been found to correlate strongly with environmental awareness or concern [Van Liere & Dunlap (1980)]. Ultimately, middle-class environmentalism is seen mostly as the expression of a greater concern of this class for the environment [Tucker (1982)].[36]

4.3.2 Distribution and Public Support of Environmental Policy

There seems to be no universal definition of the middle class in the literature. A definition that gives an idea of what is to be understood by it is given by Leigh (1994), p. 13: the middle class comprises all households earning 50% to 200% of the median earnings of all households nationwide. So the middle class is defined in economic terms as the middle-income segment.

This means that a broad middle class is not compatible with arbitrary income distributions. The emergence or existence of a middle class of significant relative size requires the distribution of income in the economy to be not more than only moderately unequal, and not polarised around its tails. So given that the middle class is characterised by a tendency to engage over-proportionally much in environmental protection and to support stricter environmental policies, and provided that consumer or voter preferences are reflected by public policy, it may be concluded that *a more equal income distribution, or one that is polarised in the middle-income region, is likely to exert a positive impact on environmental quality*.[37]

The role of the middle class in this context must not be seen too one-dimensionally. Even if its political power might not be decisive it can still play the role of a catalyst. Pasinetti (1981), for instance, writes that "there exists a very definite order of priority in consumers' wants ... This order of

---

[36] This explanation is not generally accepted. See Mohai (1985) and his references.

[37] Note that although this conclusion is similar to the one that was drawn on the basis of figure 4.1, it rests on entirely different premises. Therefore, it cannot be taken as an empirical evidence for a strictly concave "desired-tax-rate" function.

priority is particularly clear-cut at low levels of income, where satisfaction of some wants is a *conditio sine qua non* ... But the order persists at higher levels as well, where the decision process becomes more complicated only because the order itself may no longer be so obvious, and needs first to be discovered." [p. 75; italics in the original] By raising environmental issues, and pointing to the problems associated with them, green middle class members may help others to discover their want for a better environment, and hence contribute to a process that comprises greater parts of society than only the middle class.

The following sections 4.4 and 4.5 are devoted to the explanation of green middle-class environmentalism. Income distribution, but also the composition of the households' income, and private defensive expenditure are the key explanatory elements. Two distinct explanations will be offered which may complement each other. Neither of them falls back on the concern argument or requires any assumption on class-specific socio-cultural properties.

4.4 Sensitivity of Income to Environmental Policy Changes

The first of the two explanations for green middle-class elitism is based on the central assumption that the composition of income in terms of its sources varies among the different social classes. If the components of income are unequally responsive to environmental policy, changes in the composition of income will have an influence on the respective class's opportunity cost associated with a certain environmental policy.

4.4.1 Assumptions about Income Level and Composition

Suppose that the households of the economy can be grouped by their level of income or their material affluence. There are $N_U > 0$ rich households, mainly self-employed, which form the "upper class" and earn a household income equal to I_U; $N_M > 0$ "middle-class" households of employees receive I_M; and $N_L > 0$ "lower-class" worker households live on I_L. The household numbers add up to the size of the labour force: $N = N_U + N_M + N_L$. The relationship between the income levels is given by

$$I_U > I_M > I_L. \tag{4.14}$$

National or aggregate income equals $I \equiv N_U I_U + N_M I_M + N_L I_L$.

National income is still assumed to be given by (4.5). Household income consists of profits, wages and transfers, too. However, its composition may be different from that of national income. Let

$$I_i \equiv a_i(\Pi + \Gamma) + b_i wN = a_i(F - A) + (b_i - a_i)wN \tag{4.15}$$

be the income of a household of group i with $a_i>0$ and $b_i>0$ ($i=U, M, L$). (4.15) resembles (4.7) but differs in that b_i does not have to equal a_i. So (4.7) is a special case of (4.15).

For household profit and transfer income shares to add up to national income, $a_U N_U + a_M N_M + a_L N_L = 1$ and $b_U N_U + b_M N_M + b_L N_L = 1$. The multiplication of profits and transfers by the same share a_i in (4.15) means that the transfer fully compensates a household for the amount by which the firms' tax bill has reduced its profit income. For simplicity a_i and b_i will henceforth be referred to as "profit share" and "factor income share".

The factor income shares b_i can be regarded as a *labour efficiency index* which expresses the households', say hourly, work performance. A higher labour efficiency, which may be due to the higher education level or better qualification of a household group, is rewarded by the firms. $b_i w$ then represent three, possibly different, wage rates.

As before it is assumed that the households do not save. Hence consumption remains as their only use of income which means that $I_i = X_i$ if no income is wasted. According to (4.14), $X_U > X_M > X_L$.

4.4.2 The Households' Environmental Policy Choice

The households' utility function $U(X_i, Q)$ has the same properties as specified in section 4.2.1. Since by assumption $X_i = I_i = a_i(F - A) + (b_i - a_i)wN$, indirect utility equals

$$U_i = U\left[a_i(F - A) + (b_i - a_i)wN, Q(F, A)\right]. \tag{4.16}$$

This time it is the household groups, rather than every individual household, that are asked in a poll for their opinion about the appropriate pollution tax rate. Since each group is aware of the implicit abatement function $A(\tau)$ that has been derived in section 4.1.2, they take it into account when maximising (4.16) with respect to their hypothetical control τ_i. The resulting optimum condition is again (4.9), or its equivalent (4.11).

But while in section 4.2, profit share and factor income share were equal (actually they were not distinguished at all), this need not be the case any more. Household-group specific magnitudes enter τ_i in two ways: through the marginal utility of consumption which is a function of the income *level* I_i, and through the profit share a_i from which it can be inferred on the i-th household group's income *composition*, given by $a_i(\Pi+\Gamma)/I_i$.

In the following two sections, the effect of marginal changes in the households' income level (level effect) and income composition (composition effect) on τ_i will be looked at.

4.4.3 The Income Level Effect

In order to isolate the income level effect from the income composition effect, assume that the composition of I_i remains constant. This means that

$$\frac{a_i(\Pi+\Gamma)}{I_i}=\frac{va_i(\Pi+\Gamma)}{vI_i}=\frac{va_i(\Pi+\Gamma)}{va_i(\Pi+\Gamma)+vb_iwN}$$

for any arbitrary $v\neq 0$. As can be seen, a constant composition of income requires a_i to behave proportionally to b_i, that is, b_i/a_i needs to remain constant. Given this proportionality, appendix B demonstrates that

$$\left.\frac{d\tau_i}{da_i}\right|_{b_i/a_i=\text{const}}=\frac{\tau_i}{a_i\Delta_i}(\sigma_i-1) \tag{4.17}$$

where $\Delta_i\equiv 1-\frac{\partial^2 U_i}{\partial Q^2}\frac{\partial Q}{\partial A}\frac{dA}{d\tau_i}\left(a_i\frac{\partial U_i}{\partial X_i}\right)^{-1}-\frac{\partial U_i}{\partial Q}\frac{\partial^2 U_i}{\partial X_i^2}\frac{dA}{d\tau_i}\left(\frac{\partial U_i}{\partial X_i}\right)^{-1}>0$, and σ_i is given by (4.13). Implicitly in section 4.2, $b_i/a_i=1$ which is constant, too, thus (4.17) is identical to (4.12), and can therefore be expected to be positive as well. The value of a constant b_i/a_i obviously makes no difference for the sign of the income effect.

From (4.17) it can be concluded that, ceteris paribus, a household will desire the higher a pollution tax rate to be set by the government, the richer it is. Given (4.14), and provided that $b_U/a_U=b_M/a_M=b_L/a_L$ (no composition effect) this means that

$$\tau_U > \tau_M > \tau_L. \tag{4.18}$$

The reason is that the upper-class households have the lowest marginal utility of consumption, and hence the lowest marginal opportunity cost of a strict environmental policy. The lower-class households, on the other hand, would opt for a more lenient policy because their priority is to reach a higher material living standard, and a high pollution tax rate would reduce their income inacceptably much. Therefore, with all household incomes composed equally, the upper class is the environmental elite.

4.4.4 The Income Composition Effect

The households may not only differ in their income level, but also in the composition of their income, indicated by different b_i/a_i. The lower b_i/a_i is, the greater a part of the i-th household group's income consists of profits and transfers. The effect of a marginally higher profit share on the desired pollution tax rate, given a certain income level I_i, is given by

$$\left.\frac{d\tau_i}{da_i}\right|_{I_i=\text{const}} = -\frac{\tau_i}{a_i\Delta_i} < 0 \tag{4.19}$$

where $\Delta_i \equiv 1 - \frac{\partial^2 U_i}{\partial Q^2}\frac{\partial Q}{\partial A}\frac{dA}{d\tau_i}\left(a_i\frac{\partial U_i}{\partial X_i}\right)^{-1} > 0$ (see appendix C). So the greater the share of profits in household income, the lower will be the desired tax rate. The reason for this relationship is that when a_i increases, income and thus consumption of each household of group i become more sensitive to changes in $\Pi + \Gamma = F - A - wN$. Since optimal abatement A rises in response to a higher pollution tax, household income and consumption decrease when τ is set higher, and this decrease will be the more significant, the greater a_i is. Therefore, ceteris paribus, *a household's opportunity cost of a stricter environmental policy increases with its profit share a_i*. This is the income composition effect.

At a given income level I_i, an increase in a_i implies a decrease in b_i, hence from $d\tau_i/da_i < 0$, it can be inferred that $d\tau_i/db_i > 0$.

4.4.5 The Middle Class as Environmental Elite (1)

An economic explanation why the middle class may be in favour of a stricter environmental policy than the lower class poses no problem: because $I_M > I_L$, the income level effect on its own has sufficient explanatory power to account for this difference (see (4.18)). If, in addition to that, $b_L/a_L < b_M/a_M$, possibly due to a higher labour efficiency of the middle class households which is rewarded by a higher efficiency-adjusted wage rate ($b_M w > b_L w$), the difference in the desired tax rates will be even greater.

But since $I_U > I_M$, the level effect also suggests that the upper class should be expected to desire a higher pollution tax rate than the middle class. Here, the explanation of green middle-class elitism rests on the composition effect. If it is stong enough to offset and overcompensate the level effect, the middle-class households will indeed turn out to be the environmental elite. A necessary condition for this to happen is that the upper class is a class of company owners or "capitalists", whose household income is composed of relatively more profits than the middle-class households' income. In formal terms this means that $b_U/a_U < b_M/a_M$. If this applies, the rich may face a higher marginal opportunity cost of a strict environmental policy than the middle class, so that $\tau_M > \tau_U$.

4.4.6 A More General Interpretation of Assumptions and Results

The results of the last three sections have been obtained under rather specific assumptions regarding the composition of income and the households' awareness of this composition. It will now briefly be attempted to give a more general interpretation of the assumptions and the results.

In the real world a household's income may be comprised of remuneration for direct work (wage, salary), interest on savings and bonds, dividends, corporate profits, speculative profits, unemployment benefits, pensions, and more. These income components differ in numerous aspects, but the one that is of importance in the present context is their sensitivity to changes in environmental policy.

While the stream of interest payments accruing from a fixed rate government bond remains unaffected by a tax imposed on energy consumption, this does probably not apply to the profits of the energy industry.[38] It is evident that the owners or shareholders of businesses which are directly affected by stricter environmental laws and regulations face higher opportunity costs if such laws take effect than those people who own bonds and thus earn a constant income. Similarly, employees of extractive or heavy industries who would have to fear for their jobs if a certain environmental legislation was passed can be expected not to support a government policy which might impose the costs of unemployment upon them, whereas employees of the environmentally rather harmless service sector may well sympathise with the same policy because their opportunity costs are far outweighed by the benefit of a cleaner environment.

It should be clear by now that not only the level of income or consumption matters to the households' environmental policy choice but also how sensitive their individual material wellbeing is to environmental policy changes. Yet another aspect comes in when households are ill-informed. They may be unaware of the true effect which environmental policy has on their income, either under- or overestimating it. In the real world where environmental issues also involve a strong emotional component (see section 5.1.1 below) this will be the rule rather than the exception. As a consequence, their cost-benefit calculation will be biased. In this light a_i and b_i can also be seen as subjective magnitudes. Somebody not realising that her or his disposable income depends to some extent on a particular communal regulation on solid waste treatment (subjectively a_i is very low) will be in favour of tightening up this regulation (i.e. the person will state a high desired τ_i in the poll) beyond the point where marginal benefit equals *actual* marginal opportunity cost because the *subjective* marginal opportunity cost is zero.

4.5 A Private Supplement to Public Environmental Quality

The second explanation of middle-class environmentalism to be provided here is based on the assumption that households can improve their own environmental quality by mitigating the effect of pollution through *private* measures after the government has fixed τ. This is not to say that it will be those households that disagree the most with the actual level of τ which take such

[38] This does not imply that market rates of interest or the price of bonds may not be affected by such a policy measure. But for people who own bonds, interest payments remain the same.

measures. In fact, it will even turn out that the rationale underlying a household's choice of τ_i differs from the rationale behind its choice of the level of private measures to improve its own environmental quality when τ is given.

In the literature, environmental quality is often treated as a pure public good. But this is a simplification which is inappropriate in many, though certainly not all cases. Exposure to pollution, smell or noise varies from area to area, dependig on numerous natural and man-made factors. People's choice of the place of residence has a lot to to with environmental quality. It is well-known that housing sale prices reflect the differences in environmental quality variables [Johansson (1987), p. 104]. By living in a certain place one excludes others from living there, and from enjoying the environmental amenities associated with this location. Hence there is rivalry in "use", and the exclusion principle applies to some extent. Other examples include people who build swimming pools partly as substitutes for the nearby lake or river which is too polluted to be used for swimming; people who surround their houses with well-tended gardens to replace lacking natural beauty; or people who equip their house, car or office with air conditioning systems which cleanse the air of soot particles, dust and exhaust fumes.

Hirsch (1976) anticipated much of what the current literature on Environmental Kuznets Curves is concerned with, when he wrote more than twenty years ago: "So long as material privation is widespread, conquest of material scarcity is the dominant concern. As demands for purely private goods are increasingly satisfied, demands for goods and facilities with a public (social) character become increasingly active. These public demands make themselves felt through individual demands on the political system or through the market mechanism in the same way as do the demands for purely private goods. Individuals acquire both sets of goods without disaction, except where public goods are provided by public or collective action; even there, *individuals may seek to increase their own share by private purchases*." [p. 4; italics not in the original] In this last sentence, Hirsch indicates that people may find it optimal to complement, or even substitute public goods by private ones.

A classic case of private substitution of a public environmental quality good is South Korea's bottled water [Eder (1996), p. 87]. For decades the Korean government had banned the sale of bottled water because it feared that private drinking water supply would aggravate class differences. It was well-known - though denied by the government - that the publicly provided tab water was unsafe, hence an incentive existed to substitute it by bottled higher-quality water. But while the middle and upper classes could afford this private substitute the lower class was forced by its tighter budget constraint to drink from the public water system. This unequal exposure to health risks was perceived as a political risk by the government and led to the ban (which was never seriously enforced and finally struck down in 1994 by the Supreme Court). The government's sociopolitical judgement underlying the ban was an acknowledgement of the relationship between household income level and private supplementation of public environmental quality.

4.5.1 Private Defensive Expenditure

It is therefore a reasonable assumption that households can in many instances improve their own individual environmental quality without simultaneously raising it for others. For this reason environmental quality will be modelled as a *hybrid good* in this section, combining characteristics of a public and a private good. Define the quality of the environment that is enjoyed by the households of group i as

$$Q_i \equiv Q(A,F) + R(S_i) \tag{4.20}$$

where $Q(A,F)$ is the public component of Q_i, and $R(S_i) = R_i \geq 0$ is supplementary, privately supplied environmental quality, with $S_i \geq 0$ representing defensive expenditure, that is, the resources necessary to provide it. $R(S_i)$ is assumed to have the following properties:

$$R(0) = 0,\ \ R_i' > 0,\ \ R_i'' < 0,\ \ R_i'(S_i = 0) < \infty .$$

Suppose now that the government has fixed the pollution tax rate τ. Given the implicit abatement function $A(\tau)$ this means that the levels of A and Q are fully determined. Taking them as given, the households choose the levels of defensive expenditure S_i and consumption X_i such as to maximise their utility $U(X_i,Q_i)$, subject to their budget constraint

$$I_i = a_i(F - A) + (b_i - a_i)wN \geq X_i + S_i \tag{4.21}$$

and $S_i \geq 0$. The Lagrangean to the problem of household group i reads

$$\mathcal{L}_i = U(X_i, Q_i) + \mu_i\left[a_i(F - A) + (b_i - a_i)wN - X_i - S_i\right] + \psi_i S_i .$$

where ψ_i is the multiplier of the nonnegativity restriction on S_i. Since $U(\cdot)$ is strictly concave[39] and the constraints linear in the controls X_i and S_i, the first-order conditions

$$\frac{\partial \mathcal{L}_i}{\partial X_i} = 0 \Leftrightarrow \frac{\partial U_i}{\partial X_i} = \mu_i$$

$$\frac{\partial \mathcal{L}_i}{\partial S_i} = 0 \Leftrightarrow \frac{\partial U_i}{\partial Q_i} R_i' + \psi_i = \mu_i$$

are also sufficient for a unique global maximum. Complementary slackness requires that $S_i \geq 0$, $\psi_i \geq 0$, and $\psi_i S_i = 0$. The first-order conditions can be equated to yield

$$\psi_i = \frac{\partial U_i}{\partial X_i} - \frac{\partial U_i}{\partial Q_i} R_i' . \tag{4.22}$$

Like in previous chapters, the multiplier of a nonnegativity restriction can be interpreted as a marginal opportunity loss. Here ψ_i is the marginal opportunity loss of spending income on private environmental quality improvements, and it equals the difference between the marginal opportunity cost and the marginal benefit of S_i. Appendix D shows that ψ_i declines as income rises due to the falling opportunity cost of S_i, and that ψ_i will be the greater the higher τ has been set by the government. The intuition behind the latter is that a higher τ induces more pollution abatement by the firms, a higher public environmental quality, and thus a smaller incentive to take individual action because the marginal benefit of S_i is lower.

If a higher income and a lower pollution tax rate make the opportunity loss associated with S_i decline, it may be conjectured that, once ψ_i has vanished, $dS_i / dI_i > 0$ and $dS_i / d\tau < 0$. This is confirmed by appendix D. The higher the pollution tax rate is, and therefore the public component of

---

[39] Proof: The principal minors of the Hessian determinant alternate in sign, starting negative:

$$\frac{\partial^2 U_i}{\partial X_i^2} < 0 \text{ and } \begin{vmatrix} \dfrac{\partial^2 U_i}{\partial X_i^2} & \dfrac{\partial^2 U_i}{\partial X_i \partial S_i} \\ \dfrac{\partial^2 U_i}{\partial X_i \partial S_i} & \dfrac{\partial^2 U_i}{\partial S_i^2} \end{vmatrix} = \frac{\partial^2 U_i}{\partial X_i^2} \left(\frac{\partial^2 U_i}{\partial Q_i^2} R_i'^2 + \frac{\partial U_i}{\partial Q_i} R_i'' \right) > 0$$

where $\dfrac{\partial^2 U_i}{\partial X_i \partial S_i} = \dfrac{\partial^2 U_i}{\partial X_i \partial Q_i} R_i' = 0$ due to the linear separability of utility.

Q_i, the less the households spend on further improvements. And provided their marginal benefit of defensive expenditure exceeds the marginal opportunity cost, ***households with a higher income will spend more on improvements of their own environmental quality than those with a lower income***.

The latter result has a remarkable implication. It says that the composition of income has no impact whatsoever on the private initiative towards a higher individual environmental quality, i.e. the corresponding decision-making involves no composition effect. This suggests that ***the choice of the level of private defensive expenditure S_i is governed by a different rationale than the choice of a preferred pollution tax rate τ_i***. A situation may arise in which households may be willing to pay for private environmental quality improvements without supporting a policy that would provide the same environmental quality publicly.

In consequence, the income ranking $I_U > I_M > I_L$ is compatible with any ranking of desired levels of the pollution tax rate τ_i but only with a single ranking of household defensive expenditure S_i, namely

$$S_U \geq S_M \geq S_L. \tag{4.23}$$

The signs of equality only apply in the case of two or three corner solutions for S_i; otherwise the inequalities will be strict.

4.5.2 Policy Choice when Defensive Expenditure is Fixed

Before continuing, a short recapitulation will help keeping the overview of the argument so far. In a first step the households have been asked for their opinion about the appropriate environmental policy. They have come up with group-specific choices of τ_i. In a second step the government has fixed the pollution tax rate τ, indirectly determining public environmental quality Q via the firms' abatement reaction function. In a third step the households have adapted their own defensive expenditure S_i to the given Q.

Now suppose that, in a fourth step, the same households are interviewed again about their preferred level of the pollution tax. Will their statements be different from the first poll *if their S_i is fixed* for some reason?

There may be a number of reasons for defensive expenditure to be fixed, irreversible, or at least rigid over a given period of time. S_i may consist of rents, interest payments or other regular long-term obligations, resulting from an initial investment. Here, S_i represents fixed costs in the economic sense. But a fixed level of defensive expenditure may also be the consequence of people's habits, of their lack of willingness to adapt to new circumstances, or of their low geographical mobility. A household's belief that its S_i gives it some independence of the politically determined Q may induce it to keep its level of defensive expenditure even after public environ-mental policy has changed. So S_i can as well be fixed due to psychological factors.

Assume that the households of group i plan to keep their S_i constant. This means they take their previously optimised S_i as given when making up their mind on their desired level τ_i of the pollution tax rate. Taking into account the budget constraint (4.21) which includes the fixed S_i, one obtains the indirect utility function

$$U_i = U\left[a_i(F - A) + (b_i - a_i)wN - S_i, Q_i\right].$$

Maximising U_i with respect to τ_i leads to the necessary and sufficient condition

$$a_i \frac{\partial U_i}{\partial X_i} = \frac{\partial U_i}{\partial Q_i} \frac{\partial Q}{\partial A(\tau_i)} \tag{4.24}$$

which is almost identical with (4.10) except that the right-hand side contains the marginal utility of $Q_i = Q + R(S_i)$ instead of Q alone. Making use of (4.3), and rearranging gives the counterpart to (4.11):

$$\tau_i = \frac{1}{a_i} \frac{\partial U_i / \partial Q_i}{\partial U_i / \partial X_i}. \tag{4.25}$$

If I_i and a_i are the same as before, and if further $S_i = 0$ so that $Q_i = Q$, (4.25) is completely identical with (4.14). In this case the i-th group of households will state the same desired pollution tax rate in the poll.

However, if $S_i > 0$ the consumption level $X_i = I_i - S_i$ is lower and $\partial U_i / \partial X_i$ higher than in the first poll, leading to a higher marginal opportunity cost of τ_i. A positive S_i is further associated with a higher $Q_i = Q + R(S_i)$ and thus a lower $\partial U_i / \partial Q_i$ which means that the marginal benefit of a higher pollution tax rate is lower than before. So with a higher opportunity cost and a lower benefit of τ_i at the margin, ***households with positive fixed defensive expenditures will prefer a more lenient environmental policy in the second poll than in the first.***

Moreover, appendix E shows that *the higher the level of private defensive expenditure has been set, ceteris paribus, the lower will be the desired pollution tax rat in the second poll*, i.e $d\tau_i / dS_i < 0$.

4.5.3 The Middle Class as Environmental Elite (2)

Now the link to the original question, why the middle class might be "greener" than the rest of society, will be established. In order to simplify matters, and to avoid any confusion with the first explanation, assume that all profit shares a_i are the same (which causes no loss of generality since there is no income composition effect; see section 4.5.1). The ranking of the desired tax rates τ_i is determined by the ranking of income levels (4.14) alone. The resulting outcome of the *first* poll is therefore given by (4.18).

$S_i=0$ is most likely at low incomes, i.e. in the lower class. Beyond a certain threshold income level (at which $\psi_i=S_i=0$ in (4.22)), S_i rises with I_i. Therefore S_i is highest in the upper class (see (4.23)). So assume that the upper-class households have found it optimal to supplement public environmental quality by private measures, and that the corresponding defensive expenditures are fixed at $S_U > 0$, whereas the other two household groups have attached a greater priority to consumption, thus ($S_M = S_L = 0$).

In consequence only the upper class' desired level of the pollution tax will be lower in the second poll than in the first. Provided that S_U has been chosen high enough, a situation will be arise where $\tau_M > \tau_U$ which means that the middle class supports stricter environmental policy than the upper class. Again *the middle class comes out as the environmental elite*.

4.6 Concluding Remarks

This chapter has demonstrated that the distribution of income in an economy is very likely to influence the extent to which households support or reject a particular environmental policy, given a certain per capita income. Unfortunately, the direction of the influence that distributional aspects exert upon the public political opinion could not be inferred on by means of economic theory, without making rather far-reaching assumptions about functional forms which would have been hard to justify.

Contrary to the ambiguity of those theoretical results, empirical evidence suggests that the households of the middle-income segment tend to support a stricter environmental policy than other household groups. While possible economic causes of this middle-class environmental elitism - two of them have been proposed in this chapter - are not too obvious, the implication of this phenomenon for the policy-relevance of income distribution is rather clear: if a positive correlation exists between actual policy and the households' average desired environmental policy, a more equal distribution will be associated with a stronger environmental orientation of public policy than a distribution that is polarised towards its tails.

Is there a link between Environmental Kuznets Curves and the original Kuznets curve? The latter illustrates a stylised relationship between the level of per capita income and the inequality of income distribution. In Kuznets' (1955) own words: "One might thus assume a long swing in the inequality characterising the secular income structure: widening in the early phases of economic growth when the transition from the pre-industrial to the industrial civilisation was most rapid; becoming stabilised for a while; and then narrowing in the later phases." [p. 18]

One may argue that the peak of this Kuznets curve which marks an income distribution that is associated with a very small middle class, coincides with the peaks of numerous Environmental Kuznets Curves which have occurred during or shortly after industrialisation in Europe. However, a causal relationship between the Kuznets curve and Environmental Kuznets Curves would have required a century-long middle-class environmentalism. More likely it seems that the emergence of the industry sector has given rise to both, a high income inequality and high pollution levels. Hence the main causality does not run from inequality to pollution, but from the structural transformation of the economy to both of them.

Appendix

Appendix A: Sufficiency of First-Order Condition

Indirect utility $U_i = U\{a_i[F - A(\tau)], Q[F, A(\tau)]\}$ is a function of the pollution tax rate τ alone. It is to be shown that the first-order condition

$$\frac{dU_i}{d\tau}=\left(-a_i\frac{\partial U_i}{\partial X_i}+\frac{\partial U_i}{\partial Q}\frac{\partial Q}{\partial A}\right)\frac{dA}{d\tau}=0 \tag{A1}$$

is sufficient for a unique global maximum. The second-order derivative of U_i can be shown to have an ambiguous sign, hence U_i is not strictly concave. But according to (4.4) $dA/d\tau>0$, so condition (A1) can only be fulfilled if

$$-a_i\frac{\partial U_i}{\partial X_i}+\frac{\partial U_i}{\partial Q}\frac{\partial Q}{\partial A}=0. \tag{A2}$$

But this function is strictly concave in τ:

$$\frac{d}{d\tau}\left(-a_i\frac{\partial U_i}{\partial X_i}+\frac{\partial U_i}{\partial Q}\frac{\partial Q}{\partial A}\right)=a_i^{\,2}\frac{\partial^2 U_i}{\partial X_i^{\,2}}\frac{dA}{d\tau}+\Delta_i<0$$

where

$$\Delta_i\equiv\frac{\partial^2 U_i}{\partial Q^2}\left(\frac{\partial Q}{\partial A}\frac{dA}{d\tau}\right)^2+\frac{\partial U_i}{\partial Q}\frac{\partial^2 Q}{\partial A^2}\left(\frac{dA}{d\tau}\right)^2+\frac{\partial U_i}{\partial Q}\frac{\partial Q}{\partial A}\frac{d^2A}{d\tau^2}<0$$

($d^2A\,/\,d\tau^2<0$ by assumption; see footnote 33). So (A2) has at most a single solution. And since the same must also apply to (A1) its sufficiency is proved.

Appendix B: The Income Level Effect

The total differential of (4.11), taking not only τ_i but also a_i as variable, reads

$$d\tau_i=-\frac{1}{a_i^{\,2}}\frac{\dfrac{\partial U_i}{\partial Q}}{\dfrac{\partial U_i}{\partial X_i}}da_i+\frac{\dfrac{\partial^2 U_i}{\partial Q^2}\dfrac{\partial Q}{\partial A}\dfrac{dA}{d\tau_i}d\tau_i}{a_i\dfrac{\partial U_i}{\partial X_i}}+\frac{\dfrac{\partial U_i}{\partial Q}\dfrac{\partial^2 U_i}{\partial X_i^{\,2}}\dfrac{dA}{d\tau_i}d\tau_i}{\left(\dfrac{\partial U_i}{\partial X_i}\right)^2}-\frac{\dfrac{\partial U_i}{\partial Q}\dfrac{\partial^2 U_i}{\partial X_i^{\,2}}\dfrac{\partial X_i}{\partial a_i}da_i}{a_i\left(\dfrac{\partial U_i}{\partial X_i}\right)^2}$$

After sorting the terms, this becomes

$$\left[1-\frac{\dfrac{\partial^2 U_i}{\partial Q^2}\dfrac{\partial Q}{\partial A}\dfrac{dA}{d\tau_i}}{a_i\dfrac{\partial U_i}{\partial X_i}}-\frac{\dfrac{\partial U_i}{\partial Q}\dfrac{\partial^2 U_i}{\partial X_i^{\,2}}\dfrac{dA}{d\tau_i}}{\left(\dfrac{\partial U_i}{\partial X_i}\right)^2}\right]d\tau_i=\frac{1}{a_i^{\,2}}\frac{\dfrac{\partial U_i}{\partial Q}}{\dfrac{\partial U_i}{\partial X_i}}\left(-1-a_i\frac{\dfrac{\partial^2 U_i}{\partial X_i^{\,2}}}{\dfrac{\partial U_i}{\partial X_i}}\frac{\partial X_i}{\partial a_i}\right)da_i.$$

Let $\Delta_i \equiv 1 - \dfrac{\dfrac{\partial^2 U_i}{\partial Q^2}\dfrac{\partial Q}{\partial A}\dfrac{dA}{d\tau_i}}{a_i \dfrac{\partial U_i}{\partial X_i}} - \dfrac{\dfrac{\partial U_i}{\partial Q}\dfrac{\partial^2 U_i}{\partial X_i^2}\dfrac{dA}{d\tau_i}}{\left(\dfrac{\partial U_i}{\partial X_i}\right)^2} > 0$ and $\sigma_i \equiv -\dfrac{\dfrac{\partial^2 U_i}{\partial X_i^2}}{\dfrac{\partial U_i}{\partial X_i}} X_i$, then

$$\Delta_i d\tau_i = \frac{1}{a_i^2}\frac{\partial U_i / \partial Q}{\partial U_i / \partial X_i}\left(\sigma_i \frac{\partial X_i}{\partial a_i}\frac{a_i}{X_i} - 1\right) da_i .$$

Moreover, since $\dfrac{1}{a_i^2}\dfrac{\partial U_i / \partial Q}{\partial U_i / \partial X_i} = \dfrac{\tau_i}{a_i}$ and $X_i = I_i$, this can be restated as

$$\Delta_i d\tau_i = \frac{\tau_i}{a_i}\left(\sigma_i \frac{\partial I_i}{\partial a_i}\frac{a_i}{I_i} - 1\right) da_i . \tag{B1}$$

One last replacement can be made. In section 4.2, $I_i = a_i(F - A)$, thus

$$\frac{\partial I_i}{\partial a_i}\frac{a_i}{I_i} = (F - A)\frac{a_i}{I_i} = 1$$

In section 4.4.3, on the other hand, $I_i = a_i(\Pi + \Gamma) + b_i wN$. By assumption, a_i and b_i are to be held in constant proportions. This means that $\gamma_i \equiv b_i / a_i$ needs to remain constant, so that $I_i = a_i[(\Pi + \Gamma) + \gamma_i wN]$, and

$$\frac{\partial I_i}{\partial a_i}\frac{a_i}{I_i} = (\Pi + \Gamma + \gamma_i wN)\frac{a_i}{I_i} = \frac{a_i(\Pi + \Gamma) + b_i wN}{I_i} = 1 .$$

So in both cases, (B1) reduces to

$$\frac{d\tau_i}{da_i} = \frac{\tau_i}{a_i \Delta_i}(\sigma_i - 1) .$$

Appendix C: The Income Composition Effect

With τ_i and a_i assumed variable, but $X_i = I_i$ held constant, the total differential of (4.11) reads

$$d\tau_i = -\frac{1}{a_i^2}\frac{\dfrac{\partial U_i}{\partial Q}}{\dfrac{\partial U_i}{\partial X_i}} da_i + \frac{\dfrac{\partial^2 U_i}{\partial Q^2}\dfrac{\partial Q}{\partial A}\dfrac{dA}{d\tau_i}}{a_i \dfrac{\partial U_i}{\partial X_i}} d\tau_i .$$

Rearranging leads to $\dfrac{d\tau_i}{da_i} = -\dfrac{\tau_i}{a_i\Delta_i}$ where $\Delta_i \equiv 1 - \dfrac{\dfrac{\partial^2 U_i}{\partial Q^2}\dfrac{\partial Q}{\partial A}\dfrac{dA}{d\tau_i}}{a_i \dfrac{\partial U_i}{\partial X_i}} > 0.$

Appendix D: Defensive Expenditure and Its Opportunity Cost

The total differential of (4.22) equals

$$d\psi_i = \frac{\partial^2 U_i}{\partial X_i^2} dX_i - \frac{\partial^2 U_i}{\partial Q_i^2}\left(\frac{\partial Q}{\partial A}\frac{dA}{d\tau} d\tau + R_i' dS_i\right) R_i' - \frac{\partial U_i}{\partial Q_i} R_i'' dS_i.$$

In case of a corner solution for S_i which means that dS_i=0 and dX_i=dI_i this reduces to

$$d\psi_i = \frac{\partial^2 U_i}{\partial X_i^2} dI_i - \frac{\partial^2 U_i}{\partial Q_i^2}\frac{\partial Q}{\partial A}\frac{dA}{d\tau} R_i' d\tau,$$

thus $d\psi_i / dI_i < 0$ and $d\psi_i / d\tau > 0$. For an interior solution of S_i, implying that $d\psi_i = 0$ and $X_i = I_i - S_i$, one obtains

$$dS_i = \frac{\dfrac{\partial^2 U_i}{\partial X_i^2} dI_i - \dfrac{\partial^2 U_i}{\partial Q_i^2}\dfrac{\partial Q}{\partial A}\dfrac{dA}{d\tau} R_i' d\tau}{\dfrac{\partial^2 U_i}{\partial Q_i^2} R_i'^2 + \dfrac{\partial U_i}{\partial Q_i} R_i'' + \dfrac{\partial^2 U_i}{\partial X_i^2}}$$

hence $dS_i / dI_i > 0$ and $dS_i / d\tau < 0$.

Appendix E: Desired Tax Rate and Fixed Defensive Expenditure

Total differentiation of (4.25) while holding everything constant except the two controls S_i and τ_i gives

$$d\tau_i = \frac{\dfrac{\partial^2 U_i}{\partial Q_i^2}\dfrac{\partial U_i}{\partial X_i}\left(\dfrac{\partial Q}{\partial A}\dfrac{dA}{d\tau_i} d\tau_i + R_i' dS_i\right) + \dfrac{\partial U_i}{\partial Q_i}\dfrac{\partial^2 U_i}{\partial X_i^2}\left(a_i \dfrac{dA}{d\tau_i} d\tau_i + dS_i\right)}{a_i\left(\dfrac{\partial U_i}{\partial X_i}\right)^2}$$

Solving fully for $d\tau_i$, and dividing by dS_i yields

$$\frac{d\tau_i}{dS_i} = \frac{\frac{\partial^2 U_i}{\partial Q_i^2}\frac{\partial U_i}{\partial X_i}R_i' + \frac{\partial U_i}{\partial Q_i}\frac{\partial^2 U_i}{\partial X_i^2}}{a_i\left(\frac{\partial U_i}{\partial X_i}\right)^2 - \frac{\partial^2 U_i}{\partial Q_i^2}\frac{\partial U_i}{\partial X_i}\frac{\partial Q}{\partial A}\frac{dA}{d\tau_i} - \frac{\partial U_i}{\partial Q_i}\frac{\partial^2 U_i}{\partial X_i^2}a_i\frac{dA}{d\tau_i}} < 0$$

Chapter 5 Environmental Concern, Green Campaigning, and Corporate Lobbying

There are two things you shouldn't watch being made, sausage and law. Anonymous[40]

As pointed out in section 4.3, the most commonly encountered explanation of the middle class's comparatively strong engagement and involvement in environmental protection issues is its higher concern for the environment. While the last chapter avoided dealing with this psychological aspect, it constitutes a key element of the present chapter. Environmental concern, however, is not restricted to the middle class. It "tends to cut across all socioeconomic categories" [Mohai (1985), p. 821].

5.1 Environmental Concern and Public Environmental Policy

Taking this statement as a starting point, it will be attempted to answer three questions in section 5.1: What is meant by environmental concern? How does it influence people's behaviour? And how may it become relevant to the firms' pollution abatement decision?

5.1.1 Environmental Concern as a Filter of Reality

The terms environmental concern, awareness or consciousness[41] express subjectivity. They reflect a mixture of individual or collective knowledge, values and emotional affection. Knowledge about environmental issues may be acquired through one's own experience, but more importantly through education, the media, or other external sources. Since modern environmental threats are increasingly diffuse, often invisible for the lay person, and their causalities regularly poorly understood even by experts, science plays a central

---

[40] Quoted by Tietenberg (1992), p. 450

[41] These terms will be used interchangeably.

role in providing the knowledge that is needed to create consciousness for the environment [Jamison, Eyerman and Cramer (1990)].

Values are usually acquired in the course of socialisation. They determine for instance if a person takes a purely anthropocentric-utilitarian ("protect the environment to conserve its benefits for humans"), or an ecocentric ("protect the environment because all elements have a right to exist and flourish") position towards the environment [Pearce and Turner (1990), p. 229; see also section 1.1]. Emotional affection, finally, is related to values but can be stimulated rather easily and is less stable than the value system.

All three factors - knowledge, values and affection - influence the way people see the world, determine the importance they attribute to particular circumstances, and decide what they see as a problem in the first place. They represent filters through which humans perceive reality. By selecting and weighing single items the filters introduce subjectivity to people's perception. "This filtering process operates both through our five senses, and indirectly through extensions to our perceptual apparatus in the form of stories, new reports, statistics and research. These filters are essential and unavoidable, they serve as automatic pilots that largely function without people being aware of it ..." [Lidskog (1996), p. 35].

5.1.2 The Concept of Perceived Pollution

A low level of environmental awareness leads people to underestimate the harmfulness of pollution, and to perceive the quality of the environment as better than it actually is. In metaphorical terms, it is a strong filter to perception, leaving through only weak signals of the real dangers, threats and risks associated with certain environmental conditions. On the other hand, environmental concern can also amplify perception when it is excessive, leading to an exaggeratedly dramatic picture of the state of the environment.

To take a more formal approach to this issue, define ***perceived pollution*** Z, i.e. pollution as it is perceived by a household, as the product of physical or *effective pollution* P (which retains its properties specified by (4.1)) and some index $\Omega \geq 0$ of the household's environmental concern about pollution:

$$Z \equiv \Omega P. \tag{5.1}$$

Suppose that the units of Ω are defined in a way such that it expresses how "appropriate" the household's concern about pollution is relative to the level it would have under perfect information and rationality. In this ideal case $\Omega \equiv 1$, and so $Z=P$. If $0<\Omega<1$ the seriousness of P is underestimated, and perceived pollution is lower than effective pollution. $\Omega>1$ indicates an exaggeration. $\Omega=0$ means that pollution is not perceived as such at all, e.g. due to lack of information and own experience. Note, moreover, that a marginal increase in Ω at a given P has the same effect on Z as a marginal increase in P at a given Ω. A rise in Ω can hence offset a decline in P.

Provided that Z enters the household's utility, (5.1) can be interpreted as the *household production function for perceived pollution*. According to the so-called household production function approach [e.g. Michael and Becker (1973); Stigler and Becker (1977)] households derive utility from commodities which they "produce" or assemble from various inputs such as market goods, public goods, information, time, their own education, and circumstances. A telephone, for instance, is only useful for people who know how to operate it, and who have somebody to call. Hence the acquisition of a telephone, even in combination with its complement "access to a phone system" does not necessarily increase utility.

Similarly, the existence of pollution has no effect on utility unless people are aware of it or its physical consequences. In the case of pollutants that are directly and immediately harmful to human health, or which can be sensed without technical aid, awareness will build up automatically. However, people had for long been completely indifferent about emissions of CO_2 and CFCs until they were told by scientists and the media about the dangers associated with them. Awareness has been raised through the provision of information, but also through the questioning of traditional values such as commitment to laissez faire, individualism and materialism which constitute the "dominant social paradigm" [Pirages (1977); Dunlap and Van Liere (1984)], and through emotional mobilisation of the public.

In the present section 5.1 the index Ω will be assumed to depend only on factors that are determined outside of the model, such as the specific properties of pollutantants, cultural, political and other aspects of the society in question, own experience, knowledge provided by scientific research and media coverage. In later sections it will be endogenised.

5.1.3 The Household as Consumer and Voter

Perceived pollution will now be related to household utility. Assume that a single representative household forms the consumer side of the economy. It derives utility from consumption X and disutility from perceived pollution Z. The utility function $U(X,Z)$ has the properties

$$\frac{\partial U}{\partial X}>0,\ \frac{\partial^2 U}{\partial X^2}<0,\ \lim_{X\to 0}\frac{\partial U}{\partial X}=\infty,\ \frac{\partial U}{\partial Z}<0,\ \frac{\partial^2 U}{\partial Z^2}<0,\ \frac{\partial^2 U}{\partial X \partial Z}=0. \tag{5.2}$$

So unlike the utility function of earlier chapters, $U(\cdot)$ now contains perceived pollution as an argument. The replacement of environmental quality by pollution (which is by definition a measure of the abence of environmental quality) is made for analytical convenience and, as will be seen, it does not alter the behaviour of the model.

When maximising utility, the household's choice of X is constrained by its income which is again comprised of profits, transfers and wages (see (4.15)). But since there is only a single household, $a_1=b_1=1$ and $N=1$. Substution from the profit function (4.2) and the transfer $\Gamma\equiv\tau P$, household income reduces to (4.6). Since in optimum the household does not waste income, it spends everything on consumption, thus $X=I=F-A$. The effect of a marginal increase in τ on consumption is given by

$$\frac{dX}{d\tau}=-\frac{dA}{d\tau}<0 \tag{5.3}$$

the sign of which follows from (4.4).

In order to investigate how environmental concern influences the household's behaviour, the pollution tax rate τ needs once again to be treated as its hypothetical control variable. The household's indirect utility function reads $U(F-A,Z)$. Utility maximisation with respect to τ, substitution from (5.3), and division by $dA/d\tau>0$ yields the condition[42]

$$\frac{\partial U}{\partial X}-\frac{\partial U}{\partial Z}\Omega\frac{\partial P}{\partial A}=0 \tag{5.4}$$

[42] This condition is necessary and suffcient for a unique global maximum. The proof has been omitted here because $U(F-A,Z)$ is very similar to (4.8). The sufficiency of its first-order condition has been proved in appendix A of chapter 4.

which is essentially the same as the optimum condition for abatement (3.11), but extended by a dependence on environmental concern. After substitution from (4.3) it can explicitly be solved for τ:

$$\tau = -\frac{\partial U / \partial Z}{\partial U / \partial X}\Omega \qquad (5.5)$$

which shows that, ceteris paribus, *the desired pollution tax rate will be the higher the more aware of pollution the household is*.

5.1.4 Government Objective Functions and Endogenous Policy Theory

Two of the three questions from the beginning of section 5.1 concerning the meaning of environmental concern and the influence of concern on people's behaviour have been answered. It remains to address the third question about the relevance of environmental concern for the firms' pollution abatement decision. Alternatively one may look for channels through which people's demand for a better environment - which depends on their level of awareness (see (5.4) and (5.5)) - is transmitted to the firms in a way such that it enters their decision to abate.

A first transmission channel is the economic market. By choosing among close substitutes those goods which are less environmentally harmful, even if they are more expensive, or by rejecting products from eco-inefficient companies consumers create an incentive for firms to reduce the pollution associated with their products and processes. The current success of (allegedly) environmentally friendly consumer goods and services suggests that this channel exists and works to a some degree. The role of information must certainly be stressed here. The popular practice of eco-labelling, and the publishing of green consumer guides are just two examples for the response to the consumers' need of information in this context.

Another way for households to signal their demand for a better environmental quality and to transmit this demand to the firms is via the political channel, that is, through voting which ultimately leads to environmental legislation. It needs to be kept in mind, however, that "What the people get is conditioned not only by what the people want, but by whether they have one dominant party or several competitive political parties; a Presidential system or a Parlamentarian system; a free press or a controlled press; and numerous other institutional factors. It depends, in short, on their country's political structure." [Inglehard (1977), p. 6]

Under the premise that every government's overriding primary objective is to remain in power, one can derive for every type of government a set of auxiliary or secondary objectives which, when fulfilled, ensure that the primary objective is met, too. One might regard the secondary objectives as sufficient conditions, and they will vary substantially with the political framework. In a representative democracy with majority rule voting, one reasonable secondary objective of a government will be to secure the support from the majority of voters in order to be re-elected.[43]

Political competition represents an incentive for the government to orientate its policies towards the preferences of majorities or large political groups. Democracies in which governments are forced to respect their voters' will if they want to stay in office should therefore be the most promising form of political system when it comes to maximising people's utility.

In the hypothetical case of a society which is perfectly homogeneous in its political preferences, the government's optimal (in the sense of objective-function-maximising) strategy is clear. Since the party with the programme which best reflects the voting population's preferences will be favoured over all the others and win all votes, the government will aim at maximising the voters' utility through its policy. Such a scenario justifies the identity of household utility function and government objective function. This assumption will be made below. On the other hand, if the voters fall into groups of different size and with different preferences, the government's optimal strategy depends on the largest group's size and on whether coalitions can be formed. The theory of public choice deals with such kinds of problems. With a single group of voters representing the absolute majority, the government will offer a political agenda intended to maximise this biggest group's utility only, by and large neglecting all the other voters. In section 5.2 this will be supposed to be the case.

Another important aspect of a government objective function concerns the existence of special interest groups or lobbies. Not all voters have to gain or lose equally much through a certain government policy. This asymmetry is the reason why some groups of voters interfere more actively and more intensively with politics than others. However, lobbies are not only formed

---

[43] In later sections the secondary conditions will be expressed in the form of a *government objective function* the maximisation of which is taken to be sufficient to secure the government's necessary political power.

by voters with similar political preferences but also by firms and industries for which it is the only way to articulate their economic interests, often consisting in rent seeking. Group size may become but one criterion in political reasoning if efforts per group member to influence governmental policy differ significantly between the groups. Lobbies may exercise influence beyond the weight of their sheer voting power by materially supporting political parties. Such contributions can be used by the parties to finance their promotion and public relations work up to entire election campaigns.

Given that voters do not possess perfect information on the different parties' precise political activities, and therefore have to rely on the information provided by the media, the lobbies, and the parties themselves, there is a large potential for manipulation of voters. So if it is not alone the political programme that counts in winning votes but also the way the programme is presented and communicated, the government may deviate in its actual policy to some degree from what its voters expect it to do without losing its support. In that case the government's objective function will include both the utility of its electorate and the contributions from lobbies. It will then have to trade off two possibly opposing interests against each other [see Grossman and Helpman (1994), (1995) for a similar discussion in the context of trade policy]. Sections 5.3 and 5.4 will consider this type of objective function.

Magee et al. (1989), p. 47, draw parallels between a competitive economy and politics: "in both economic and political markets, there is a process for resolving conflicting goals: In economic markets the desired quantities traded by buyers and sellers are equilibrated by the price mechanism; in political markets, the levels of power exercised by conflicting groups are balanced by the policies that are enacted. Policies in political markets are like prices in economic markets: They are equilibrating mechanisms that adjust to balance opposing forces." So just like prices which are determined "endogenously" in economic equilibrium, also policies as power-maximising political measures or strategies can be derived endogenously. This is the core message of *endogenous policy theory*.

One interesting implication of this approach for politics is that democratic governments will tend to be pushed into a passive role. Magee et al. (1989) write: "Ironically, since the parties cannot select the policies that are in the best interests of the country, we have the *powerless politician effect*: *Government policies are outside of policymaker control.*" [p. 5; italics in the original.] "The assertion that politicians are powerless is supported by the observation that barriers to entry by challengers are low. There is a highly elastic supply of politicians at low prices" [p. 59] which ensures a high degree of political competition and efficiency of the political market.

5.1.5 The Government's Environmental Policy

Returning to the formal model, the pollution tax rate τ which has so far been treated as exogenously given will now be modelled as the outcome of the government's optimising behaviour. According to the discussion in the last section, it will be assumed that the government is democratically elected, and that its overriding objective is to stay in office. Since all households are identical by assumption, the government maximises its political support by pursuing a policy that maximises the households' utility. Therefore, its objective function must be

$$G = U(X, Z) \tag{5.6}$$

The government's policy instrument is the tax rate τ with respect to which it maximises its objective function. But since the resulting optimisation problem is identical with the household's hypothetical utility maximisation in section 5.1.3, the results are identical, too, namely (5.4) or (5.5).

Just like (3.11) or (3.20), condition (5.4) suggests that those environmental problems will be tackled first which have the most immediate impact on people's wellbeing, and those which can be mitigated or resolved at relatively low marginal cost. But furthermore, the model predicts that environmental problems which fulfil neither of the two conditions - a characteristic of many modern pollutants - might still be addressed if they attract sufficient public attention. This attention will in most cases be the result of broad media coverage, inducing public awareness or concern about the problem in question.

Typical examples are acid rain or "electro smog". Carbon emissions fall into the same category, but avoidance costs appear to be prohibitive. Presumably for the same reason of induced environmental concern one observes today that problems of local relevance in the developing world often meet some form of willingness to pay in rich countries far away, usually cases which "sell well", such as whale hunting or the killing of baby seals. The rejection of nuclear energy by large parts of the public in some countries also seems to be more the result of exogenously generated, subjective concern than of personal experience through exposure.

(5.5) is the government's optimal policy choice, given its objective function. It implies that τ is, inter alia, an increasing function of Ω. In fact, this relationship establishes the ***link between perception and environmental policy*** which will play an important role in the following sections. To conclude it can be said that within the framework of this model, rising environmental concern is good for the environment.

5.1.6 A Simple Functional Forms Example

In order to prepare the ground for the sections 5.2 - 5.4, the pollution and utility functions will now be assigned specific forms. They will be chosen in a way such that the level of output and the efficiency of abatement drop out as a determinants of environmental policy. Since their effect on optimal pollution and abatement levels has already been analysed in chapter 3, they can be sacrificed to Occam's Razor. The resulting model will highlight the particular role of public environmental concern for policy-making and all variables that are affected by policy. It will also be simple enough to allow for various extensions while maintaining its transparency.

Suppose that the demand side of the economy is comprised of a constant number of identical households. Let this number be normalised to unity, so that aggregate and per capita magnitudes coincide. Household utility is given by the linearly separable form

$$U(X,Z) = \ln X - Z^2 \tag{5.7}$$

which fulfils all assumptions made in (5.2). Household income equals (4.6). Gross emissions are proportional to output F. The amount of gross emissions avoided through abatement is proportional to abatement spending A. The resulting net emissions $F-A$ affect the environment at an increasing scale, that is, every unit of net emission causes a greater damage than the previous unit. Pollution here must therefore be understood not as the sum of emissions but rather as a damage function. Suppose that this pollution rises quadratically with net emissions, so that the pollution function can be written as

$$P = 0.5(F - A)^2. \tag{5.8}$$

For $F>A$ this function possesses all properties that have been postulated in (4.1) except the infinite efficiency of abatement when $A=0$. This this last property which rules out corner solutions of A is replaced in the present model by the assumption that $A>0$.

Substitution from (5.8) into the firms' optimum condition (4.3) reveals that $\tau(F-A)=1$ which can be solved for abatement:

$$A = F - \tau^{-1}. \tag{5.9}$$

So A is increasing in F and τ. From (4.6) it follows that income equals

$$I = \tau^{-1}. \tag{5.10}$$

The households spend their entire income on consumption: $X = I = \tau^{-1}$. Note that this consumption function does not contain ouput as argument. Substitution from (5.9) into (5.8) yields the indirect pollution function

$$P = 0.5\tau^{-2}. \tag{5.11}$$

Given X and P as functions of τ, the government's objective function reads

$$G = U = \ln(\tau^{-1}) - 0.25\Omega^2\tau^{-4}. \tag{5.12}$$

Its maximisation with respect to τ yields the optimum condition

$$\frac{\partial G}{\partial \tau} = \frac{\partial U}{\partial \tau} = -\tau^{-1} + \Omega^2\tau^{-5} = 0 \tag{5.13}$$

which can be solved for

$$\tau = \Omega^{1/2}. \tag{5.14}$$

In optimum the tax rate is increasing and strictly concave in Ω. Substituting from (5.14) into (5.9)-(5.11) shows that

$$A = F - \Omega^{-1/2} \tag{5.15}$$

$$I = \Omega^{-1/2} \tag{5.16}$$

$$P = 0.5\Omega^{-1}. \tag{5.17}$$

From (5.15) one can see that the assumption made above that $0<A<F$ implies that $F^{-2} < \Omega < \infty$.

The striking simplicity of the above relationships is the result of the particular choice of functional forms. Although some generality is lost, especially through the elimination of the output level as determinant of pollution and policy, and through the assumption of a single representative household these simple functions will still allow for a number of conclusions in what follows.

5.2 Green Campaigning

In the simple model just developed, all variables are functions of Ω alone since F has been assumed constant. A rise in Ω for exogenous reasons induces the government to pursue a stricter environmental policy through setting a higher pollution tax rate. The firms react by increasing their efforts to abate pollution at the cost of reducing the households' income which lowers their consumption level. Now environmental concern will be endogenised to some degree. An obvious way to do this would be to make Ω a function of personal exposure to, or experience with, pollution. But since, over time, Ω would simply tend to unity this would not provide any new insight.

More interesting, and increasingly important in the context of highly complex, imperceptible, or not yet generally recognised environmental problems, is the role of different interest groups within society and their interaction with the objective to manipulate public concern about pollution.

Environmental protection issues have figured prominently in recent political debates. Parties, governmental and non-governmental organisations, firms and private initiatives, many of which with strongly diverging ideas about the best environmental strategy, pursue activities that are aimed directly or indirectly at influencing other members of society in their sense. Greenpeace is probably the best-known manipulator of public environmental concern on an international level but locally many small groups are at least as active in directing public interest towards environmental problems, or in mobilising the public against individual polluters.

Big firms, professional associations and corporate interest groups, on the other hand, aim at keeping environmental regulations and the associated compliance costs at moderate levels by counteracting the greens' public relations efforts, and by engaging in lobbying with the government. Such activities, for simplicity called "green campaigning"[44] and "corporate lobbying", will now be looked at.

5.2.1 Green Core and Grey Households

Suppose that the demand side of the functionally specified model economy considered in section 5.1.6 now consists of households falling into two groups which differ in their concern about the environment. The bigger group, referred to as "*grey households*" or simply "*the greys*", is characterised by a level of concern equal to Ω with $F^{-2} < \Omega < \overline{\Omega} < \infty$. The greys correspond to the households of the section 5.1.6 model. However, their Ω is not constant. The greys do not actively inform themselves about the latest state of scientific knowledge regarding environmental risks and threats, but they passively - and perhaps uncritically - absorb what they are being told by the media and through other channels. This behaviour which might be due to high information and search costs may be exploited to manipulate their Ω through selected information, public relations efforts and campaigns.

The remaining smaller group of households has a higher concern about environmental issues, given by the constant $\overline{\Omega}$, which may be due to a higher degree to which they are exposed to, or physically affected by, pollution; to their education, knowledge and personal experience; or to their attitudes and moral views. These environmentalist households will be called the "*green core*" of society, "*green households*" or the "*greens*". Their share in the total number of households, which is again normalised to unity, is constant at $0<\varepsilon<0.5$.

The grey households' only use of income is consumption, hence $I=X$. They reach a utility of $U = \ln X - Z^2 = \ln X - (\Omega P)^2$ which exceeds the green households' utility $U_G = \ln X_G - Z_G^2 = \ln X_G - (\overline{\Omega} P)^2$ even if $X = X_G$ because of the difference in the perception of effective pollution.

5.2.2 Government Policy

In section 5.1, with only a single type of household or voter, the government's objective function was taken to be identical with this household's utility function. Utility maximisation by the government was ment to buy

---

[44] Green campaigning in this study is not to be understood as election campaign activities for a green party, but as party-independent, issue-related information and PR work.

votes. With two distinct groups of households, the government's objective function may now take various forms. One may still imagine a government that tries to maximise utility but takes into account the composition of the electorate, that is, it could be thought to maximise a welfare function combining both groups' utility.

However, in a parlamentarian multiparty democracy this will not be a majority-securing strategy if there is at least one other party offering a programme that is utility-maximising for the greys only. The result will be that the government is formed by the party with the "grey" programme which is supported by a share $1-\varepsilon$ of households or voters. If a third party supports the greens' objectives, it will receive a share ε of votes and do the opposition work in parlament. The joint-utility maximising party will be out of the race with zero votes. Therefore, with the assumed composition of households, and voting under the majority rule, the government's objective function must again be given by (5.6) which it maximises subject to the greys' budget constraint.

Since the resulting optimisation problem is identical with that of section 5.1.6, the pollution tax rate will be the same as before, namely (5.14), implying the relationships (5.15)-(5.17).

5.2.3 Optimal Campaigning

The grey households' utility, expressed as a function of τ and Ω, is given by (5.12). Since in optimum $\partial U/\partial\tau=0$ (see (5.13)) their utility could not be increased by a different pollution tax rate than the one set by the government. Hence the greys feel perfectly represented and have no incentive to interfere with politics in other ways than by voting.

Assuming for the moment that also the green core households spend their income only on consumption, so that $X_G = I = \tau^{-1}$ (see (5.10)), their utility equals

$$U_G = \ln(\tau^{-1}) - 0.25\overline{\Omega}^2\tau^{-4}. \tag{5.18}$$

Differentiation and substitution from (5.14) shows that utility could be increased by a higher tax rate:

$$\frac{\partial U_G}{\partial \tau} = -\tau^{-1} + \overline{\Omega}^2\tau^{-5} = -\Omega^{-1/2}(1-\overline{\Omega}^2\Omega^{-2}) > 0.$$

This indicates that the greens are not satisfied with the government's policy. There exists a preference among them for a stricter environmental policy. It will now be looked at how they may go about to achieve such a policy.

The green households are aware of the government's objective function, hence they realise how the pollution tax is adjusted to Ω. Their aim is to make use of the functional relationship (5.14), and to employ it in their own interest by raising Ω through environmental campaigning. The greens act cooperatively among themselves because they are sufficiently small a group to discourage free-riding, and they are convinced that only by standing together they can make a difference. Note that in this setting it would be no reasonable strategy for the greens to try and influence policy by overstating their preferences for a better environment.

Let H denote green campaign spending, and assume that $H \geq 0$. Then the green households face the budget constraint $I \geq X_G + H$ where X_G and H are their two control variables. Since it can be expected that no income is wasted, the budget constraint will hold as a strict equality in optimum. Moreover, it has been shown that $I = \Omega^{-1/2}$ (see (5.16)), hence the budget constraint can be rewritten as $X_G = \Omega^{-1/2} - H$ and used immediately to eliminate X_G from the utility function which then reads

$$U_G = \ln(\Omega^{-1/2} - H) - 0.25\overline{\Omega}^2\Omega^{-2}. \tag{5.19}$$

Now the effect of H on Ω needs to be defined. Let $h \equiv \varepsilon H$ represent total campaign expenditure in the economy. It is assumed that Ω depends on h in the following way:

$$\frac{\partial \Omega}{\partial h} > 0, \ \frac{\partial^2 \Omega}{\partial h^2} < 0, \ \lim_{h \to 0} \frac{\partial \Omega}{\partial h} < \infty \quad \text{for } h > 0.$$

The first two assumptions say that the marginal efficiency of campaigning is positive but diminishing, and the limit expression states that it has a finite upper bound. The initial or autonomous level of the grey households' Ω, denoted Ω_0, will be assumed to exert the following influence:

$$\frac{\partial \Omega}{\partial \Omega_0} > 0 \text{ and } \frac{\partial^2 \Omega}{\partial h \, \partial \Omega_0} < 0.$$

The greens' objective is to choose their H in a way such that it maximises their utility (5.19), subject to the nonnegativity of H. The Lagrangean corresponding to this problem reads

$$\mathscr{L} = \ln(\Omega^{-1/2} - H) - 0.25\overline{\Omega}^2\Omega^{-2} + \psi H,$$

leading to the first-order condition

$$\frac{\partial \mathscr{L}}{\partial H} = -\frac{0.5\varepsilon\Omega^{-3/2}\frac{\partial\Omega}{\partial h}+1}{\Omega^{-1/2}-H} + 0.5\varepsilon\overline{\Omega}^2\Omega^{-3}\frac{\partial\Omega}{\partial h} + \psi = 0. \tag{5.20}$$

Note that $\partial\Omega/\partial H = (\partial\Omega/\partial h)(\partial h/\partial H) = \varepsilon(\partial\Omega/\partial h)$. The complementary slackness conditions require that $\psi \geq 0$, $H \geq 0$ and $\psi H = 0$. Here ψ is the Lagrangean multiplier associated with the nonnegativity restriction on H and represents the marginal opportunity loss of campaigning. If $\psi > 0$ and hence $H = 0$, differentiation of (5.20) with respect to Ω_0 shows that

$$\frac{d\psi}{d\Omega_0} > 0 \tag{5.21}$$

(see appendix A). This means that *campaigning will only be regarded optimal if* Ω_0 *is not too high*. Intuitively, this was to be expected because the lower Ω_0, the more the government's environmental policy deviates from what the green core would like it to be.

Also the share of green households in the economy influences the opportunity loss, and hence the campaigning decision. The greater ε, the lower will be ψ (see appendix A), implying that *if the green households represent a significant part of society, they are more likely to engage in campaigning activities* at a given level of Ω_0 than if they are only a very small minority (provided their group-internal discipline which prevents free-riding does not break down). The reason lies in the public good character of the campaign impact. Campaigning costs per green household for achieving a certain environmental awareness among the grey households are the lower, the more greens join in and contribute.

Turning to campaign spending, if Ω_0 is low enough for a given ε so that campaigning becomes attractive, ψ vanishes, and (5.20) turns into an implicit campaign function. Appendix B shows that

$$\frac{dH}{d\Omega_0} < 0. \tag{5.22}$$

The relationship between H and the green core's share ε, however, is ambiguous. The reason is that both the marginal benefit and the marginal opportunity cost of campaigning are increasing in ε. On the one hand, a higher ε causes to the public-good effect already identified above: the more green households there are, the less each of them has to spend on campaigns to achieve a certain level of environmental awareness among the greys. On the other hand, a higher ε means that a given campaign contribution per green household achieves a higher Ω, leading to a lower income $I = \Omega^{-1/2}$ which reduces consumption possibilities, thereby raising the opportunity cost of campaigning.

But it is not only campaigning that influences the level of income. The opposite is also true. To see this, let $I_0 \equiv \Omega_0{}^{-1/2}$ (see (5.16)) be the *initial* household income, i.e. income per capita *before* the green households make their campaigning decision. Since $dI_0 / d\Omega_0 = -0.5\Omega_0{}^{-3/2} < 0$, it follows from (5.21) and (5.22) that

$$\text{sgn}\frac{d\psi}{dI_0} = -\text{sgn}\frac{d\psi}{d\Omega_0} < 0 \quad \text{and} \quad \text{sgn}\frac{dH}{dI_0} = -\text{sgn}\frac{dH}{d\Omega_0} > 0.$$

Thus a higher initial income is associated with a lower marginal opportunity loss of campaigning, or with a higher optimal level of campaign spending, ceteris paribus. In other words, *campaigning will only be regarded optimal if* I_0 *is not too low,* and if this is the case *campaign spending is increasing in* I_0. Growing per capita income means a rising I_0, and hence favours campaigning. It can can hence be concluded that *economic growth in the sense of a rising* I_0 *is likely to result in an increasing environmental concern among the grey households, and via the democratic process in a higher pollution tax rate, and a better environmental quality.*

5.2.4 External Effects of Campaigning

When deciding upon the privately optimal level of H, the green core households neglect the effect that their campaigning has on the grey households' utility. Basically three effects can be distinguished. First of all, with some given level of effective pollution P, a rise in Ω causes additional disutility to the grey households because they perceive the same effective pollution more intensively. Green campaigning thus involves a first ***negative*** externality.

Secondly, the grey households benefit from the same effect as the green core, namely that their rising Ω makes more abatement and thus a lower effective pollution level optimal. Less effective pollution implies less perceived pollution, ceteris paribus. This is a ***positive*** externality of green campaigning. In general it cannot be said whether the positive or the negative effect will dominate. In the present model, however, the net effect is always zero. The reason is that pollution as perceived by the grey households is given by $Z \equiv \Omega P = 0.5\Omega\Omega^{-1} = 0.5$. It turns out that any change in Ω is exactly offset by an opposite change in P. Thus the grey households' perceived pollution is completely inelastic to changes in environmental concern.

A third externality concerns the grey households' consumption level. A stricter environmental policy induces the firms to spend more on pollution abatement, thereby reducing all households' income. The greens take this effect on their own consumption level into account when trading off X_G against H, but they ignore the effect on the greys' consumption. The value of this third externality equals

$$\frac{\partial \ln X}{\partial H} = \frac{\partial \ln(\Omega^{-1/2})}{\partial H} = -0.5\varepsilon\Omega^{-1}\frac{\partial \Omega}{\partial h} < 0$$

per grey household. Hence campaigning is a source of social inefficieny.

But there is yet another, less conventional way of looking at the effect of campaigning. If $\overline{\Omega}$ does not exceed unity, i.e. if the greens do not perceive the state of the environment to be worse than it actually is, then $\Omega<1$ because by assumption $\Omega < \overline{\Omega}$. This means that the grey households underestimate the true harmfulness of (effective) pollution, e.g. for their health, making them support an environmental policy that is too lenient from an informed point of view.[45] Since an increase in Ω induces a stricter, and hence

[45] In philosophy [e.g. Kymlicka (1990), pp. 16-18; Hausman and McPherson (1994)], two kinds of preferences are distinguished. Preferences which take perfect information into account are called ***informed***. Their satisfaction increases welfare for sure. Individuals, on the other hand, usually do not have access to perfect information or do not inform themselves to the necessary extent, and instead rely on their subjective, possibly false perceptions and beliefs. Their preferences are referred to as ***uninformed***. The satisfaction of uninformed preferences may or may not increase utility. (continues on next page)

an objectively more "appropriate" policy from which also the greys benefit, *even if they do not realise it*, campaigning may be said to cause a positive externality.

5.2.5 A Tax on Campaigning?

At this point it is worth stressing the parallels between the firms' and the green core's activities. *Both groups raise the grey households' perceived pollution*, the firms by emitting effective pollution, the green core by influencing perception. The effective pollution caused by the firms is subject to a tax which is aimed at maximising the greys' utility by discouraging pollution emissions. Given the government's objective function, it seems only consequent also to expect a tax on campaigning.

Provided that $H>0$, the effect of such a tax, denoted by ν, on campaigning would have to be negative: $\partial H/\partial \nu<0$. The optimum campaign tax rate would maximise the grey households' utility $U = \ln(\Omega^{-1/2}) - 0.25$:

$$\frac{\partial U}{\partial \nu} = -0.5\varepsilon\Omega^{-1}\frac{\partial \Omega}{\partial h}\frac{\partial H}{\partial \nu} = 0.$$

If $\varepsilon>0$ and $\Omega<\infty$ there are two ways how this condition can be met. First of all, if the greens did not intend to engage in campaigning ($H=0$) anyway because they would incur a positive opportunity loss, $\partial H/\partial \nu=0$ since H cannot be reduced further. Clearly, a positive campaign tax would make no sense in this case.

The second way to meet the condition presupposes that campaigning *would* take place if $\nu=0$. This time, $\partial H/\partial \nu=0$ is achieved by setting the campaign tax at a level sufficiently high to render campaigning inefficient for the greens under all circumstances. The optimum level of ν is prohibitive for campaigning and enforces a corner solution for H.

In mainstream economics, however, it is assumed that preferences are stable over time. New information, for instance about a commodity, does not change the consumers' preferences (i.e. the utility function) but alters the characteristics of the commodity in question. In this sense every commodity is a vector, composite, or bundle of various characteristics. This is exactly the idea behind the household production function approach mentioned in section 5.1.2

So in both cases *the optimum level of campaigning from the greys' point of view is zero*. Only if the campaign tax revenues were redistributed to the greys by the government, campaigning activities might not be suppressed completely.

In real-world democracies, however, no such thing as a campaign tax can be found. Attempts to influence the public opinion through political, environmental or other campaigns, public relations efforts, advertisements and the media take place almost unrestrictedly. If taxing or otherwise discouraging such activities is a feasible strategy for a government what might be the reason for it not to be pursued?

The answer lies in the intrinsic value of the *freedom of speech* that would be curtailed by such measures. Freedom of speech, along with the freedom of the press and other rights, is a precondition for democracy to work. People must be allowed to utter their opinion, even with the objective of convincing others of it. Punishing those who create awareness and spread concern about the state of the environment would be like killing the messenger (though in this case, the message is partly a product of the messenger).

5.3 Corporate Lobbying

Not only the grey households are affected negatively by a higher environmental awareness level Ω, but also the firms. Upon substitution from (5.9), (5.11) and (5.14), their profits function (4.2) (where $N=1$) reads

$$\Pi = 0.5\Omega^{-1/2} - w. \tag{5.23}$$

Successful campaigning leads to declining profits:

$$\frac{\partial \Pi}{\partial H} = -0.25\varepsilon\Omega^{-3/2}\frac{\partial \Omega}{\partial h} < 0.$$

However, different from the passive group of grey households, the firms as active profit maximisers do not simply put up with the green core's activities. They look for ways to influence policy on their own. One way to do this is to engage in campaigning themselves, but with the opposite objective: to play down environmental hazards and risks, to distract public attention from real problems, to cool down hot issues, thus to draw a nicer picture of their operations and of the state of the environment.

On the other hand, especially if the green core has already gained some public profile, it will be very costly for the firms to start a successful countercampaign of their own. It would be rather easy for the greens - who may claim to be the moral conscience of society - to turn the firms' public relations work against them by accusing them of misleading and deceiving the public. So the firms' own campaigning will tend to be rather cautious, employed to accompany and support other measures.

Another way for the firms to exert influence on governmental policy consists in lobbying, i.e. pursuing activities aimed at raising the likelyhood that the outcome of political processes is favourable for the firms. A key feature of lobbying is that it does not involve swaying voters; instead, the targets are politicians, but also other influencial people. Besides providing information and arguments for their position, lobbies often use incentives to win politicians for their cause. For example, a lobby may offer to cooperate in issue B if the government supports its position on issue A. Equally well, it can offer incentives in the form of financial contributions to the party's budget, e.g. in return for a lower pollution tax rate. Financial contributions of any kind have the great advantage of being much less obvious to the general public, and harder to detect as well for the greens.

5.3.1 Government Policy

So suppose that, for the reasons given in section 5.1.4, the government's objective is not any more simply to maximise the grey households' utility, but to maximise a function that combines the grey's utility $U = \ln X - 0.25\Omega^2\tau^{-4}$ and the firms' lobbying contributions $L \geq 0$. This way, the government faces a proper trade-off, and its "policies play the same role in politics as prices play in an economy: Both are equilibrating variables that adjust until opposing forces are balanced" [Magee et al. (1989), p. 3].

At first glance one might be inclined to expect the government having to strike a balance between its own income L from donations, and the grey households' income and consumption level $I = X = \tau^{-1} - L$. But although L does reduce household income ceteris paribus, there is no trade off. The reason is that the firms will only spend resources on influencing the government if that increases their profits

$$\Pi = 0.5\tau^{-1} - L - w. \qquad (5.24)$$

This ensures that the households' income will not decline either, but rise as a consequence of lobbying: L induces a lower tax rate τ, less abatement A, and ultimately a higher household income. Hence the real trade-off that the government's objective function implies, exists between the households' disutility from increasing pollution and the benefit the government derives from a higher L.

A number of plausible forms for the government's new objective function may be found, but many of them have either no analytical solution at all, or lead to solutions that cannot be solved explicitly for τ. To avoid an unnecessary complication of the model, a particular functional form will be assumed that will turn out to produce quite manageable results. It reads

$$G = \ln(\tau^{-1})(1+L)^{4\beta} - 0.25\Omega^2\tau^{-4} \tag{5.25}$$

where $\beta > 0$. The first term is the grey households' utility of consumption when $L=0$, multiplied by a weight. This function can be interpreted in the following way. The government offers the firms to ignore the deduction of L from the households' income (which would drive up the tax instead of lowering it), provided that the firms pay this L to the government as a "compensation". It knows that consumptionwise the greys will be better off with lobbying, so at least from this side it does not have to fear a decline of its popularity among its voters. On the other hand, the lower τ, the greater will be the utility loss through higher perceived pollution $-0.25\Omega^2\tau^{-4}$. The factor $(1+L)^{4\beta}$, finally, gives some extra weight to the first term, expressing the value which the government attaches to financial contributions relative to the grey households' disutility of perceived pollution. The higher L, the more the government is willing to sacrifice environmental quality, and the voters' utility associated with it, to increase its own income. If the firms decide to refrain from lobbying, (5.25) reduces to $G = \ln(\tau^{-1}) - 0.25\Omega^2\tau^{-4}$ which is the familiar version (5.12) of the government objective function.

When deciding on its policy, the government takes L as given. It makes its policy contingent on the firms' contribution, that is, it offers the firms a flexible political programme which is only fully determined after they have made up their mind on how much they are willing to donate. The condition for the government's optimum choice of τ,

$$\frac{\partial G}{\partial \tau} = -\tau^{-1}(1+L)^{4\beta} + \Omega^2\tau^{-5} = 0,$$

can be solved to yield

$$\tau = \Omega^{1/2}(1+L)^{-\beta}. \tag{5.26}$$

Like in its original form as given by (5.14), the tax rate is increasing and concave strictly in Ω. In fact, if $L=0$ (5.26) turns into (5.14). But the tax rate is now also decreasing in lobbying efforts L, opening the firms a new way to influence their pollution tax bill.

5.3.2 Optimal Lobbying

With τ being a function of Ω and L, the firms can now make use of their second control variable besides abatement. They maximise their profits (5.24) with respect to L, subject to $L \geq 0$. The pollution tax rate τ is now given by (5.26), so profits equal

$$\Pi = 0.5\Omega^{-1/2}(1+L)^{\beta} - L - w, \tag{5.27}$$

and the Lagrangean associated with the firms' lobbying problem reads

$$\mathcal{L} = 0.5\Omega^{-1/2}(1+L)^{\beta} - L - w + \theta L.$$

The optimal L has to fulfil the first-order condition

$$\frac{\partial \mathcal{L}}{\partial L} = 0.5\beta\Omega^{-1/2}(1+L)^{\beta-1} - 1 + \theta = 0 \tag{5.28}$$

and meet the complementary slackness conditions $\theta \geq 0$, $L \geq 0$ and $\theta L = 0$. The multiplier θ of the nonnegativity restriction on L is the opportunity loss of lobbying. As long as $\theta > 0$, lobbying has a corner solution. This will be the case if Ω exceeds a certain threshold level Ω_L which is found by setting $L=\theta=0$ in (5.28). One finds that

$$\Omega_L = 0.25\beta^2. \tag{5.29}$$

As long as $\Omega > \Omega_L$, the opportunity loss θ will be positive and increasing in Ω. However, if $\Omega < \Omega_L$, the firms will engage in lobbying. The profit-maximising level of L is obtained by setting $\theta=0$ and solving (5.28):

$$L = b^{-1/\beta}\Omega^{1/(2\beta-2)} - 1 \tag{5.30}$$

where $b \equiv (2/\beta)^{-\beta/(\beta-1)} > 0$ is a constant. Substitution into (5.26) yields

$$\tau = b\Omega^{1/(2-2\beta)} \tag{5.31}$$

In connection with (5.25), β has already been restricted to positive values. Now an upper limit can be fixed as well. To ensure that $\partial\tau/\partial\Omega > 0$ it must hold that $1/(2-2\beta) > 0$ or $\beta < 1$, so taken together $0 < \beta < 1$. It follows that the firms' profit function is strictly concave in L, and that optimal lobbying L is strictly decreasing in Ω.

This last result can be rephrased to highlight its implications: ***the higher the greys' environmental concern is, the less will the firms lobby for a lower tax*** or, if $L=0$ already, the higher will be the opportunity loss of lobbying. This result is not counter-intuitive if the properties of the profit function (5.27) are considered. Without lobbying, a rising Ω causes a decline in profits but at a diminishing rate ($\partial\Pi/\partial\Omega < 0$ and $\partial^2\Pi/\partial\Omega^2 > 0$). Thus the marginal profit reduction through $d\Omega > 0$ is greatest when Ω is low (namely if $\Omega < \Omega_L$). This is the situation when lobbying is efficient. However, if $\Omega > \Omega_L$, a further marginal increase in Ω hardly lowers the firms' profits, at least not as much as lobbying would do.

5.3.3 Lobbying: External Effects and Taxation

Just like green campaigning, lobbying involves external effects which do not only concern the grey, but also the green households. A lower pollution tax rate due to lobbying allows the firms to shift part of their production costs to the households. These costs take the form of reduced abatement efforts or of an increasing undersupply of environmental quality which represents a misallocation of resources. Therefore, lobbying is socially ineffient.

Moreover, both green and grey households have an incentive to push for a ban on this kind of lobbying. Similar to the tax-on-campaigning example of section 5.2.5, it could be shown that a prohibitively high lobby tax would be optimal from the point of view of both household groups. In fact, in real politics, bribing is illegal, and other lobbying activities are restricted by the law, or observed and regulated by official authorities. These legal constraints on lobbying might be expressed in terms of a differentiated lobby tax system that would achieve the same result.

Yet by far not all hypothetical lobby tax rates would be prohibitively high, for lobbying does take place. Again one reason may be that a higher good is to be protected, in this case perhaps not so much the freedom of speech than the right of those concerned by the consequences of legislation to articulate and promote their interests, a right which is characteristic especially of parliamentarian democracies.

A more pragmatic reason not to ban lobbying seems to consist in the lack of a clear criterion that would allow the unambiguous identification of lobbying. For instance, if a large car manufacturer announces that it would have to cease its domestic production if a pollution tax was introduced, it will be hard to decide whether this statement is aimed at influencing environmental policy, which would make it a lobbying activity, or whether it is simply the result of an internal calculation. The information and transaction cost of investigating every possible case of lobbying would probably not be justified by the benefit of a ban on lobbying.

5.4 Green Campaigning Revisited

Through their campaigning, the green core households aim at achieving an environmental policy that reflects their own perception of pollution more appropriately. Their campaigning optimum as given by (5.20) was obtained under the premise that $L=0$, that is, in absence of corporate lobbying. However, if the firms engage in lobbying activities, the premise is violated, and the results of section 5.2 have to be reconsidered. Therefore, the steps of section 5.2 will now be reworked, but based on the tax rate with lobbying (5.26). The objective is to establish the main properties of the campaigning reaction function $H(\Omega, L)$.

All households earn an income of $I = \Omega^{-1/2}(1+L)^{\beta} - L$. In equilibrium, the greys spend it entirely on consumption, whereas the green core's consumption level is given by $X_G = \Omega^{-1/2}(1+L)^{\beta} - L - H$. As to effective pollution, it follows from (5.11) that $P = 0.5\Omega^{-1}(1+L)^{2\beta}$. The greens aim at maximising their utility

$$U_G = \ln\left[\Omega^{-1/2}(1+L)^{\beta} - L - H\right] - 0.25\overline{\Omega}^2\Omega^{-2}(1+L)^{4\beta}$$

with respect to campaigning efforts H, subject to $H \geq 0$. The Lagrangean corresponding to their decision problem reads

$$\mathscr{L} = \ln\left[\Omega^{-1/2}(1+L)^{\beta} - L - H\right] - 0.25\overline{\Omega}^2\Omega^{-2}(1+L)^{4\beta} + \psi H,$$

giving rise to the optimum condition

$$\frac{\partial \mathscr{L}}{\partial H} = -\frac{0.5\varepsilon\Omega^{-3/2}(1+L)^{\beta}\frac{\partial\Omega}{\partial h}+1}{\Omega^{-1/2}(1+L)^{\beta} - L - H} + 0.5\varepsilon\frac{\overline{\Omega}^2}{\Omega^3}(1+L)^{4\beta}\frac{\partial\Omega}{\partial h} + \psi = 0. \quad (5.32)$$

If $L=0$ this condition boils down to (5.20). Hence (5.32) is simply a generalisation of the former. In the case of a corner solution of H, the opportunity loss of campaigning ψ is positive, increasing in the grey households' initial level of environmental concern Ω_0, and decreasing in the green core's share ε. This was already found in section 5.2.3. But now ψ can also be differentiated with respect to lobbying L which reveals that the opportunity loss of campaigning declines as L gets higher (see appendix C). Hence the more the firms engage in lobbying, the more likely it is that the green households become active themselves.

If $\psi=0$, an interior solution for campaigning occurs. Differentiation shows again that H is decreasing in Ω_0 and ambiguously related to ε. New is the result that $H(\Omega,L)$ is increasing but concave in L (see appendix D), saying that the *optimal campaign level is the higher, the more the firms spend on lobbying*, but that H only rises at a diminishing rate with L.

Of course the Lagrangean could as well have been formulated based on the optimal level of L as given by (5.30) straight away, so that the pollution tax rate (5.31) would have had to be used instead of (5.26). This shows that *the order in which firms and green households decide upon their activities is irrelevant for the outcome as long as each group is aware of the respective other group's reaction*. Every group maximises its objective function, given that the other one does so, too. The outcome is a Cournot equilibrium.

5.5 Concluding Remarks

In an attempt to investigate the role of politico-economic factors on the quality of the environment, three main aspects have been addressed: public environmental concern, green campaigning and corporate lobbying. In a democratic political system the first element of this list tends to add a subjective component to the link between economic activity and environmental impact. In the presence of imperfect knowledge about the true harmfulness of many pollutants, and in the face of regular emotion-laden public controversies on environmental topics such a component must not be omitted in a positive analysis.

Environmental concern also represents the base and the precondition for the other two aspects considered. Campaigning would make no sense if people were perfectly aware of all environmental problems. There would be no reason for controversy, and hence nobody would engage in campaigning in the first place. Similarly, if everybody was in possession of some "ultimate environmental truth", no elected government could allow itself to give in to the temptation of financial and other incentives offered by lobbies, and to pursue a policy that violates the interests of the majority of its voters.

But both phenomena, campaigning and lobbying, are being observed, and to a significant extent do influence actual policy-making. Therefore, in order to understand why environmental problems are approached or not approached in certain ways, and to be able to make predictions on what has to be expected in terms of environmental quality in the future, a broader view on the economy-environment nexus must be adopted. Pollution is only partly a technologically determined by-product of economic activity, and also the voters' environmental preferences have only got a limited weight when influential interest groups enter the political arena. The constellation of, and the interaction between these groups as well as the institutional framework are at least as important.

Appendix

Appendix A: The Opportunity Loss of Campaigning

Setting $H=0$ and solving (5.20) for ψ yields

$$\psi = 0.5\varepsilon\Omega^{-1}\frac{\partial\Omega}{\partial h} + \Omega^{1/2} - 0.5\varepsilon\overline{\Omega}^{2}\Omega^{-3}\frac{\partial\Omega}{\partial h}$$

Its partial derivative with respect to Ω_0 equals

$$\frac{\partial\psi}{\partial\Omega_0} = -0.5\varepsilon\Omega^{-2}\frac{\partial\Omega}{\partial\Omega_0}\frac{\partial\Omega}{\partial h} + 0.5\varepsilon\Omega^{-1}\frac{\partial^2\Omega}{\partial h\,\partial\Omega_0} + 0.5\Omega^{-1/2}\frac{\partial\Omega}{\partial\Omega_0}$$
$$+1.5\varepsilon\overline{\Omega}^2\Omega^{-4}\frac{\partial\Omega}{\partial\Omega_0}\frac{\partial\Omega}{\partial h} - 0.5\varepsilon\overline{\Omega}^2\Omega^3\frac{\partial^2\Omega}{\partial h\,\partial\Omega_0}$$
$$= 0.5\varepsilon\Omega^{-2}\frac{\partial\Omega}{\partial\Omega_0}\frac{\partial\Omega}{\partial h}\left(3\overline{\Omega}^2\Omega^{-2} - 1\right) + 0.5\varepsilon\Omega^{-1}\frac{\partial^2\Omega}{\partial h\,\partial\Omega_0}\left(1 - \overline{\Omega}^2\Omega^2\right)$$
$$+0.5\Omega^{-1/2}\frac{\partial\Omega}{\partial\Omega_0}$$

Since $\overline{\Omega}^2\Omega^{-2} > 1$ and $\partial\Omega / (\partial h\,\partial\Omega_0) < 0$ this derivative is positive. The partial derivative with respect to the green core's share in the number of households is given by

$$\frac{\partial\psi}{\partial\varepsilon} = 0.5\Omega^{-1}\frac{\partial\Omega}{\partial h} - 0.5\overline{\Omega}^2\Omega^{-3}\frac{\partial\Omega}{\partial h} = 0.5\Omega^{-1}\frac{\partial\Omega}{\partial h}\left(1 - \overline{\Omega}^2\Omega^{-2}\right) < 0.$$

Appendix B: Optimal Campaigning

If $\psi=0$, (5.20) can be solved for H to give

$$H = \Omega^{-1/2} - \frac{\Omega^{3/2}}{\overline{\Omega}^2} - \frac{2\Omega^3}{\varepsilon\overline{\Omega}^2}\left(\frac{\partial\Omega}{\partial h}\right)^{-1}$$

Its partial derivative with respect to Ω_0 reads

$$\frac{\partial H}{\partial\Omega_0} = -0.5\Omega^{-3/2}\frac{\partial\Omega}{\partial\Omega_0} - 1.5\frac{\Omega^{1/2}}{\overline{\Omega}^2}\frac{\partial\Omega}{\partial\Omega_0} - 6\frac{\Omega^2}{\varepsilon\overline{\Omega}^2}\frac{\partial\Omega}{\partial\Omega_0}\left(\frac{\partial\Omega}{\partial h}\right)^{-1}$$
$$+\frac{2\Omega^3}{\varepsilon\overline{\Omega}^2}\left(\frac{\partial\Omega}{\partial h}\right)^{-2}\frac{\partial^2\Omega}{\partial h\,\partial\Omega_0}$$

which is negative since $\partial\Omega / (\partial h\,\partial\Omega_0) < 0$. The partial derivative with respect to ε equals

$$\frac{\partial H}{\partial\varepsilon} = -0.5H\Omega^{-3/2}\frac{\partial\Omega}{\partial h} - 1.5H\frac{\Omega^{1/2}}{\overline{\Omega}^2}\frac{\partial\Omega}{\partial h} - 6H\frac{\Omega^2}{\varepsilon\overline{\Omega}^2} + 2\frac{\Omega^3}{\varepsilon^2\overline{\Omega}^2}\left(\frac{\partial\Omega}{\partial h}\right)^{-1}$$
$$+2H\frac{\Omega^3}{\varepsilon\overline{\Omega}^2}\left(\frac{\partial\Omega}{\partial h}\right)^{-2}\frac{\partial^2\Omega}{\partial h^2}$$

All terms are negative except the last term of the first line which is positive. Since nothing is known about the magnitudes of the terms the sign of the whole expression remains ambiguous.

Appendix C: Lobbying and the Opportunity Loss of Campaigning

During the following steps one needs to keep in mind a few important relationships. The determination of $\partial\psi/\partial L$ makes no sense if L has a corner solution. For L not to have a corner solution it must be given that $\theta=0$ (see (5.28)). But $\theta=0$ only if Ω is not greater than $\Omega_L = 0.25\beta^2$ (see (5.29)). All these conditions are assumed to hold.

By setting $H=0$, (5.32) reduces to

$$\psi = \frac{0.5\varepsilon\Omega^{-3/2}(1+L)^{\beta}\frac{\partial\Omega}{\partial h}+1}{\Omega^{-1/2}(1+L)^{\beta}-L} - 0.5\varepsilon\frac{\overline{\Omega}^2}{\Omega^3}(1+L)^{4\beta}\frac{\partial\Omega}{\partial h}.$$

Differentiating with respect to lobbying L gives

$$\begin{aligned}
\frac{\partial\psi}{\partial L}\Delta = {} & 0.5\beta\varepsilon\Omega^{-2}(1+L)^{2\beta-1}\frac{\partial\Omega}{\partial h} - 0.5\beta\varepsilon\Omega^{-3/2}(1+L)^{\beta-1}L\frac{\partial\Omega}{\partial h} \\
& -0.5\beta\varepsilon\Omega^{-2}(1+L)^{2\beta-1}\frac{\partial\Omega}{\partial h} + 0.5\varepsilon\Omega^{-3/2}(1+L)^{\beta}\frac{\partial\Omega}{\partial h} \\
& -2\beta\varepsilon\overline{\Omega}^2\Omega^{-4}(1+L)^{6\beta-1}\frac{\partial\Omega}{\partial h} + 4\beta\varepsilon\overline{\Omega}^2\Omega^{-7/2}(1+L)^{5\beta-1}L\frac{\partial\Omega}{\partial h} \\
& -2\beta\varepsilon\overline{\Omega}^2\Omega^{-3}(1+L)^{4\beta-1}L^2\frac{\partial\Omega}{\partial h} \\
& +1-\beta\Omega^{-1/2}(1+L)^{\beta-1}
\end{aligned}$$

where the common denominator is $\Delta \equiv [\Omega^{-1/2}(1+L)^{\beta} - L]^2$. The first elements of the first and the second line can be eliminated against each other. From condition (5.28) one can further see that the sum in the last line equals $-0.5\beta\Omega^{-1/2}(1+L)^{\beta-1}$ since $\theta=0$. After rearranging one obtains

$$\frac{\partial\psi}{\partial L}\Delta = 4\beta\varepsilon\overline{\Omega}^2\Omega^{-7/2}(1+L)^{5\beta-1}\frac{\partial\Omega}{\partial h}\left[L-0.5\Omega^{-1/2}(1+L)^{\beta}\right]$$

$$+0.5\varepsilon\Omega^{-1}(1+L)^{\beta}\frac{\partial\Omega}{\partial h}\left[\Omega^{-1/2}-\Omega^{-1/2}\frac{\beta L}{1+L}-4\beta\frac{\overline{\Omega}^2}{\Omega^2}(1+L)^{3\beta-1}L^2\right]$$

$$-0.5\beta\Omega^{-1/2}(1+L)^{\beta-1}$$

The bracketed term in the first line is exactly $-\Pi$, so the first line is negative, just like the third line. The sign of the bracket in line two is ambiguous. If L is large then the term containing L^2 dominates and the whole expression is negative. However, if L tends to zero, the second parenthesis and thus the whole second line will be positive. Nevertheless, the negative sign of the entire expression remains unaffected by a positive second line because

$$\lim_{L\to 0}\left(\frac{\partial\psi}{\partial L}\Delta\right) = -2\beta\varepsilon\overline{\Omega}^2\Omega^{-4}\frac{\partial\Omega}{\partial h}+0.5\varepsilon\Omega^{-3/2}\frac{\partial\Omega}{\partial h}-0.5\beta\Omega^{-1/2}$$

$$=0.5\varepsilon\Omega^{-3/2}\frac{\partial\Omega}{\partial h}\left(1-4\beta\overline{\Omega}^2\Omega^{-5/2}\right)-0.5\beta\Omega^{-1/2}$$

is always negative. The reason is that $1-4\beta\overline{\Omega}^2\Omega^{-5/2}<0$ for any given $0<\beta<1$ as long as $0<\Omega\leq\Omega_L=0.25\beta^2$. Therefore, $\partial\psi/\partial L<0$.

Appendix D: The Effect of Lobbying on Optimal Campaigning

If $\psi=0$ (5.32) can be solved for

$$H=\Omega^{-1/2}(1+L)^{\beta}-L-\frac{\Omega^{3/2}}{\overline{\Omega}^2}(1+L)^{-3\beta}-\frac{2\Omega^3}{\varepsilon\overline{\Omega}^2}(1+L)^{-4\beta}\left(\frac{\partial\Omega}{\partial h}\right)^{-1}$$

Differentiation with respect to lobbying yields

$$\frac{\partial H}{\partial L}=0.5\beta\Omega^{-1/2}(1+L)^{\beta-1}-1+3\beta\frac{\Omega^{3/2}}{\overline{\Omega}^2}(1+L)^{-3\beta-1}$$

$$+4\beta\frac{2\Omega^3}{\varepsilon\overline{\Omega}^2}(1+L)^{-4\beta-1}\left(\frac{\partial\Omega}{\partial h}\right)^{-1}$$

Optimal lobbying requires that $0.5\beta\Omega^{-1/2}(1+L)^{\beta-1}-1=0$ if L has no corner solution (see (5.28)), hence only the last two terms of the sum remain which are both positive, so $\partial H/\partial L>0$. The second-order derivative

$$\frac{\partial^2 H}{\partial L^2} = (-9\beta^2 - 3\beta)\frac{\Omega^{3/2}}{\overline{\Omega}^2}(1+L)^{-3\beta-2}$$
$$-(16\beta^2 + 4\beta)\frac{2\Omega^3}{\varepsilon\overline{\Omega}^2}(1+L)^{-4\beta-2}\left(\frac{\partial\Omega}{\partial h}\right)^{-1}$$

is negative.

Chapter 6 Endogenous Environmental Policy and its Effects on a Growing Economy

There is only one pollution ... People.

J. Lovelock[46]

In section 2.1 a distinction was made between absolute and relative emission reductions. Declining emissions in absolute terms mean that the *level* of emissions falls over a given period of time, as opposed to declining emissions in relative terms which signify a fall in the emission *intensity* or the emission *per unit of output*.[47] Environmental Kuznets Curves have been defined as to comprise two intervals of per capita income. In the lower-income interval the absolute pollution level increases with per capita income, and in the upper-income interval it decreases. Provided that the rate of pollution assimilation or decay is constant, the inverted U-curve of pollution must be the result of a similar inverted U-shaped pattern of emission levels (see section 2.5.3). From this it can be inferred that, given a nondeclining population size, Environmental Kuznets Curves automatically imply declining emission intensities of output (or of income) in the upper-income interval.

In Grossman's terminology that was introduced in section 2.1, changing emission intensities in a particular sector are a *technique effect*. In the models of the previous chapters, a decreasing emission intensity was only achieved through pollution control activities. Emission intensity reductions were thus limited to an economy's environment phase. This was the consequence of the rather simple structure of the models used. But, as has been emphasised in chapter 2, the technique effect can have various sources, including the substi-

---

[46] Lovelock (1979), p. 122

[47] In the case of only a single good or sector there are no problems of comparing different emission intensities. The reference unit with respect to which the intensity is expressed (e.g. emissions per ton of physical output, or per dollar worth of output) is more or less arbitrary. With several goods or sectors, however, a common denominator is needed to allow cross-sectoral emission intensity comparisons. Usually the value of one unit of the numeraire good is chosen as reference. For instance, if gross domestic product is the unit of account, then emission intensities express how much emission is associated with a sectoral output that is worth one unit of GDP. Therefore, "output" should henceforth be understood as "value of output" or "output in terms of the numeraire".

tution of "dirty" by "clean(er)" production inputs. And Grossman's identity (2.2) highlights yet another possibility for relative emission reductions to occur, namely through changes in the sectoral structure of the economy that were referred to as the *composition effect*. Substitutional and sectoral dynamics are two aspects that will be concentrated upon in this chapter.

The objectives pursued are twofold. First of all, it will be demonstrated how a government chooses its environmental policy in a dynamic context, given its particular objective function, and how this endogenously determined policy changes in the course of economic growth. Policy will again take the form of a pollution tax. The government's objective function which reflects the political structure of the country in question (see the discussion of section 5.1.4) will turn out to be central for the behaviour of the entire model.

The second objective consists in investigating the ways in which the government's environmental policy affects the rates of consumption growth and capital accumulation, prices, demand, the sectoral structure, factor intensities, emission intensities, and the quality of the environment. To keep the model, that will be developed for this purpose, manageable and transparent, specific functional forms will be used, and technological change will not be considered, but only briefly addressed at the end of the chapter.

In section 6.1 the model is constructed step by step by stating the basic assumptions about the consumer side, production, pollution, as well as the use of output, and by deriving the households' and firms' optimal decisions, taking the government's environmental policy as given. Section 6.2 is concerned with the government's objective function and shows how the pollution tax rate must be fixed optimally at every moment of time. With this groundwork done, section 6.3 isolates and analyses various effects that the pollution tax rate introduces into the model when no abatement is carried out by the firms. Section 6.4 adresses the same question but then with abatement taking place. Section 6.5, finally, sums up the results and relates them to those of earlier chapters.

6.1 A Multi-Sector Growth Model with Pollution

The model to be developed will borrow elements from earlier models of this study. The dynamics will be similar to those of the model in section 3.3. Some functional forms will be taken from chapters 3 and 5. The decentralised decision making structure will be the same as in chapter 5. But the second objective of this chapter requires a more detailed modelling of the economy's internal structure than in chapters 2 and 3. At least two factor inputs are necessary to allow for substitution effects in production. Furthermore, at least two consumer goods must be considered to enable the occurrence of substitution effects in consumption.

6.1.1 Assumptions about the Consumer Side

Suppose that the consumer side of the economy consists of a single representative household which is equipped with perfect foresight. It possesses some initial endowment of assets in the form of capital goods worth $K(0)>0$ which it rents to the firms at an interest rate of r. Since the household owns the firms, it also earns their profits Π. Finally, it receives a transfer $\Gamma\geq 0$ from the government. Income $rK+\Pi+\Gamma$ can be saved which increases the assets K, and hence the capital stock available to the firms, or used for consumption

$$X \equiv p_1 X_1 + p_2 X_2. \tag{6.1}$$

X_i and p_i ($i=1,2$) are the quantities and prices of the goods consumed. X represents total consumption spending. The household's budget constraint can thus be written as

$$\dot{K} = rK + \Pi + \Gamma - X. \tag{6.2}$$

Subject to the restriction of its initial endowment $K(0)>0$ and its budget constaint, the household aims at maximising its welfare

$$\int_0^\infty U(X_1, X_2, P)\exp(-\rho t)\,dt$$

with respect to consumption X_i and savings $\dot{K}$. $P\geq 0$ is the level of pollution, and $\rho>0$ is the constant rate of time preference. Assume further that at time $t=0$

$$r(0)>\rho. \tag{6.3}$$

The implications of this assumption will be pointed out in the course of the following sections. Let instantaneous utility be given by

$$U(X_1, X_2, P) \equiv \omega_1 \ln X_1 + \omega_2 \ln X_2 - 0.5P^2 \tag{6.4}$$

where $\omega_i > 0$ and $\omega_1 + \omega_2 = 1$. This utility function corresponds closely to the functional form already used in chapter 5. Effectively, it only differs from (5.7) by the inclusion of two instead of only a single consumer good. Note that (6.4) implies strictly positive levels of both X_1 and X_2 because the logarithm is not defined for nonpositive values.

6.1.2 Welfare Maximisation

Given the objective function and the dynamic constraint, the current-value Hamiltonian to the households' optimisation problem reads

$$\mathcal{H} = \omega_1 \ln X_1 + \omega_2 \ln X_2 - 0.5P^2 + \mu(rK + \Pi + \Gamma - p_1 X_1 - p_2 X_2) \tag{6.5}$$

where μ is the costate variable associated with the state variable K. Its equation of motion is given by (6.2), but in (6.5) X has been replaced by (6.1). Maximisation leads to the optimum conditions

$$\frac{\partial \mathcal{H}}{\partial X_i} = 0 \Leftrightarrow \mu = \frac{\omega_i}{p_i X_i} \tag{6.6}$$

$$\frac{\partial \mathcal{H}}{\partial K} = \mu\rho - \dot{\mu} \Leftrightarrow \hat{\mu} = \rho - r \tag{6.7}$$

The transversality condition for this infinite-horizon problem reads

$$\lim_{t \to \infty} \mu K \exp(-\rho t) = 0$$

which is identical with (3.7). Substitution from (6.6) into (6.1) gives

$$\mu = \frac{\omega_1 + \omega_2}{X} = \frac{1}{X}. \tag{6.8}$$

Logarithmic differentiation shows that $\hat{\mu} = -\hat{X}$ which can be equated with the Euler equation (6.7) to yield a differential equation for consumption:

$$\dot{X} = X(r - \rho) \tag{6.9}$$

Given assumption (6.3), this equation shows that consumption spending must rise at least initially. Integration leads to

$$X(t) = X(0)\exp\left\{\int_0^t [r(s) - \rho]ds\right\}. \tag{6.10}$$

By making use of (6.8) and (6.10), one can restate the transversality condition as

$$\lim_{t\to\infty} \frac{K}{X(0)}\exp\left\{-\int_0^t [r(s) - \rho]ds\right\}\exp(-\rho t) = \lim_{t\to\infty} \frac{K}{X(0)}\exp\left[-\int_0^t r(s)ds\right] = 0.$$

or, provided that $X(0)>0$,

$$\lim_{t\to\infty} K\exp\left[-\int_0^t r(s)ds\right] = 0 \tag{6.11}$$

which is the so-called No-Ponzi-Game condition [see Blanchard & Fischer (1989), p. 49]. From this condition and the the budget constraint (6.2) one obtains the following relationship (see appendix A):

$$X = \rho(K + \Theta) \tag{6.12}$$

where

$$\Theta(t) \equiv \int_t^\infty [\Pi(s) + \Gamma(s)]\exp\left[-\int_t^s r(u)du\right]ds$$

is the present value of the future flow of profits and transfer income. It can be regarded as wealth in the sense of representing a claim on future profits and government transfers, just like K is wealth, deriving its value from its future productive use. So consumption is a linear function of total wealth $K+\Theta$, and ρ is the marginal propensity to consume out of wealth. X may also be interpreted as "interest" on $K+\Theta$ where ρ represents the "interest rate". Since the households possess perfect foresight they anticipate their future income in their current consumption and saving decisions.

After replacing X by (6.12), the households' budget constraint (6.2) reads $\dot{K} = (r-\rho)K + \Pi + \Gamma - \rho\Theta$, and since $\dot{\Theta} = r\Theta - \Pi - \Gamma$ it can be written as a proper equation of motion of total wealth:

$$\dot{K} + \dot{\Theta} = (K + \Theta)(r - \rho).$$

As was to be expected, total wealth grows at the same rate as consumption spending.

6.1.3 Assumptions about Production, Pollution, and the Use of Output

The production side of the economy is assumed to consist of many profit-maximising firms acting under perfect competition. Production takes place in five sectors. Sector i=1,2 supplies consumer good i, sector 3 the capital good C, sector 4 the capital good D, and sector 5 the capital good A.

Output of sector k=1,...,5 comprises goods and pollution. The sectoral production function for goods is given by

$$F_k = \Phi_k(C_k, D_k) = D_k \phi_k(z_k) > 0 \tag{6.13}$$

if $C_k > 0$ and $D_k > 0$, and $F_k = \Phi_k(0, D_k) = \Phi_k(C_k, 0) = 0$. Φ_k is a linearly homogeneous, neoclassical production function. $\phi_k(z_k) \equiv \Phi_k(C_k / D_k, 1)$ is its intensive form.[48] $z_k \equiv C_k / D_k$ is the factor intensity of production in the k-th sector. C_k and D_k are physical quantities or stocks of the respective capital goods employed in sector k as factor inputs.

Pollution is taken to be a flow. The sectoral pollution function takes the admittedly simple form

$$P_k = \xi D_k - \zeta A_k. \tag{6.14}$$

where A_k is the physical amount of ***abatement capital*** (rather than abatement spending like in previous models) allocated to sector k. (6.14) corresponds closely to the environmental quality function (3.25). The parameters retain their interpretations: ξ>0 is the constant pollution coefficient of "dirty"

---

[48] A neoclassical production function implies that production is increasing and strictly concave in both arguments. It follows for its intensive form that $\phi_k' > 0$ and $\phi_k'' < 0$.

capital, and $\zeta>0$ is the constant efficiency of abatement. Note that these parameters are the same in each sector.

The only important difference between capital goods of type C and type D is that the use of D in production contributes to pollution ("dirty" capital) whereas C does not ("clean" capital). So C may be thought of as human capital, a knowledge stock, or intellectual property such as patents or blueprints.

The sectoral capital stocks are constrained by

$$0 \le \sum_{k=1}^{5} C_k \le C, \quad 0 \le \sum_{k=1}^{5} D_k \le D \quad \text{and} \quad 0 \le \sum_{k=1}^{5} A_k \le A. \tag{6.15}$$

Assuming that in equilibrium these constraints hold as equalities, the economy-wide or aggregate pollution level can be written as

$$P = \sum_{k=1}^{5} P_k = \sum_{k=1}^{5} (\xi D_k - \zeta A_k) = \xi D - \zeta A \tag{6.16}$$

This simple aggregation highlights the great advantage of a pollution function that is not only linearly separable in total D and total A, but also in the respective sectoral capital stocks. Suppose finally that the government levies a tax $\tau \ge 0$ on each unit of pollution generated.

In equilibrium the representative household purchases the *entire* output of the firms. Consumer goods $i=1,2$ are bought for consumption purposes: $F_i = X_i > 0$. The strict positivity is implied by the utility function (6.4), and has already been pointed out in section 6.1.1. It follows that *both* p_i *are equilibrium prices* because the X_i have interior solutions. The value of output of the first two sectors of the economy equals total consumption spending:

$$p_1 F_1 + p_2 F_2 = p_1 X_1 + p_2 X_2 = X. \tag{6.17}$$

Due to the assumptions of perfect competition and linear homogeneity in production, the consumer good prices equal their respective unit costs: $p_i = c_i$.

The purchase of newly produced capital goods by the household represents its saving because it adds them to the existing stocks of capital goods the aggregate value of which represents its assets K. In equilibrium $F_3 = \dot{C} \ge 0$, $F_4 = \dot{D} \ge 0$, and $F_5 = \dot{A} \ge 0$. The increase in K can thus be written as

$$p_3F_3 + p_4F_4 + p_5F_5 = p_3\dot{C} + p_4\dot{D} + p_5\dot{A} = \dot{K} \tag{6.18}$$

If (but not only if) the output level of a sector $j=3,4,5$ is positive then the purchasing price p_j is an equilibrium price which must again equal the corresponding unit cost: $p_j=c_j$. On the other hand, if an $F_j=0$ it does not matter whether the p_j is an equilibrium price or not, since it drops out of the equation.

Within the limit set by the household's savings, namely that the increase in household assets K equals the value of output of the capital-goods producing sectors, it is up to the firms to decide which amount of each capital good they produce, and in which sectors these goods are employed. However, both decisions are irreversible in the sense that one type of capital good cannot be converted into another, and capital of a certain type cannot be moved from one sector to another, once it has been employed somewhere in a production process.[49] Therefore, the only way for the firms to influence the capital structure is through additions to the capital stocks.

This irreversibility of decisions entails a certain rigidity of the capital structure. It cannot be adapted instantaneously to rapid or discontinuous changes in economic conditions, with the consequence that temporary or even permanent imbalances or disequilibria of the capital structure may occur. A *balanced capital structure* can be defined as the particular composition and allocation of aggregate capital which ensures that the return r on (or the marginal net private benefit of) any type of capital in any sector and use is the same. This does not mean that there must be positive stocks of all types of capital or in all sectors, but if a positive stock has been built up it must yield the same return as all other positive stocks.

In order to allow such a balanced capital structure to prevail at every moment of time, and thus to avoid complications which are unnecessary for the purpose of this chapter, it will be taken that initially a balanced capital structure exists, and that economic conditions do not change faster than the firms can adapt the capital structure.

---

49 This assumption resembles the so-called "putty-clay" case of the vintage approach in the earlier theory of economic growth [e.g. Johansen (1959)]. Roughly speaking, it asserts that the capital-labour ratio in production can be chosen more or less freely *before* production is started. However, once being used in production, factors are fixed, and the formerly substitutional technology becomes limitational. So "putty-clay" stands for ex ante substitutability and ex post limitationality.

In equilibrium, a stock is valued at the price (or value) of its marginal unit. Therefore, the entire capital stock of one type must be valued at the corresponding price p_j of the last capital good added. This price is an equilibrium price, equal to the corresponding unit cost c_j, for otherwise $F_j=0$ which would mean that either the capital stock in question has not been built up in the first place, or that the return on this capital stock would differ from that of others. The latter would conflict with the assumption about the balanced capital structure, and can therefore be excluded. The value of the aggregate or total capital stock is thus given by

$$K = p_3C + p_4D + p_5A \tag{6.19}$$

which is effectively the integral of (6.18), prices being held constant. Since $X_i = F_i = \Phi_i(C_i, D_i) > 0$ it can be concluded that also $C>0$ and $D>0$. Hence like p_1 and p_2, also p_3 *and* p_4 *will always be equilibrium prices*. However, since $A=0$ cannot be ruled out, p_5 *may but need not be an equilibrium price.*

One more simplifying assumption concerns the production functions of the sectors $j=3,4,5$. It is rather strong, but not necessary for the main points of this chapter. By eliminating numerous price and substitution effects it enhances the transparency and tractability of the model considerably. Suppose that all capital goods are produced with the same technology, hence $\Phi_3 = \Phi_4 = \Phi_5$ and $\phi_3 = \phi_4 = \phi_5$.

Provided that each factor price (not the purchasing price) is the same in all sectors[50], identical linearly homogeneous production technologies in the sectors $j=3,4,5$ have three fundamental implications. First, the unit cost c_j of producing any type of capital good is the same.[51] Second, due to the assumption of perfect competition, $c_j=p_j$ if p_j is an equilibrium price, so

$$p_3 = p_4 \qquad \text{always} \tag{6.20a}$$

$$p_3 = p_4 = p_5 \qquad \text{if and only if } p_5 \text{ is an equilibrium price} \tag{6.20b}$$

---

[50] This does not mean that all factor prices need to be equal; factor prices can and will differ in this model. It only means that employing one unit of a factor, say C, costs the same, no matter in which sector the factor is used.

[51] Linear homogeneity in production gives rise to scale-independent marginal costs which are called unit costs.

And third, the factor intensities z_j are equal if p_j is an equilibrium price, so

$$z_3 = z_4 \qquad \text{always} \tag{6.21a}$$
$$z_3 = z_4 = z_5 \qquad \text{if and only if } p_5 \text{ is an equilibrium price} \tag{6.21b}$$

By choosing capital goods of type C and D as numeraire, and setting $p_3 = p_4 \equiv 1$, (6.19) reduces to $K = C + D + p_5 A$. If p_5 is an equilibrium price then according to (6.18b) $p_3 = p_4 = p_5 = 1$ and thus

$$K=C+D+A, \tag{6.22}$$

and if this is not the case, the value of p_5 does not matter because $A=0$, so (6.22) still applies. Note that (6.22) is an aggregation of values, not of physical units.

In contrast to the capital-goods producing sectors, technologies in the sectors $i=1,2$ will be assumed to differ. More concretely, the production of consumer good 1 is taken to be more "C-intensive" than the production of consumer good 2 an any factor price ratio:

$$z_1 > z_2 \tag{6.23}$$

Apart from excluding factor intensity reversals, this assumption does not entail a loss of generality.

6.1.4 Profit Maximisation and Optimal Capital Allocation

Profits in the k-th sector ($k=1,...,5$) are given by the value of output, less factor costs in the form of interest payments for capital services, less the tax bill:

$$\Pi_k = p_k F_k - r(C_k + D_k + A_k) - \tau P_k \tag{6.24}$$

Taking the factor market to be cleared in equilibrium (that is, the restrictions (6.15) hold as equalities), the Lagrangean corresponding to the allocation problem faced by the firms of sector k reads

$$\mathcal{L}_k = p_k F_k - r(C_k + D_k + A_k) - \tau P_k - \theta_k F_k + \lambda_k A_k$$

where θ_k and λ_k are the multipliers of the nonnegativity restrictions on F_k and A_k. Maximisation of $\mathcal{L}_k$ with respect to the firms' controls leads to a set of conditions determining the optimal allocation of capital:

$$\frac{\partial \mathcal{L}_k}{\partial C_k} = 0 \Leftrightarrow r = (p_k - \theta_k)\frac{\partial F_k}{\partial C_k}$$

$$\frac{\partial \mathcal{L}^k}{\partial D_k} = 0 \Leftrightarrow r = (p_k - \theta_k)\frac{\partial F_k}{\partial D_k} - \tau\frac{\partial P_k}{\partial D_k} = (p_k - \theta_k)\frac{\partial F_k}{\partial D_k} - \tau\xi$$

$$\frac{\partial \mathcal{L}_k}{\partial A_k} = 0 \Leftrightarrow r = -\tau\frac{\partial P_k}{\partial A_k} + \lambda_k = \tau\zeta + \lambda_k \tag{6.25}$$

In addition to that, the complementary slackness conditions $\theta_k \geq 0$, $F_k \geq 0$, $\theta_k F_k = 0$, $\lambda_k \geq 0$, $A_k \geq 0$ and $\lambda_k A_k = 0$ must be met. If $\theta_k > 0$ it means that p_k is no equilibrium price, and that the return on capital that could be earned in sector k is lower than elsewhere in the economy. In this case it would be inefficient to allocate capital to sector k, and therefore $F_k = C_k = D_k = 0$. As can be seen, among all sectors with $\theta_k = 0$, a balanced capital structure is efficient.

(6.25) implies that all λ_k are equal, so let $\lambda \equiv \lambda_k$. The income earned by A consists in avoided tax payments. Since λ represents the opportunity loss associated with investing in the stock A, $\lambda > 0$ means that the return on A, given by $\tau\zeta$, is lower than on C and D, and that therefore no abatement capital stock is accumulated. The phase of economic growth where this holds can again be called *development phase* (see chapters 2 and 3). Moreover, zero investment in A means that the output of the fifth sector of the economy is not demanded. Hence *in the development phase* $\theta_5 > 0$, $F_5 = C_5 = D_5 = 0$, *and* p_5 *is not an equilibrium price*.

The above conditions can be summarised compactly by

$$r = (p_k - \theta_k)\frac{\partial F_k}{\partial C_k} = (p_k - \theta_k)\frac{\partial F_k}{\partial D_k} - \tau\xi = \tau\zeta + \lambda . \tag{6.26}$$

From this condition one obtains the standard efficiency condition for factor allocation, requiring the equality of the factor price ratio and the marginal rate of transformation in optimum:

$$y \equiv \frac{r+\xi\tau}{r} = \frac{\partial F_k / \partial D_k}{\partial F_k / \partial C_k} \tag{6.27}$$

which holds of course only for those sectors with interior solutions ($\theta_k = 0$). The factor prices in this model are obviously r for one unit of C, and $r+\xi\tau$ for one unit of D. The tax on pollution drives a wedge equal to $\xi\tau$ between them. As can be seen, this wedge is responsible for a level of y greater than unity. y determines how sectoral investment dK_k is divided between dC_k and dD_k. When y is given, or taken as given by the firms, the total differential of (6.27) can be solved for

$$\frac{dC_k}{dD_k} = \frac{\dfrac{\partial^2 F_k}{\partial D_k^2} - y\dfrac{\partial^2 F_k}{\partial C_k \partial D_k}}{y\dfrac{\partial^2 F_k}{\partial C_k^2} - \dfrac{\partial^2 F_k}{\partial C_k \partial D_k}} > 0,$$

saying that an expansion of a sector's total capital stock is always associated with an increase in *both* types of capital. If this relationship holds for each sector individually, it must also apply on aggregate or economy-wide level, therefore $dC/dD > 0$. If $dA = 0$ and thus $dK = dC + dD$ it follows that $dK/dD = dC/dD + 1$ or, alternatively,

$$\frac{dD}{dK} = \left(1 + \frac{dC}{dD}\right)^{-1} > 0. \tag{6.28}$$

This relationship will be of some use later on in this chapter. Another expression that will be needed below can be derived from the aggregate profit function

$$\Pi \equiv \sum_{k=1}^{5} \Pi_k = \sum_{k=1}^{5} \left[p_k F_k - r(C_k + D_k + A_k) - \tau P_k\right].$$

In equilibrium, the constraints (6.15) hold as strict equalities. Recall further that $K = A + C + D$ (see (6.22)), then total profits can be written as

$$\Pi = \sum_{k=1}^{5} p_k F_k - rK - \tau P \tag{6.29}$$

Due to the linear homogeneity in production, the value of aggregate or total output can be stated in a more useful way by making use of Euler's theorem and (6.26):[52]

$$\sum_{k=1}^{5} p_k F_k = r(C+D) + \tau\xi D, \tag{6.30}$$

Upon substitution into (6.29) one obtains $\Pi = \tau\xi D - rA - \tau P$. Replacing P by (6.16) and r by (6.26) gives $\Pi = \tau\xi D - (\tau\zeta + \lambda)A - \tau(\xi D - \zeta A) = \lambda A$, and since complementary slackness requires that $\lambda A = 0$, profits reduce to $\Pi = 0$.

6.1.5 Two Lemmas

The following two lemmas emphasise the central role of governmental policy in this model. Their proofs have been relegated to the appendices B and C, respectively.

Lemma 1:
Return on capital is a decreasing function of the pollution tax rate:

$$\frac{dr}{d\tau} < 0$$

Lemma 2:
The unit cost ratio of the consumer goods 1 *and* 2 *is a decreasing function of the pollution tax rate*:

$$\frac{d(c_1/c_2)}{d\tau} < 0$$

52 The steps are:

$$\sum_{k=1}^{5} p_k F_k = \sum_{k=1}^{5} p_k \left(\frac{\partial F_k}{\partial C_k} C_k + \frac{\partial F_k}{\partial D_k} D_k \right) = \sum_{k=1}^{5} \left[r C_k + (r + \tau\xi) D_k \right]$$
$$= r(C+D) + \tau\xi D$$

6.2 Government Objective and Policy

In line with the discussion in section 5.1.4 suppose that the government's overriding objective is to be re-elected. Industry lobbies and other powerful interest groups are assumed not to exist. Since there is only a single representative household, the government maximises its chances of being re-elected by making the household's objective function its own. With the household maximising welfare, i.e. the present value of the future flow of utility, a dynamic component enters also the government's policy choice.

In order to choose the appropriate environmental policy the government must maximise its (and in the present context the household's) objective function subject to the same constraint that is faced by the household, namely the flow budget constraint (6.2). But different from the household which is ignorant about the structure of the production side of the economy, the government is able to take the composition of profit income into account.

Replacing Π in the budget constraint (6.2) by the profit function (6.29), and cancelling Γ and τP against each other - Γ is once again the transfer by which the government redistributes its pollution tax revenue τP - gives

$$\dot{K} = \sum_{k=1}^{5} p_k F_k - X. \tag{6.31}$$

Apart from this modification, the current-value Hamiltonian corresponding to the government's optimisation problem is identical with the household's Hamiltonian (6.5):

$$\mathcal{H} = \omega_1 \ln X_1 + \omega_2 \ln X_2 - 0.5P^2 + \mu\left(\sum_{k=1}^{5} p_k F_k - p_1 X_1 - p_2 X_2\right) \tag{6.32}$$

In chapters 4 and 5, different objective functions have been maximised with respect to the government's control τ. The problems addressed there were static in nature, and corner solutions for A had been excluded (i.e. the models were only concerned with the environment phase). The government's present optimisation problem, however, involves both dynamic aspects (it influences the household's saving behaviour), and the possible nonoptimality of abatement (due to the bounded efficiency of abatement). Now the maximisation of $\mathcal{H}$ with respect to τ would be insufficient for two reasons: it would only yield a static optimum condition, and this condition would not provide enough information to derive a unique level of τ in the development phase.

The condition determining the optimal dynamics of a Hamiltonian system is the Euler equation. For the Hamiltonian (6.32) it reads

$$\frac{\partial \mathcal{H}}{\partial K} = \mu\rho - \dot{\mu}$$

$$\Leftrightarrow \hat{\mu} = \rho + PX\left(\xi\frac{dD}{dK} - \zeta\frac{dA}{dK}\right) - \sum_{k=1}^{5} p_k\left(\frac{\partial F_k}{\partial C_k}\frac{dC_k}{dK} + \frac{\partial F_k}{\partial D_k}\frac{dD_k}{dK}\right) \quad (6.33)$$

where μ has been replaced by $1/X$ (see (6.8)). In order to find the optimal dynamic governmental policy, it is this condition which all further considerations must be based on. First, assume a corner solution for A, so that $dA=0$ and $(dC+dD)/dK=1$. After a number of steps (see appendix D), (6.33) reduces to

$$\hat{\mu} = \rho - r + \xi\frac{dD}{dK}(PX - \tau).$$

From (6.7) it is known that $\hat{\mu} = \rho - r$. Since $\xi>0$ by assumption, and $dD/dK>0$ according to (6.28), one can conclude that

$$\tau = PX. \quad (6.34)$$

Now suppose that A has an interior solution, so that $dA>0$ and $(dA+dC+dD)/dK=1$. After summing over all changes of sectoral capital stocks, and substituting from (6.26), the Euler equation (6.33) becomes

$$\hat{\mu} = \rho + PX\left(\xi\frac{dD}{dK} - \zeta\frac{dA}{dK}\right) - r\left(\frac{dC}{dK} + \frac{dD}{dK}\right) - \xi\tau\frac{dD}{dK}.$$

With an interior solution for A, $\lambda=0$ in (6.26), and hence $\zeta=r/\tau$. Moreover, $(dC+dD)/dK=1-dA/dK$ and $\xi dD-\zeta dA=dP$, so that the Euler equation can be written as

$$\hat{\mu} = \rho - r + (PX - \tau)\frac{dP}{dK}.$$

For this to reduce to $\hat{\mu} = \rho - r$, it is necessary that either $dP/dK=0$ or $\tau=PX$ or both. For the choice of the correct condition, a few considerations are necessary. In the environment phase $r=\tau\zeta$, hence $dr/d\tau=\zeta>0$. But this contradicts lemma 1 which states that $dr/d\tau<0$. The only way for τ to meet both requirements is to remain constant from the moment when λ vanishes. But if τ is constant, so are the return on capital r, and the consumption growth rate $\hat{X}=r-\rho>0$ (see (6.9)). Now suppose that $\tau=PX$, then a growing X and a constant τ imply a declining pollution level P. It follows that policy (6.34) and $dP/dK=0$ are mutually exclusive.

It has been shown that *any* optimal policy induces X to grow at a constant rate, starting from its initial value in the environment phase. Given this unique optimal consumption time path, policy alternatives only differ with respect to the pollution they are associated with. Here it becomes clear the welfare-maximising policy is the one that makes pollution decline rather than keeping it constant. Therefore, (6.34) *is the government's optimal policy choice*.

Consumption expenditure X in (6.34) represents the inverse of the opportunity cost of capital accumulation: the higher X, the lower the current marginal utility that is foregone through additional saving. At higher consumption levels the household is willing to support a stricter environmental policy (a higher τ) because its opportunity cost is lower.

Now the model is specified to an extent that allows to demonstrate in detail which effects governmental policy triggers off. It is important to keep in mind, however, that the form of the public policy as given by (6.34) hinges decisively upon the particular government objective function assumed here. Since policy is determined endogenously, a different government objective function, e.g. one that includes lobby contributions or bribes, or one that gives the welfare of a particular group of agents priority over others', would result in a different tax rate formula.

6.3 The Development Phase

In section 2.4.2 the phase of economic growth characterised by a positive opportunity loss of abatement, i.e. by $\lambda>0$ in condition (6.26), has been titled *development phase* because economic activity is solely concerned with increasing material prosperity. Since $A=0$ in the development phase, the pollution function (6.16) reduces to $P=\xi D$, and the optimal pollution tax rate equals $\tau=\xi DX$.

6.3.1 Optimal Growth and Stability

Two differential equations describe the dynamics of the economy: the equations of motion of consumption and capital. The former is given by (6.9), the latter by the household's flow budget constraint (6.2). Since $\Pi=0$ and $\Gamma = \tau P = P^2 X = (\xi D)^2 X$, the differential equation for capital can be restated as

$$\dot{K} = rK + (\xi D)^2 X - X. \tag{6.35}$$

Appendix E shows that the system's equilibrium where $\dot{X} = \dot{K} = 0$, given the boundary conditions (3.7) and $K(0)>0$, is *globally saddle point stable*. Moreover, it proves that

$$\frac{\dot{X}}{\dot{K}} = \frac{dX}{dK} > 0 \tag{6.36}$$

everywhere along the two stable arms of this equilibrium, one of which is optimal trajectory for X and K. According to (6.3) and (6.9), $dX>0$. It follows from (6.36) that also $dK>0$. So ultimately it is assumption (6.3) which ensures that the economy starts with a capital stock $K(0)$ *lower* than the stationary state stock. Moreover, since $dD/dK>0$ by (6.28), also $dD>0$, and with a rising "dirty" capital stock, and increasing consumption, as well the pollution tax rate $\tau=\xi DX$ rises over time. This is the key feature of the government's environmental policy in the development phase: *each unit of pollution is subject to an endogenously rising tax as the economy grows.*

According to lemma 1, a rising τ is associated with a declining return on capital in the development phase. But return on capital is the households' only incentive to save, and capital accumulation is the only source of growth in this economy. It follows that the government's enviromental policy discourages saving and, in consequence, exercises a *growth-dampening effect*. This effect explains why in the development phase growth slows down as the economy asymptotically approaches its saddle point.

6.3.2 Goods Prices, Demand and Sectoral Structure

Under perfect competition, prices equal marginal costs of production. With linearly homogeneous technologies, marginal costs are unit costs which are scale-independent. Lemma 2 states that the unit cost ratio c_1 / c_2 of the consumer goods 1 and 2 is a decreasing function of τ alone. It follows that since τ increases in the course of growth, the price ratio p_1 / p_2 declines or, equivalently, that

$$\hat{p}_1 - \hat{p}_2 < 0. \tag{6.37}$$

So consumer good 1 the production of which is more intensive in "clean" capital C (see (6.23)), becomes cheaper relative to good 2 when environmental policy gets stricter. Since the pollution tax rate rises endogenously as the economy grows, this price effect accompanies growth in the development phase.

Replacing μ in (6.6) by $1/X$ (see (6.8)), and solving leads to the consumption demand function $X_i = \omega_i X / p_i$. Logarithmic differentiation of the ratio of demand functions $X_2 / X_1 = (\omega_2 p_1) / (\omega_1 p_2)$ yields

$$\hat{X}_2 - \hat{X}_1 = \hat{p}_1 - \hat{p}_2 < 0. \tag{6.38}$$

This means that the C-intensive consumer good is demanded and produced (since supply must equal demand in equilibrium) in relatively increasing *amounts* as the economy grows, and τ rises with it. Output of sector 1 grows relative to the output of sector 2. Therefore, government policy can be said to have a sectoral *composition effect* on the economy, favouring the environmentally friendlier good over the other. Note, however, that in terms of *value* of their respective outputs the two sectors remain in fixed proportion: $(p_2 X_2) / (p_1 X_1) = \omega_2 / \omega_1$. This characteristic is due to the particular form of the assumed utility function, and will not hold for other utility functions.

Since by assumption the production of all capital goods has the same factor intensity, no composition effect exists among them.

6.3.3 Factor Intensity

Generally, the cost a firm faces when employing a unit of capital is its rental rate r. Due to government intervention, however, the cost of "dirty" capital exceeds r by the "wedge" $\tau\xi$. Economic intuition tells one to expect the relatively more expensive factor to be increasingly substituted by the other the more their costs differ or, in other words, the greater τ gets. Formally this can be shown by differentiating the factor price ratio $y \equiv (r + \tau\xi)/r = 1 + \tau\xi / r$ to obtain

$$\frac{dy}{d\tau} = \frac{\xi}{r} - \frac{\tau\xi}{r^2}\frac{dr}{d\tau} > 0. \tag{6.39}$$

The sign follows from lemma 1. Based on this result, appendix F proves that $dz_k / dy > 0$, so that

$$\frac{dz_k}{d\tau} = \frac{dz_k}{dy}\frac{dy}{d\tau} > 0 \tag{6.40}$$

which confirms that production in every sector does become more intensive in "clean" capital in response to a stricter environmental policy. This third consequence of government policy may be called *substitution effect* because "clean" capital gradually substitutes "dirty" capital in production.

6.3.4 Pollution Intensity

In accordance with Grossman's identity (2.2), the pollution intensity of sector k is defined as

$$e_k \equiv \frac{P_k}{p_k F_k} = \frac{\xi D_k}{p_k D_k \phi_k(z_k)} = \frac{\xi}{p_k \phi_k(z_k)}.$$

From the inclusion of the price p_k in the denominator it can be seen that the pollution intensity is the amount of pollution associated with the production of output *worth one unit of the numeraire*. This normalisation ensures the comparability of pollution intensities of different sectors. Differentiation of e_k while keeping p_k fixed indicates that *a stricter environmental policy leads to less pollution emitted per unit of output in each sector by exploiting the substitution effect*:

$$\frac{de_k}{d\tau} = -\frac{\xi}{p_k[\phi_k(z_k)]^2}\phi_k{'}\left.\frac{dz_k}{d\tau}\right|_{p_k=\text{const}} < 0.$$

Hence a falling pollution intensity does not depend on abatement but can also be achieved by cost-minimising factor substitution which here occurs in response to environmental policy.

However, despite a *declining pollution intensity*, the absolute pollution level $P=\xi D$ still rises strictly monotonically along the optimal path in the development phase since $\dot{D}>0$, reaching its maximum in the stationary state. Hence *in the development phase the scale effect dominates the combined composition and substitution effects*.

6.4 The Environment Phase

By definition the *environment phase* is characterised by an opportunity loss of abatement of zero. When $\lambda=0$ in (6.26), return on capital in abatement equals the return on capital in production. Optimal capital allocation requires the firms to ensure that this equality is maintained in the course of further economic growth.

Substitution from the aggregate pollution function (6.16) into the pollution tax function (6.34) gives $\tau=(\xi D-\zeta A)X$. Using this to replace τ in (6.26) one obtains the abatement capital function

$$A=\frac{\xi}{\zeta}D-\frac{r}{\zeta^2 X}. \tag{6.41}$$

So abatement is increasing in "dirty" capital and consumption, and decreasing in the return on capital. Substituting this abatement function back into the pollution function (6.16) yields

$$P=\frac{r}{\zeta X}, \tag{6.42}$$

from which it follows immediately that

$$\tau=\frac{r}{\zeta}. \tag{6.43}$$

This expression has already been used earlier in this chapter. It results directly from (6.26) when λ is set equal to zero. (6.43) can be employed to prove that *the factor price ratio is constant in the environment phase*:

$$y\equiv\frac{\partial F_k/\partial D_k}{\partial F_k/\partial C_k}=\frac{r+r\xi/\zeta}{r}=1+\frac{\xi}{\zeta}. \tag{6.44}$$

This alone does not prove that the return on capital r is constant as well. However, if y is constant but r was not, then an increase in $r=\partial F_k / \partial C_k$ would have to be accompanied by a proportional increase in $r+\tau\xi/\zeta = \partial F_k / \partial D_k$. Here a contradiction occurs because the two marginal productivities of F_k cannot rise at the same time. Therefore, *a constant y is only compatible with a single r which is constant in the environment phase.*

According to (6.43) *a constant r implies a constant τ.*[53] Given (6.40), $d\tau=0$ means that also the capital intensity in every sector remains constant. Since further the composition effect vanishes when τ is constant (which follows from lemma 2 and section 6.3.2), the sectoral structure does not change either, implying that the overall capital intensity C/D is constant, too.

With τ being constant, not only the capital intensity and the sectoral structure, but also prices, the growth rate of consumption, and the pollution intensity of output remain the same. Only asymptotically constant, however, are the ratios A/C and A/D as well as the growth rate of total capital K. This can be shown as follows. With r constant, X rising at a constant rate, and D rising at a positive rate, abatement function (6.41) implies that $A/D<\xi/\zeta$ but $\lim_{t\to\infty}A/D=\xi/\zeta$, and hence that $\lim_{t\to\infty}\hat{A}=\hat{D}=\hat{C}$.

Upon substitution from (6.30), the budget constraint (6.32) reads $\dot{K}=r(C+D)+\tau\xi D-X=rK+\tau\xi D-rA-X$. By (6.41) and (6.26), the two terms in the middle of this expression can be written as

$$\tau\xi D-rA=\tau\xi D-r\left(\frac{\xi}{\zeta}D-\frac{r}{\zeta^2 X}\right)=\tau\xi D-\tau\xi D+\frac{\tau^2}{X}=\frac{\tau^2}{X}.$$

Since X grows at a constant, positive rate in the environment phase, this expression vanishes asymptotically as time goes to infinity. Therefore, the households' flow budget constraint *asymptotically* takes the form

$$\dot{K}=rK-X.$$

Given the constant r, it is not difficult to show that if this holds, both X and K grow at the same rate. The asymptotic form of the present endogenous growth model strongly resembles the "AK"-model used in section 3.3.

---

[53] Recall that the constancy of τ and r in the environment phase has already been pointed out in section 6.2, but based on different arguments.

The last property of the model in the environment phase to be looked at is the behaviour of the aggregate pollution level. For r to remain constant, (6.42) requires that

$$\hat{P} = -\hat{X} < 0$$

which means that in optimum the pollution level declines at a constant rate (see also section 6.2). Just like in the functionally specified model versions in chapter 3, pollution rises in the development phase, and falls once abatement is carried out. Hence also *the present model produces an Environmental Kuznets Curve*.

6.5 Concluding Remarks

To conclude the analysis of the model it can be said that embedded in its development phase are all three effects which Grossman (1993) identified as determining the level of pollution generated by an economy (see section 2.1). But while scale effect, composition effect and technique effect in Grossman's decomposition can have various different causes and, in particular, involve both intentional and unintentional factors, all effects in the present model of optimal growth are exclusively *intentional*.

First, the scale effect of output which ultimately leads to a rise in the pollution level is counteracted by the government's policy through increasingly discouraging savings, capital accumulation, and thus growth. The growth-dampening effect of governmental policy works against the scale effect. Second, the composition of demand, physical output and thus the sectoral proportions change in the course of growth not due to exogenous structural change but only in response to policy. Third, input substitution as a special category of Grossman's technique effect is induced by relative price shifts on the factor markets, these shifts being intended by the government, and not the result of fluctuating world market prices or natural scarcity.

The environment phase sees the pollution level decline as the economy asymptotically converges to a balanced growth path with a positive, constant rate of growth. Sustainable growth is feasible because abatement, induced by public policy, overcomes the conflict between economic growth and the environment.

For simplicity, the government objective function and its constraint have been assumed identical with the household's objective function and its budget restriction. Therefore, optimal public policy must be welfare-maximising and identical with the socially optimal policy. The pollution tax rate chosen by the government thus coincides with a Pigovian tax rate. However, if a different government objective function is postulated this will not hold anymore. In the face of the results of chapter 5, for instance, it can be conjectured that if firms engaged in lobbying for a lower tax rate, and the government traded off household welfare against income from lobby contributions, the resulting tax rate would be lower than the Pigovian one, giving rise to weaker growth-dampening, composition and substitution effects on the economy.

Technological change, endogenously induced by environmental policy, have not been considered. The modelling of a research and development sector which supplies blueprints for more efficient abatement technologies, for example, would have increased the complexity of the model considerably. Positive externalities arising from environmental protection efforts, such as learning effects ("learning by abating"), leading to nondecreasing returns to abatement could have been included more easily in the model. Clearly, these extensions provide interesting and important areas for further research.

Appendix

Appendix A: Consumption and Total Wealth

Define $\Xi(T) \equiv \exp\left[\int_0^T r(t)dt\right]$, then integration of the budget constraint (6.2) yields

$$K(T) = \Xi(T)\left[K(0) + \int_0^T \frac{\Pi(t)+\Gamma(t)-X(t)}{R(t)}dt\right]$$

or, after substitution from (6.10),

$$K(T) = \Xi(T)\left[K(0) + \int_0^T \frac{\Pi(t)+\Gamma(t)}{R(t)}dt\right] + \Xi(T)\frac{X(0)}{\rho}\left[\exp(-\rho T)-1\right]. \quad \text{(A1)}$$

Let $T \to \infty$ and substitute from (A1) into the No-Ponzi-Game condition (6.11) to obtain

$$\frac{X(0)}{\rho} = K(0) + \int_0^\infty \frac{\Pi(t) + \Gamma(t)}{\Xi(t)} dt .$$

Substituting back into (A1) results in

$$K(T) = \frac{X(T)}{\rho} - \Xi(T) \int_T^\infty \frac{\Pi(t) + \Gamma(t)}{\Xi(t)} dt .$$

After defining

$$\Theta(T) \equiv \Xi(T) \int_T^\infty \frac{\Pi(t) + \Gamma(t)}{\Xi(t)} dt = \int_T^\infty [\Pi(t) + \Gamma(t)] \exp\left[-\int_T^t r(s) ds \right] dt$$

this can be written as $X = \rho(K + \Theta)$.

Appendix B: Proof of Lemma 1

The capital goods produced in sector j=3,4 have been defined as numeraire, and their price was set equal to one. Making use of the intensive form of the production function,

$$\phi_j(z_j) \equiv \Phi_j(C_j / D_j, 1),$$

it follows from (6.26) that if $\theta_j = 0$,

$$r = \phi_j' \quad \text{and} \quad r + \tau\xi = \phi_j - z_j \phi_j' \tag{B1}$$

where $z_j \equiv C_j / D_j$. Differentiation of (B1) yields

$$\frac{dr}{dz_j} = \phi_j'' \quad \text{and} \quad \frac{dr + \xi d\tau}{dz_j} = -z_j \phi_j''.$$

Division of the latter by the former gives

$$\frac{dr + \xi d\tau}{dz_j} \bigg/ \frac{dr}{dz_j} = 1 + \frac{\xi d\tau}{dr} = -z_j$$

which can be solved for

$$\frac{dr}{d\tau} = -\frac{\xi}{1+z_j} < 0. \tag{B2}$$

Appendix C: Proof of Lemma 2

Linear homogeneity in production gives rise to marginal costs which are scale-independent unit costs, given by

$$c_k = \min\left[ra_{Ck} + (r+\tau\xi)a_{Dk}:\ \Phi_k(a_{Ck}, a_{Dk}) = 1\right] \tag{C1}$$

where a_{Ck} and a_{Dk} are input coefficients representing the cost-minimising amount of the respective factors necessary to produce one unit of good k. Differentiation of (C1) gives

$$dc_k = a_{Ck}dr + rda_{Ck} + a_{Dk}(dr + \xi d\tau) + (r+\tau\xi)da_{Dk}. \tag{C2}$$

By taking rental rates as given and minimising costs, firms ensure that

$$rda_{Ck} + (r+\tau\xi)da_{Dk} = 0.$$

Substituting this into (C2) leads to

$$dc_k = a_{Ck}dr + a_{Dk}(dr + \xi d\tau).$$

Division by $c_k = ra_{Ck} + (r+\tau\xi)a_{Dk}$ yields the growth rate

$$\hat{c}_k = \frac{a_{Dk}(z_k dr + dr + \xi d\tau)}{a_{Dk}(z_k r + r + \tau\xi)} = \frac{z_k dr + dr + \xi d\tau}{rz_k + r + \tau\xi}.$$

where $z_k \equiv a_{Ck} / a_{Dk}$. From (B2) it is known that $dr + \xi d\tau = -z_j dr$, hence

$$\hat{c}_k = \frac{z_k - z_j}{rz_k + r + \tau\xi} dr.$$

The difference between the unit cost growth rates of goods 1 and 2 equals

$$
\begin{aligned}
\hat{c}_1 - \hat{c}_2 &= \frac{z_1 - z_j}{rz_1 + r + \tau\xi} dr - \frac{z_2 - z_j}{rz_2 + r + \tau\xi} dr \\
&= \frac{(z_1 - z_j)(rz_2 + r + \tau\xi) - (z_2 - z_j)(rz_1 + r + \tau\xi)}{(rz_1 + r + \tau\xi)(rz_2 + r + \tau\xi)} dr \\
&= \frac{z_1(r + \tau\xi) - rz_j z_2 - z_2(r + \tau\xi) + rz_j z_1}{(rz_1 + r + \tau\xi)(rz_2 + r + \tau\xi)} dr \\
&= \frac{(z_1 - z_2)(r + \tau\xi + rz_j)}{(rz_1 + r + \tau\xi)(rz_2 + r + \tau\xi)} dr
\end{aligned}
$$

where j=3,4,5. According to (B2) $dr = -\xi d\tau / (1 + z_j)$, hence

$$
\hat{c}_1 - \hat{c}_2 = \frac{(z_2 - z_1)(r + \tau\xi + rz_j)}{(rz_1 + r + \tau\xi)(rz_2 + r + \tau\xi)} \frac{\xi}{1 + z_j} d\tau
$$

Finally, since $\hat{c}_1 - \hat{c}_2 = d(c_1 / c_2) / (c_1 / c_2)$ one can write

$$
\frac{d(c_1 / c_2)}{d\tau} = \frac{c_1}{c_2} \frac{(z_2 - z_1)(r + \tau\xi + rz_j)}{(rz_1 + r + \tau\xi)(rz_2 + r + \tau\xi)} \frac{\xi}{1 + z_j} < 0.
$$

The sign follows from the assumption that $z_1 > z_2$ (see (6.23)).

Appendix D: The Pollution Tax Equation in the Development Phase

In the development phase $A = dA = F_5 = C_5 = D_5 = 0$. The Euler equation (6.33) thus reduces to

$$
\hat{\mu} = \rho + PX\xi \frac{dD}{dK} - \sum_{k=1}^{4} p_k \left(\frac{\partial F_k}{\partial C_k} \frac{dC_k}{dK} + \frac{\partial F_k}{\partial D_k} \frac{dD_k}{dK} \right).
$$

Upon substitution from (6.26), where $\theta_1 = \ldots = \theta_4 = 0$ because the prices $p_1 = \ldots = p_4 = 0$ are equilibrium prices (see section 6.1.3), this becomes

$$
\hat{\mu} = \rho + PX\xi \frac{dD}{dK} - r \sum_{k=1}^{4} \frac{dC_k}{dK} - (r + \tau\xi) \sum_{k=1}^{4} \frac{dD_k}{dK}.
$$

In the development phase $\sum_{k=1}^{4} dC_k = dC$ and $\sum_{k=1}^{4} dD_k = dD$, hence

$$\hat{\mu} = \rho + PX\xi \frac{dD}{dK} - r\frac{dC}{dK} - (r + \tau\xi)\frac{dD}{dK}.$$

Considering that $dC = dK - dD$, one obtains

$$\hat{\mu} = \rho + PX\xi \frac{dD}{dK} - r\frac{dK - dD}{dK} - (r + \tau\xi)\frac{dD}{dK} = \rho - r + \xi \frac{dD}{dK}(PX - \tau)$$

which, with the assumptions made, implies (6.34).

Appendix E: Stability in the Development Phase

This appendix is divided in three parts. In a first part, the local saddle-point stability of the model is proved. In a second part, the global convergence to the equilibrium point is shown to be the only optimal outcome. The third part demonstrates that changes in X and K always have the same sign.

Part 1: The system of differential equations describing the dynamics of the economy is given by

$$\dot{K} = rK + (\xi D)^2 X - X \tag{6.35}$$

$$\dot{X} = X(r - \rho). \tag{6.9}$$

Since this system is nonlinear it needs to be linearised around the equilibrium. The linear approximation system reads

$$\begin{bmatrix} \dot{K} \\ \dot{X} \end{bmatrix} = \Lambda \begin{bmatrix} K - \tilde{K} \\ X - \tilde{X} \end{bmatrix}$$

(a tilde marks an equilibrium value) with the coefficient matrix

$$\Lambda = \begin{bmatrix} \partial\dot{K} / \partial K & \partial\dot{K} / \partial X \\ \partial\dot{X} / \partial K & \partial\dot{X} / \partial X \end{bmatrix} = \begin{bmatrix} B + K\dfrac{\partial r}{\partial K} & K\dfrac{\partial r}{\partial X} + (\xi D)^2 - 1 \\ X\dfrac{\partial r}{\partial K} & r - \rho + X\dfrac{\partial r}{\partial X} \end{bmatrix}$$

where $B \equiv r + 2\xi^2 DXdD / dK$. In a stationary state it must hold that $\dot{K} = \dot{X} = 0$. The trivial solution is characterised by $X=K=0$, but if $K(0)>0$ then $X(0)>0$ by (6.12), and any trajectory leading to $X=0$ must violate (6.9) through a jump in X. Hence the trivial solution cannot be an optimum. The nontrivial solution is given by $rK=[1-(\xi D)^2]X$ and $r=\rho$ or, combining both conditions, $\rho K=[1-(\xi D)^2]X$ with $X>0$ and $K>0$. In this equilibrium, $B=\rho+2\xi^2 DXdD/dK$ which is positive because according to (6.28) $dD/dK>0$.

The Jacobian determinant $|\Lambda|$ evaluated at the nontrivial equilibrium equals

$$|\Lambda| = \begin{vmatrix} B+K\dfrac{\partial r}{\partial K} & K\dfrac{\partial r}{\partial X}-\dfrac{\rho K}{X} \\ X\dfrac{\partial r}{\partial K} & X\dfrac{\partial r}{\partial X} \end{vmatrix} = X\frac{\partial r}{\partial X}\left(B+K\frac{\partial r}{\partial K}\right)-X\frac{\partial r}{\partial K}\left(K\frac{\partial r}{\partial X}-\frac{\rho K}{X}\right)$$

$$= BX\frac{\partial r}{\partial X}+X\frac{\partial r}{\partial X}K\frac{\partial r}{\partial K}-X\frac{\partial r}{\partial K}K\frac{\partial r}{\partial X}+X\frac{\partial r}{\partial K}\frac{\rho K}{X}$$

$$= BX\frac{\partial r}{\partial X}+\rho K\frac{\partial r}{\partial K}$$

Since $\tau=PX$ (see (6.34)), $P=\xi D$, $dD/dK>0$, and $dr/d\tau<0$ (see lemma 1), the two partial derivatives on which the sign of the determinant depends can be rewritten as

$$\frac{\partial r}{\partial X}=\frac{dr}{d\tau}\frac{\partial \tau}{\partial X}=P\frac{dr}{d\tau}<0$$

$$\frac{\partial r}{\partial K}=\frac{dr}{d\tau}\frac{\partial \tau}{\partial D}\frac{dD}{dK}=\xi X\frac{dr}{d\tau}\frac{dD}{dK}<0.$$

Therefore the determinant is negative. This sign implies one positive and one negative root, so that the linear approximation system is globally saddle point stable. According to the Liapunov theorem [Takayama (1994), p. 414] it follows that the original system must be locally saddle point stable.

Part 2: The Hamiltonian (6.5) on which the dynamics of the model are based is strictly concave in the state K and the controls X_i, C and D, so that any optimum, provided it exists, must be global and unique. Both stable branches of the saddle-point equilibrium are feasible, but there can be only one which meets both the initial condition and the transversality condition. This branch is the unique optimal trajectory.

Step 3: The zero-motion lines $\dot{X}=0$ and $\dot{K}=0$ divide the (X, K) phase plane into four isosectors in each of which the direction of motion is uniquely determined. In the two isosectors characterised by $\dot{X}/\dot{K}=dX/dK<0$ motions diverge from the equilibrium whereas in the remaining sectors where $\dot{X} / \dot{K} = dX / dK > 0$ motions converge. Any trajectory strictly converging to the saddle-point equilibrium - and the two stable branches of the equilibrium are the only ones there are - must therefore pass through the latter isosectors, hence along the optimal trajectory $dX/dK>0$.

Appendix F: Factor Intensity and Factor Price Ratio

By making use of the intensive form of the production function one obtains from (6.26)

$$r = p_k \phi_k' \quad \text{and} \quad r + \tau\xi = p_k(\phi_k - z_k \phi_k').$$

for all k with $\theta_k = 0$. The factor price ratio $y \equiv (r + \tau\xi) / r$ can thus be written as

$$y = \frac{\phi_k}{\phi_k'} - z_k.$$

Total differentiation yields

$$dy = \frac{\phi_k'}{\phi_k'} dz_k - \frac{\phi_k \phi_k''}{(\phi_k')^2} dz_k - dz_k = -\frac{\phi_k \phi_k''}{(\phi_k')^2} dz_k$$

which can be solved for

$$\frac{dz_k}{dy} = -\frac{(\phi_k')^2}{\phi_k \phi_k''} > 0.$$

Chapter 7 Environmental Kuznets Curves: Limitations and Opportunities

All flesh is grass.
Isaiah 40:8

This last chapter is not intended to repeat what has already been said in the "Concluding Remarks" sections of chapters 2 - 6. It will, however, take up once more some of the main issues of the study, relate them to a common context, and try to join them to a single whole. Moreover, the most serious limitations of, or obstacles to, Environmental Kuznets Curves will be summarised in order to avoid the impression that the inverted U-shaped pattern could be expected for all kinds of environmental problems, and to indicate potentially fruitful directions of future research in this field. Finally, it will be attempted to give the development phase and the environment phase an interpretation that goes beyond their purely technical aspects.

7.1 A Simple Concept and its Complex Realisation

The key assumption underlying most parts of this study has been that, in general, Environmental Kuznets Curves do not occur accidentally, but are largely the result of some at least near-optimal behaviour. Their occurrence can be explained by a rather simple cost-benefit argument that has been derived using basic economic theory. It holds that economic activity is associated with various forms of environmental impact. At its early stages of development, an economy is still too small to cause serious harm to the environment, and the free initial endowment of environmental quality, combined with a low consumption level, renders inefficient the allocation of available resources to pollution avoidance or mitigation activities. More immediate needs such as food, clothing, shelter, or general material wellbeing are given higher priority.

But as the economy grows, its impact on the natural habitat increases. At some point, environmental quality may become so scarce, and hence valuable relative to alternative goods, that the marginal benefit of a better environment is no longer smaller than the marginal cost of achieving it. This presupposes that the marginal abatement cost is finite, i.e. pollution control must be feasible. Taking away resources from productive or consumptive uses, and employing them in pollution reduction then becomes the optimal strategy. If abatement technologies are efficient enough, environmental deterioration can be reversed.

This argument, which was developed in chapters 2 and 3, has a strong intuitive appeal, but its transfer and application to the real world in a straight-forward way causes difficulties. First of all, polluters and the victims of pollution need not coincide, which means that even if a demand for a better environment arises among the latter, there is no immediate incentive for the former to satisfy it. And secondly, even if polluters and pollutees did coincide, the public-good character of many types of pollution would still not make private pollution abatement activities an individually rational strategy. These objections to the Environmental Kuznets Curve hypothesis indicate that the simple theoretical concept sketched above can hardly be the full story. Since there is no market for environmental quality[54], the link between the demand for pollution reductions and their supply is still missing.

In chapter 5 it has been argued that this missing link may consist in the political market of democracy. The pollutees, in this study the households, can vote for a government that promises to take measures aimed at satisfying the demand for a better environment. Although the individual household will, in one way or another, pay for such measures, it can be sure that all the other households will bear part of the cost as well. The problem of free-riding associated with the provision of public goods can thus be overcome. The government's incentive to take the demand for a stricter environmental policy seriously is the next election if it wants to stay in power.

With the analysis of the political processes that give rise to a certain environmental policy, and of the role of the different agents involved in these processes, one enters the domain of political economy. The originally simple concept of Environmental Kuznets Curves turns into a highly complex issue when a multitude of interest groups, each with its own objective function, set of constraints, and control variables, is taken into account. Chapter 4 has

---

54 There are markets on which environmental quality is reflected by prices. The housing market has already been mentioned earlier. In the tourism and recreation industry, a high air and water quality, an intact vegetation, and places of natural beauty permit fetching higher prices. But on these markets, environmental quality is a characteristic of the goods traded, and not the good itself.

shown that already an unequally distributed national income may give rise to a large diversity of different political positions among the households. When the various groups start interacting with each other, when side-payments (or, more generally, lobbying activities) are considered, and subjective factors such as the concern about the environment are taken into account like in chapter 5, it gets increasingly hard to identify the common fundamental trend pattern underlying this complexity, namely that a growing material prosperity keeps fuelling the demand for a better environment.

Nevertheless, in the models of chapters 4 and 5, these trends can clearly be observed: the figures 4.1 and 4.2, and the income level effect described in section 4.4.3 document that a household's desired pollution tax rate increases with the household's income level. In section 5.2.3, campaign spending is found to be increasing in the greens' per capita income, inducing a higher environmental awareness of the grey households, and via the democratic process leading to a stricter environmental policy.

In the model of chapter 6 which retains the basic decentralised decision-making structure of the previous models, but adds an intertemporal aspect to public environmental policy, the positive correlation between household income and the pollution tax rate is obvious, reflecting the rising demand for a better environment in the course of economic growth per capita. However, the emphasis of this chapter is not so much on the processes that lead to a certain policy, than on the processes which are triggered off by policy, such as sectoral and substitutional dynamics. The model gives an idea of the complex effects which environmental policy induces in real-world economies with their several sectors, technologies, substitution possibilities, factors of production, intermediate goods, and pollutants.

7.2 Environmental Kuznets Curves: Not a Cure-All

Much of what has been said about Environmental Kuznets Curves may create the impression that, in the long run, environmental problems will all be tackled, probably even solved, depending only on sufficiently high a per capita income. This is certainly not the case. The first objection to viewing Environmental Kuznets Curves as a cure-all is that, already by definition, they fail to exist for irreversible environmental damage such as biodiversity loss, or the removal of primary rainforest cover.

Secondly, it has been emphasized repeatedly that for actual improvements of environmental conditions to be optimal, given the marginal benefit of such improvements, abatement technology needs to be efficient enough, or sufficient substitution possibilities must be available. The avoidance of CO_2 emissions, for instance, seems not to meet this technological feasibility criterion, at least today.

A third limitation of Environmental Kuznets Curves is associated with the lack of knowledge about the hazards of certain types of pollution, about threshold effects, and about the joint effects of combinations of pollutants, often leading to an underestimation of their true harmfulness. As chapter 5 has demonstrated, a low level of concern among the public about an objectively serious environmental problem may lead to a situation in which the technological circumstances are favourable for a proper environmental turn-around, but a reduction of hazardous pollution is not considered a worthwhile objective. In consequence, nothing is done to prevent this problem from aggravating further. More generally speaking, an Environmental Kuznets Curve is the more unlikely to occur, the less people are concerned about the pollutant in question.

The level of concern does not only seem to depend on information, but also on being personally affected. The motto "out of sight, out of mind" summarises well the last limitation of Environmental Kuznets Curves to be addressed here. If the voters or decision makers do not themselves suffer from the consequences of pollution, they will not demand or order pollution reductions, unless they have other motives for doing so. Long-term environmental problems such as the deposition of radioactive waste are characterised by an intertemporal separation of those who decide about the emission level, and those who suffer from its consequences decades or even centuries later. Apart from non-use related motives, such as compassion, ethical commitment, or a sense of responsibility for posterity, there is no incentive for the polluters of earlier generations to spend resources on avoiding this pollution. So due to the particular incentive structure associated with one-directional externalities, intertemporal environmental problems tend to lack an important precondition for the occurrence of Environmental Kuznets Curves.

Clearly, to remove these obstacles to environmental turn-arounds must be a prime concern of future research. But while the role of natural scientists and engineers in this context is rather self-evident, the economic and general social science profession will have to concentrate more than in the past on the development of special incentive systems that can be applied to handle environmental problems involving highly unequal distributions of benefits and costs among polluters and pollutees. Global pollutants emitted by the economies of souvereign states are the first main problem in this area, inter-temporal pollutants are the second.

7.3 From Cowboy Economy to Spaceman Economy

The vanishing of the opportunity loss of abatement in the environment phase does not only mark the point at which it becomes efficient to abate pollution. It may also have another environment-related significance which might help overcoming some limitations of Environmental Kuznets Curves.

The development phase of an Environmental Kuznets Curve has been defined as the phase during which active environmental protection would be inefficient or non-optimal. Available resources are better employed in other activities which yield a higher benefit at the margin. The reason for this non-optimality of pollution abatement lies in the abundance of environmental quality relative to other goods, which is the result of the free initial supply of environmental services such as clean air and water, pollution sinks, biodegradation capacity, intact ecosystems supplying food, building material, biomass fuel, and so forth. In the development phase, there is no need to economise on these services, and their price of zero encourages their wasteful exploitation.

In his famous article "The Economics of the Coming Spaceship Earth", Boulding (1966) calls an economy, which manages its natural and environmental resources in this way, a *cowboy economy*, "the cowboy being symbolic of the illimitable plains and also associated with reckless, exploitative, romantic, and violent behaviour ..." [p. 11].

The environment phase, on the other hand, starts when the quality of the environment has become so low, scarce, and precious relative to other goods, that people are willing to trade off increases in the consumption of the latter against further decreases in the former. The finiteness of the initial endowment of environmental quality puts an end to its free availability.

Boulding contrasts his image of the cowboy on the open plain by the image of a spaceman who is fully dependent on a closed, small, and fragile life support system. He writes that "... the earth has become a single spaceship, without unlimited reservoirs of anything, either for extraction or for pollution, and in which, therefore, man must find his place in a cyclical ecological system ..." [ib.] Boulding's *spacemen economy* is thus an economy (or rather the planet-wide economy) which remains within its natural boundaries set by the condition of sustainability, or long-term life support.

Does an economy's entrance into an environment phase represent an advancement towards the spaceman economy? First of all, there is the technical side of the question which has been dealt with throughout this study: pollution abatement may or may not suffice to reverse the trend of decreasing environmental quality. It may simply be argued that if pollution declines in the environment phase, economic activity has become sustainable, and sustainability is the spaceman's prime concern.

But besides this technical side, there also seems to be a psychological side of the question. The cowboy and the spaceman differ in their profession, in their habitat, but above all they differ in their *attitude towards their respective habitat*. To draw a parallel, in the early environment phase people, who are still cowboys in the metaphorical sense, are for the first time confronted with the scarcity of environmental quality. This newly experienced scarcity changes the way they manage their environmental resources, but it can further be expected to change their perspective of, and their attitude towards, the place they live in. In other words, the experience of environmental scarcity may well turn people into spacemen, not only in deed, but also in mind.

Symbols and Abbreviations

Index Symbols

G	green core households
i, j, k	general index variables; in chapter 6: $i=1,2$; $j=3,4,5$; $k=1,...,5$
L	lower class
M	middle class
U	upper class

Greek Symbols

α	constant productivity of capital in the "AK"-model
β	parameter of the utility function in chapter 3, and of the government objective function in chapter 5
Γ	transfer income
Δ, Δ_i	auxiliary variable
δ	constant rate of natural pollution "decay"
ε	share of green core households in total number of households
γ_i	auxiliary constant
ζ	constant marginal efficiency of abatement
H	Hessian matrix
$\lvert \mathrm{H}_i \rvert$	i-th principal minor of the Hessian determinant
Θ	present value of future profits and transfer income
θ, θ_i	Lagrangean multiplier
Λ	Jacobian matrix
λ, λ_i	Lagrangean multiplier; opportunity loss of abatement
$\tilde{\lambda}$	opportunity loss of abatement in the stationary state
μ	costate variable; shadow price of capital
ν	rate of a hypothetical tax on campaigning
ξ	constant marginal pollution coefficient of capital
Ξ	discount factor
Π (Π_i)	profit function or level (of sector i)
ρ	constant rate of pure time preference
σ (σ_i)	elasticity of marginal utility with respect to consumption (of a household of group i)
T	desired-pollution-tax-rate function
τ	pollution tax rate

τ_i	pollution tax rate desired by household i or by a household of group i
$\bar{\tau}$	arithmetic mean of the households' desired pollution tax rates
Φ_i	production function of sector i
ϕ_i	intensive form of Φ_i
χ	costate variable; shadow price of environmental quality
ψ	Lagrangean multiplier
Ω	(the grey households') environmental concern
$\bar{\Omega}$	the green households' constant environmental concern
Ω_0	pre-campaign level of environmental concern
Ω_L	level of Ω below which corporate lobbying is efficient
ω_i	parameter of a utility function

Latin Symbols

A	abatement expenditure; in chapter 6 abatement capital stock
A_i	abatement of pollution of type i in chapter 3; abatement capital allocated to sector i in chapter 6
a	marginal abatement cost, fixed at a constant level
a_i	national income share of household i or profit share of a household of group i
a_{Ci}, a_{Di}	input coefficients of the unit cost function
B	auxiliary variable
b_i	factor income share of a household of group i
C (C_i)	"clean" capital (employed in sector i)
c_i	unit cost function, or unit cost of sector i's output
D (D_i)	"dirty" capital (employed in sector i)
E	emission function or level
e_i	emissions per unit of output (emission intensity) in sector i
F (F_i)	output (of sector i)
G	government objective function
H	green campaign spending per household
h	total campaign spending, $h=\varepsilon H$
$\mathcal{H}$	current-value Hamiltonian function
$\mathcal{H}^*$	optimised Hamiltonian
I	nonsaved income or total expenditure
I_i	income of household i or of a household of group i
I_0	pre-campaign income level

K (K_i)	real, physical, or man-made capital; in chapter 6 the aggregate of A, C and D (allocated to sector i)
$\tilde{K}$	stationary-state capital stock
L	lobbying contributions: the firms' donations to a political party
$\mathcal{L}$, $\mathcal{L}_i$	Lagrangean function
m_i	share of emissions of sector i in total emissions
N	number of households, size of the labour force
n	number of ... (various applications)
P	pollution function or level
P_i	pollution function or level of type i in chapter 3, or of sector i in chapter 6
$\tilde{P}$	stationary-state pollution level
P^*	level of P when the economy enters the environment phase
p_i	price of good i or of the good produced in sector i
Q	environmental quality function or level
$\mathbf{Q}$	n-vector of different dimensions of environmental quality
Q_i	i-th dimension of environmental quality (chapter 3), or environmental quality enjoyed by a household of group i (chapter 4)
$\overline{Q}$ $(\overline{Q}_i)$	highest achievable environmental quality (of dimension i)
q_1, q_2, q_3	accounting prices of environmental quality
R	supply function of private supplementary environmental quality
R_i	supplementary, privately supplied environmental quality of a household of group i; $R_i = R(S_i)$
R_+^2 (R_{++}^2)	nonnegative (strictly positive) quadrant of the two-dimensional real space
r	rental rate of capital; in chapter 3 social return on capital
S_i	defensive expenditure of a household of group i
s	auxiliary variable
s_i	share of output of sector i in total output
t	time
X	consumption level; in chapter 6 total consumption expenditure $X = p_1X_1 + p_2X_2$
X_i	consumption level of household i or of a household of group i; in chapter 6 the amount of good i consumed
$\tilde{X}$	stationary-state consumption level
X^*	level of X when the economy enters the environment phase

$\overline{X}$	arithmetic mean of the households' consumption
U (U_i)	utility function or level (of household i or of a household of group i)
u, v	auxiliary variables
w	wage rate
y	factor price ratio
Z (Z_G)	perceived pollution; $Z = \Omega P$ ($Z_G = \overline{\Omega} P$)
z_i	factor intensity $z_i = C_i/D_i$ in sector i

Abbreviations

CFCs	chlorofluorocarbons
CO	carbon monoxide
CO_2	carbon dioxide
e.g.	example given (exempli gratia)
GDP	gross domestic product
GEMS	Global Environmental Monitoring System
GNNP	"green" net national product
ib.	in the same place (ibidem)
i.e.	that is to say (id est)
NGO	non-governmental organisation
NNP	net national product
NO_2	nitrous dioxide
NO_X	nitrous oxides
OLS	ordinary least squares
OPEC	Organization of Petroleum Exporting Countries
PR	public relations
SO_2	sulphur dioxide
SPM	suspended particulate matter

Figures

References

Barro, R. J. and Sala-i-Martin, X. (1995): *Economic Growth*, New York

Baumol, W. J. (1967): Macroeconomics of Unbalanced Growth: The Anatomy of Urban Crisis, *American Economic Review*, vol. 57, pp. 415-426

Baumol, W. J. and Oates, W. E. (1979): *Economics, Environmental Policy and the Quality of Life*, Hampshire/UK

Beckerman, W. (1972): Economic Development and the Environment: A False Dilemma, *International Conciliation*, no. 586, pp. 57-71

------ (1977): The Case for Economic Growth, in: H. J. Leonard, , J. C. Davies III and G. Binder (eds.): *Business and Environment - Toward Common Ground*, Washington, D.C., pp. 240-246

------ (1992): *Economic Development and the Environment: Conflict or Complementarity?* World Bank Policy Research Paper no. 961, Washington, D.C.

------ (1993): The Environmental Limits to Growth: A Fresh Look, in: H. Giersch (ed.): *Economic Progress and Environmental Concern*, Berlin, pp. 3-23

Blanchard, O. J. and Fischer, S. (1989): *Lectures on Macroeconomics*, Cambridge/Mass.

Boulding, K. (1966): The Economics of Coming Spaceship Earth, in: *Environmental Quality in a Growing Economy - Essays from the 6th RFF Forum*, Baltimore/Md., pp. 3-14

Chiang, A. C. (1984): *Fundamental Methods of Mathematical Economics*, 3rd ed., Singapore

------ (1992): *Elements of Dynamic Optimization*, Singapore

Commoner, B. (1972): The Environmental Cost of Economic Growth, in: *Chemistry in Britain*, vol. 8, no. 2, pp. 52-65

Daly, H. E. (1992): *Steady-State Economics*, 2nd ed., London

Dasgupta, P. (1993): *An Inquiry into Well-Being and Destitution*, Oxford, 1993

Dasgupta, P. (1995): Economic Development and the Environment: Issues, Policies, and Political Economy, in: M. G. Quibria (ed.): *Critical Issues in Asian Development*, Hong Kong, pp. 160-185

Dasgupta, P. and Mäler, K.-G. (1994): *Poverty, Institutions, and the Environmental-Resource Base*, World Bank Environment Paper no. 8, Washington, D.C.

Devarajan, S. and Fisher, A. C. (1981): Hotelling's "Economics of Exhaustible Resources" Fifty Years Later, *Journal of Economic Literature*, vol. 19, pp. 65-73

Diani, M. (1989): Italy: The "Liste Verdi", in: F. Müller-Rommel (ed.): *New Politics in Western Europe. The Rise and Success of Green Parties and Alternative Lists*, Boulder, pp. 113-122

Dorfman, R. (1969): An Economic Interpretation of Optimal Control Theory, *American Economic Review*, vol. 59, pp. 817-831

Dunlap, R. E. and Van Liere, K. D. (1984): Commitment to the Dominant Social Paradigm and Concern for Environmental Quality, *Social Science Quarterly*, vol. 65, pp. 1013-1028

Economist, The (1991): Animal Rights, November 16th, pp. 25-30

Eder, N. (1996): *Poisoned Prosperity. Development, Modernization, and the Environment in South Korea*, Armonk/N.Y.

Ehrlich, P. R. and Ehrlich, A. H. (1991): *Healing the Planet: Strategies for Resolving the Environmental Crisis*, Reading/Mass.

Ehrlich, P. R. and Holdren, J. (1971): The Impact of Population Growth, *Science*, vol. 171, no. 3977, pp. 1212-1217

Engel, E. (1857): Die Productions- und Consumptionsverhältnisse des Königreichs Sachsen, originally in *Zeitschrift des Statistischen Bureaus des Königlich Sächsischen Ministerium des Inneren*, no. 8/9, reprinted in: *Bulletin de l'Institut International de Statistique*, vol. 9 (1895)

Fisher, A. G. B. (1939): Production, Primary, Secondary, Tertiary, *The Economic Record*, vol. 15, pp. 24-38

Forster, B. (1973): Optimal Capital Accumulation in a Polluted Environment, *Southern Economic Journal*, vol. 34, pp. 544-547

Fourastié, J. (1969): *Le Grand Espoir du XXe Siècle*, Paris

Frankland, E. G. (1989): Federal Republic of Germany: "Die Grünen", in: F. Müller-Rommel (ed.): *New Politics in Western Europe. The Rise and Success of Green Parties and Alternative Lists*, Boulder, pp. 61-79

Fuller, R. B. and Dil, A. (1983): *Humans in Universe*, New York

Georgescu-Roegen, N. (1975): Energy and Economic Myths, *Southern Economic Journal*, vol. 41, pp. 347-381

Grossman, G. M. (1995): Pollution and Growth: What Do We Know?, in: I. Goldin and L. A. Winters (eds.): *The Economics of Sustainable Development*, Cambridge/UK, pp. 19-46

Grossman, G. M. and Helpman, E. (1994): Protection for Sale, *American Economic Review*, vol. 84, pp. 833-850

------ (1995): Trade Wars and Trade Talks, *Journal of Political Economy*, vol. 103, pp. 675-708

Grossman, G. M. and Krueger, A. B. (1991): *Environmental Impacts of the North American Free Trade Agreement*, National Bureau of Economic Research Working Paper no. 3914, Cambridge/Mass.

------ (1993): Environmental Impacts of the North American Free Trade Agreement, in: P. Garber, (ed.): *The US-Mexico Free Trade Agreement*, Cambridge/Mass., pp. 353-378

------ (1995): Economic Growth and the Environment, *Quarterly Journal of Economics*, vol. 110, pp. 353-377

Grossman, G. M., Krueger, A. B. and Laity, J. (1994): *Determinants of Air Pollution in U.S. Counties*, Discussion Papers in Economics no. 169, Woodrow Wilson School, Princeton University, Princeton

Hartwick, J. M. (1990): Natural Resources, National Accounting and Economic Depreciation, *Journal of Public Economics*, vol. 43, pp. 291-304

------ (1992): Deforestation and National Accounting, *Environmental and Resource Economics*, vol. 2, pp. 513-521

Hartwick, J. M. and Olewiler, N. D. (1986): *The Economics of Environmental Resource Use*, New York

Hausman, D. and McPherson, M. (1994): Preference, Belief and Welfare, *American Economic Review - Papers and Proceedings*, vol. 84, pp. 396-400

Heilbroner, R. L. (1973): Economics as a "Value-Free" Science, *Social Research*, vol. 40, pp. 129-143

Hettige, H., Lucas, R. E. B. and Wheeler, D. (1992): The Toxic Intesity of Industrial Production: Global Patterns, Trends, and Trade Policy, *American Economic Review - Papers and Proceedings*, vol. 82, pp. 478-481

Hirsch, F. (1976): *Social Limits to Growth*, London

Höffe, O. (1993): *Moral als Preis der Moderne*, 2nd ed., Frankfurt a.M.

Holtz-Eakin, D. and Selden, T. M. (1995): Stoking the Fires? CO_2 Emissions and Economic Growth, *Journal of Public Economics*, vol. 57, pp. 85-101

Houthakker, H. S. (1957): An International Comparison of Household Expenditure Patterns, Commemorating the Centenary of Engel's Law, *Econometrica*, vol. 25, pp. 532-551

Inglehart, R. (1977): *The Silent Revolution; Changing Values and Political Styles Among Western Publics*, Princeton

Jamison, A., Eyerman, R. and Cramer, J. (1990): *The Making of the New Environmental Consciousness. A Comparative Study of the Environmental Movements in Sweden, Denmark and the Netherlands*, Edinburgh

Johansen, L. (1959): Substitution vs. Fixed Production Coefficients in the Theory of Economic Growth: A Synthesis, *Econometrica*, vol. 27, pp. 229-248

Johansson, P.-O. (1987): *The Economic Theory and Measurement of Environmental Benefits*, Cambridge/UK

King, A. and Schneider, B. (1991): *The First Global Revolution*, New York

Kuznets, S. (1955): Economic Growth and Income Inequality, *American Economic Review*, vol 45, pp. 1-28

Kymlicka, W. (1990): *Contemporary Political Philosophy*, Oxford

Leontief, W. (1970): Environmental Repercussions and the Economic Structure: An Input-Output Approach, *Review of Economics and Statistics*, vol. 52, pp. 262-271

Lidskog, R. (1996): In Science We Trust? On the Relation Between Scientific Knowledge, Risk Consciousness and Public Trust, *Acta Sociologica*, vol. 39, pp. 31-54

Lovelock, J. E. (1979): *Gaia: A New Look on Earth*, Oxford

Maddala, G. S. (1992): *Introduction to Econometrics*, 2nd ed., New York

Magee, S. P., Brock, W. A. and Young, L. (1989): *Black Hole Tariffs and Endogenous Policy Theory*, New York

Mäler, K.-G. (1991): National Accounts and Environmental Resources, *Environmental and Resource Economics*, vol. 1, pp. 1-15

Marrewijk, C. v., Ploeg, F. v. d., and Verbeek, J. (1993): *Is Growth Bad for the Environment? Pollution, Abatement, and Endogenous Growth*, World Bank Policy Research Working Paper no. 1151, Washington, D.C.

Martínez-Alier, J. (1995): The Environment as a Luxury Good or "Too Poor to be Green"?, *Economie Appliquée*, vol. 48, pp. 215-230

Meadows, D. H., Meadows, D. L., Randers, J. and Behrens III, W. (1972): *The Limits to Growth*, New York

Meadows, D. H., Meadows, D. L., and Randers, J. (1992): *Beyond the Limits*, Post Mills/Vermont

Michael, R. T. and Becker, G. S. (1973): On the New Theory of Consumer Behaviour, *Swedish Journal of Economics*, vol. 75, pp. 378-396

Mohai, P. (1985): Public Concern and Elite Involvement in Environmental Conservation Issues, *Social Science Quarterly*, vol. 66, pp. 820-838

Motz, L. and Weaver, J. H. (1993): *The Story of Mathematics*, New York

Mulligan, C. B. and Sala-i-Martin, X. (1991): *A Note on the Time-Elimination Method for Solving Recursive Dynamic Economic Models*, National Bureau of Economic Research, Technical Working Paper no. 116

Oak Ridge National Laboratory (1992): *Trends '91: A Compendium of Data on Global Change*, Oak Ridge/Tennessee

O'Neill, O. (1997): Environmental Values, Anthropocentrism and Speciesism, *Environmental Values*, vol. 6, pp. 127-142

Panayotou, T. (1993): *Empirical Tests and Policy Analysis of Environmental Degradation at Different Stages of Economic Development*, Working Paper no. 238, Technology and Employment Programme, International Labour Office, Geneva

Pasinetti, L. L. (1981): *Structural Change and Economic Growth*, Cambridge/ U.K.

Pearce, D. W. and Turner, R. K. (1990): *Economics of Natural Resources and the Environment*, New York

Pearson, P. J. G. (1994): Energy, Externalities, and Environmental Quality: Will Development Cure the Ills it Creates?, *Energy Studies Review*, vol. 6, pp. 199-216

Pezzey, J. (1989): *Economic Analysis of Sustainable Growth and Sustainable Development*, Working Paper no. 15, World Bank Environment Department, Washington, D.C.

Pirages, D. C. (1977): A Social Design for Sustainable Growth, in: D. C. Pirages (ed.): *The Sustainable Society*, New York, pp. 1-13

Poguntke, T. (1989): The "New Politics Dimension" in European Green Parties, in: F. Müller-Rommel (ed.): *New Politics in Western Europe. The Rise and Success of Green Parties and Alternative Lists*, Boulder, pp. 175-195

Radetzki, M. (1992): Economic Growth and the Environment, in: P. Low, (ed.): *International Trade and the Environment*, World Bank Discussion Paper no. 159, Washington D.C., pp. 121-136

Rebelo, S. (1991): Long-Run Policy Analysis and Long-Run Growth, *Journal of Political Economy*, von. 99, pp. 500-521

Roberts, J. T. and Grimes, P. E. (1997): Carbon Intensity and Economic Development 1962-91: A Brief Exploration of the Environmental Kuznets Curve, *World Development*, vol. 25, pp. 191-198

Schipper, L. and Meyers, S. (1992): *World Energy: Building a Sustainable Future*, published by the Stockholm Environment Institute, Stockholm

Selden, T. M. and Song, D. (1994): Environmental Quality and Development: Is there a Kuznets Curve for Air Pollution Emissions?, *Journal of Environmental Economics and Management*, vol. 27, pp. 147-162

------ (1995): Neoclassical Growth, the J Curve for Abatement, and the Inverted U Curve for Pollution, *Journal of Environmental Economics and Management*, vol. 29, pp. 162-168

Sengupta, R. (1996): *Economic Development and CO_2-Emission: Economy - Environment Relation and Policy Approach to Choice of Emission Standard for Climate Control*, Discussion Paper no. 75, Institute for Economic Development, Boston University

Shafik, N. (1994a): Economic Development and Environmental Quality: An Econometric Analysis, *Oxford Economic Papers*, vol. 46, pp. 757-773

------ (1994b): Macroeconomic Causes of Deforestation: Barking Up the Wrong Tree?, in: K. Brown and D. W. Pearce (eds.): *The Causes of Tropical Deforestation*, London, pp. 86-95

Shafik, N. and Bandyopadhyay, S. (1992): *Economic Growth and Environmental Quality*, World Bank Policy Research Working Paper no. 904, Washington, D.C.

Slade, M. E. (1982): Trends in Natural-Resource Commodity Prices: An Analysis of the Time Domain, *Journal of Environmental Economics and Management*, vol. 9, pp. 122-137

Smith, K. R. (1990): The Risk Transition, *International Environmental Affairs*, vol. 2, pp. 227-251

Solow, R. M. (1986): On the Intergenerational Allocation of Natural Resources, *Scandinavian Journal of Economics*, vol. 88, npp. 141-149

Stern, D. I. (1996): *Progress on the Environmental Kuznets Curve?*, Working Paper in Ecological Economics no. 9601, Australian National University, Canberra

Stern, D. I., Common, M. S. and Barbier, E. B. (1996): Economic Growth and Environmental Degradation: The Environmental Kuznets Curve and Sustainable Development, *World Development*, vol. 24, no. 7, pp. 1151-1160

Stigler, G. J. and Becker, G. S. (1977): De Gustibus non est Disputandum, *American Economic Review*, vol. 67, pp. 76-90

Summers, R. and Heston, A. (1991): The Penn World Table (Mark 5): An Expanded Set of International Comparisons, 1950-1988, *Quarterly Journal of Economics*, vol. 106, pp. 327-368

Takayama, A. (1994): *Analytical Methods in Economics*, New York

Tietenberg, T. (1992): *Environmental and Natural Resource Economics*, 3rd ed., New York

Tucker, W. (1982): *Progress and Privilege: America in the Age of Environmentalism*, Garden City/N.Y.

Van Liere, K. D. and Dunlap, R. E. (1980): The Social Bases of Environmental Concern: A Review of Hypotheses, Explanations and Empirical Evidence, *Public Opinion Quarterly*, vol. 44, pp. 181-197

Varian, H. (1993): *Intermediate Microeconomics*, 3rd ed., New York

Weitzman, M. (1976): On the Welfare Significance of National Product in a Dynamic Economy, *Quarterly Journal of Economics*, vol. 90, pp. 156-162

World Bank (1992): *World Development Report 1992 - Development and the Environment*, New York

World Resources Institute (1991): *World Resources 1990-91: A Guide to the Global Environment*, New York

Lecture Notes in Economics and Mathematical Systems

For information about Vols. 1–284
please contact your bookseller or Springer-Verlag

Vol. 285: Toward Interactive and Intelligent Decision Support Systems. Volume 1. Proceedings, 1986. Edited by Y. Sawaragi, K. Inoue and H. Nakayama. XII, 445 pages. 1987.

Vol. 286: Toward Interactive and Intelligent Decision Support Systems. Volume 2. Proceedings, 1986. Edited by Y. Sawaragi, K. Inoue and H. Nakayama. XII, 450 pages. 1987.

Vol. 287: Dynamical Systems. Proceedings, 1985. Edited by A.B. Kurzhanski and K. Sigmund. VI, 215 pages. 1987.

Vol. 288: G.D. Rudebusch, The Estimation of Macroeconomic Disequilibrium Models with Regime Classification Information. VII,128 pages. 1987.

Vol. 289: B.R. Meijboom, Planning in Decentralized Firms. X, 168 pages. 1987.

Vol. 290: D.A. Carlson, A. Haurie, Infinite Horizon Optimal Control. XI, 254 pages. 1987.

Vol. 291: N. Takahashi, Design of Adaptive Organizations. VI, 140 pages. 1987.

Vol. 292: I. Tchijov, L. Tomaszewicz (Eds.), Input-Output Modeling. Proceedings, 1985. VI, 195 pages. 1987.

Vol. 293: D. Batten, J. Casti, B. Johansson (Eds.), Economic Evolution and Structural Adjustment. Proceedings, 1985. VI, 382 pages.

Vol. 294: J. Jahn, W. Knabs (Eds.), Recent Advances and Historical Development of Vector Optimization. VII, 405 pages. 1987.

Vol. 295. H. Meister, The Purification Problem for Constrained Games with Incomplete Information. X, 127 pages. 1987.

Vol. 296: A. Börsch-Supan, Econometric Analysis of Discrete Choice. VIII, 211 pages. 1987.

Vol. 297: V. Fedorov, H. Läuter (Eds.), Model-Oriented Data Analysis. Proceedings, 1987. VI, 239 pages. 1988.

Vol. 298: S.H. Chew, Q. Zheng, Integral Global Optimization. VII, 179 pages. 1988.

Vol. 299: K. Marti, Descent Directions and Efficient Solutions in Discretely Distributed Stochastic Programs. XIV, 178 pages. 1988.

Vol. 300: U. Derigs, Programming in Networks and Graphs. XI, 315 pages. 1988.

Vol. 301: J. Kacprzyk, M. Roubens (Eds.), Non-Conventional Preference Relations in Decision Making. VII, 155 pages. 1988.

Vol. 302: H.A. Eiselt, G. Pederzoli (Eds.), Advances in Optimization and Control. Proceedings, 1986. VIII, 372 pages. 1988.

Vol. 303: F.X. Diebold, Empirical Modeling of Exchange Rate Dynamics. VII, 143 pages. 1988.

Vol. 304: A. Kurzhanski, K. Neumann, D. Pallaschke (Eds.), Optimization, Parallel Processing and Applications. Proceedings, 1987. VI, 292 pages. 1988.

Vol. 305: G.-J.C.Th. van Schijndel, Dynamic Firm and Investor Behaviour under Progressive Personal Taxation. X, 215 pages.1988.

Vol. 306: Ch. Klein, A Static Microeconomic Model of Pure Competition. VIII, 139 pages. 1988.

Vol. 307: T.K. Dijkstra (Ed.), On Model Uncertainty and its Statistical Implications. VII, 138 pages. 1988.

Vol. 308: J.R. Daduna, A. Wren (Eds.), Computer-Aided Transit Scheduling. VIII, 339 pages. 1988.

Vol. 309: G. Ricci, K. Velupillai (Eds.), Growth Cycles and Multisectoral Economics: The Goodwin Tradition. III, 126 pages. 1988.

Vol. 310: J. Kacprzyk, M. Fedrizzi (Eds.), Combining Fuzzy Imprecision with Probabilistic Uncertainty in Decision Making. IX, 399 pages. 1988.

Vol. 311: R. Färe, Fundamentals of Production Theory. IX, 163 pages. 1988.

Vol. 312: J. Krishnakumar, Estimation of Simultaneous Equation Models with Error Components Structure. X, 357 pages. 1988.

Vol. 313: W. Jammernegg, Sequential Binary Investment Decisions. VI, 156 pages. 1988.

Vol. 314: R. Tietz, W. Albers, R. Selten (Eds.), Bounded Rational Behavior in Experimental Games and Markets. VI, 368 pages. 1988.

Vol. 315: I. Orishimo, G.J.D. Hewings, P. Nijkamp (Eds), Information Technology: Social and Spatial Perspectives. Proceedings 1986. VI, 268 pages. 1988.

Vol. 316: R.L. Basmann, D.J. Slottje, K. Hayes, J.D. Johnson, D.J. Molina, The Generalized Fechner-Thurstone Direct Utility Function and Some of its Uses. VIII, 159 pages. 1988.

Vol. 317: L. Bianco, A. La Bella (Eds.), Freight Transport Planning and Logistics. Proceedings, 1987. X, 568 pages. 1988.

Vol. 318: T. Doup, Simplicial Algorithms on the Simplotope. VIII, 262 pages. 1988.

Vol. 319: D.T. Luc, Theory of Vector Optimization. VIII, 173 pages. 1989.

Vol. 320: D. van der Wijst, Financial Structure in Small Business. VII, 181 pages. 1989.

Vol. 321: M. Di Matteo, R.M. Goodwin, A. Vercelli (Eds.), Technological and Social Factors in Long Term Fluctuations. Proceedings. IX, 442 pages. 1989.

Vol. 322: T. Kollintzas (Ed.), The Rational Expectations Equilibrium Inventory Model. XI, 269 pages. 1989.

Vol. 323: M.B.M. de Koster, Capacity Oriented Analysis and Design of Production Systems. XII, 245 pages. 1989.

Vol. 324: I.M. Bomze, B.M. Pötscher, Game Theoretical Foundations of Evolutionary Stability. VI, 145 pages. 1989.

Vol. 325: P. Ferri, E. Greenberg, The Labor Market and Business Cycle Theories. X, 183 pages. 1989.

Vol. 326: Ch. Sauer, Alternative Theories of Output, Unemployment, and Inflation in Germany: 1960–1985. XIII, 206 pages. 1989.

Vol. 327: M. Tawada, Production Structure and International Trade. V, 132 pages. 1989.

Vol. 328: W. Güth, B. Kalkofen, Unique Solutions for Strategic Games. VII, 200 pages. 1989.

Vol. 329: G. Tillmann, Equity, Incentives, and Taxation. VI, 132 pages. 1989.

Vol. 330: P.M. Kort, Optimal Dynamic Investment Policies of a Value Maximizing Firm. VII, 185 pages. 1989.

Vol. 331: A. Lewandowski, A.P. Wierzbicki (Eds.), Aspiration Based Decision Support Systems. X, 400 pages. 1989.

Vol. 332: T.R. Gulledge, Jr., L.A. Litteral (Eds.), Cost Analysis Applications of Economics and Operations Research. Proceedings. VII, 422 pages. 1989.

Vol. 333: N. Dellaert, Production to Order. VII, 158 pages. 1989.

Vol. 334: H.-W. Lorenz, Nonlinear Dynamical Economics and Chaotic Motion. XI, 248 pages. 1989.

Vol. 335: A.G. Lockett, G. Islei (Eds.), Improving Decision Making in Organisations. Proceedings. IX, 606 pages. 1989.

Vol. 336: T. Puu, Nonlinear Economic Dynamics. VII, 119 pages. 1989.

Vol. 337: A. Lewandowski, I. Stanchev (Eds.), Methodology and Software for Interactive Decision Support. VIII, 309 pages. 1989.

Vol. 338: J.K. Ho, R.P. Sundarraj, DECOMP: An Implementation of Dantzig-Wolfe Decomposition for Linear Programming. VI, 206 pages.

Vol. 339: J. Terceiro Lomba, Estimation of Dynamic Econometric Models with Errors in Variables. VIII, 116 pages. 1990.

Vol. 340: T. Vasko, R. Ayres, L. Fontvieille (Eds.), Life Cycles and Long Waves. XIV, 293 pages. 1990.

Vol. 341: G.R. Uhlich, Descriptive Theories of Bargaining. IX, 165 pages. 1990.

Vol. 342: K. Okuguchi, F. Szidarovszky, The Theory of Oligopoly with Multi-Product Firms. V, 167 pages. 1990.

Vol. 343: C. Chiarella, The Elements of a Nonlinear Theory of Economic Dynamics. IX, 149 pages. 1990.

Vol. 344: K. Neumann, Stochastic Project Networks. XI, 237 pages. 1990.

Vol. 345: A. Cambini, E. Castagnoli, L. Martein, P Mazzoleni, S. Schaible (Eds.), Generalized Convexity and Fractional Programming with Economic Applications. Proceedings, 1988. VII, 361 pages. 1990.

Vol. 346: R. von Randow (Ed.), Integer Programming and Related Areas. A Classified Bibliography 1984–1987. XIII, 514 pages. 1990.

Vol. 347: D. Ríos Insua, Sensitivity Analysis in Multi-objective Decision Making. XI, 193 pages. 1990.

Vol. 348: H. Störmer, Binary Functions and their Applications. VIII, 151 pages. 1990.

Vol. 349: G.A. Pfann, Dynamic Modelling of Stochastic Demand for Manufacturing Employment. VI, 158 pages. 1990.

Vol. 350: W.-B. Zhang, Economic Dynamics. X, 232 pages. 1990.

Vol. 351: A. Lewandowski, V. Volkovich (Eds.), Multiobjective Problems of Mathematical Programming. Proceedings, 1988. VII, 315 pages. 1991.

Vol. 352: O. van Hilten, Optimal Firm Behaviour in the Context of Technological Progress and a Business Cycle. XII, 229 pages. 1991.

Vol. 353: G. Ricci (Ed.), Decision Processes in Economics. Proceedings, 1989. III, 209 pages 1991.

Vol. 354: M. Ivaldi, A Structural Analysis of Expectation Formation. XII, 230 pages. 1991.

Vol. 355: M. Salomon. Deterministic Lotsizing Models for Production Planning. VII, 158 pages. 1991.

Vol. 356: P. Korhonen, A. Lewandowski, J . Wallenius (Eds.), Multiple Criteria Decision Support. Proceedings, 1989. XII, 393 pages. 1991.

Vol. 357: P. Zörnig, Degeneracy Graphs and Simplex Cycling. XV, 194 pages. 1991.

Vol. 358: P. Knottnerus, Linear Models with Correlated Disturbances. VIII, 196 pages. 1991.

Vol. 359: E. de Jong, Exchange Rate Determination and Optimal Economic Policy Under Various Exchange Rate Regimes. VII, 270 pages. 1991.

Vol. 360: P. Stalder, Regime Translations, Spillovers and Buffer Stocks. VI, 193 pages . 1991.

Vol. 361: C. F. Daganzo, Logistics Systems Analysis. X, 321 pages. 1991.

Vol. 362: F. Gehrels, Essays in Macroeconomics of an Open Economy. VII, 183 pages. 1991.

Vol. 363: C. Puppe, Distorted Probabilities and Choice under Risk. VIII, 100 pages . 1991

Vol. 364: B. Horvath, Are Policy Variables Exogenous? XII, 162 pages. 1991.

Vol. 365: G. A. Heuer, U. Leopold-Wildburger. Balanced Silverman Games on General Discrete Sets. V, 140 pages. 1991.

Vol. 366: J. Gruber (Ed.), Econometric Decision Models. Proceedings, 1989. VIII, 636 pages. 1991.

Vol. 367: M. Grauer, D. B. Pressmar (Eds.), Parallel Computing and Mathematical Optimization. Proceedings. V, 208 pages. 1991.

Vol. 368: M. Fedrizzi, J. Kacprzyk, M. Roubens (Eds.), Interactive Fuzzy Optimization. VII, 216 pages. 1991.

Vol. 369: R. Koblo, The Visible Hand. VIII, 131 pages.1991.

Vol. 370: M. J. Beckmann, M. N. Gopalan, R. Subramanian (Eds.), Stochastic Processes and their Applications. Proceedings, 1990. XLI, 292 pages. 1991.

Vol. 371: A. Schmutzler, Flexibility and Adjustment to Information in Sequential Decision Problems. VIII, 198 pages. 1991.

Vol. 372: J. Esteban, The Social Viability of Money. X, 202 pages. 1991.

Vol. 373: A. Billot, Economic Theory of Fuzzy Equilibria. XIII, 164 pages. 1992.

Vol. 374: G. Pflug, U. Dieter (Eds.), Simulation and Optimization. Proceedings, 1990. X, 162 pages. 1992.

Vol. 375: S.-J. Chen, Ch.-L. Hwang, Fuzzy Multiple Attribute Decision Making. XII, 536 pages. 1992.

Vol. 376: K.-H. Jöckel, G. Rothe, W. Sendler (Eds.), Bootstrapping and Related Techniques. Proceedings, 1990. VIII, 247 pages. 1992.

Vol. 377: A. Villar, Operator Theorems with Applications to Distributive Problems and Equilibrium Models. XVI, 160 pages. 1992.

Vol. 378: W. Krabs, J. Zowe (Eds.), Modern Methods of Optimization. Proceedings, 1990. VIII, 348 pages. 1992.

Vol. 379: K. Marti (Ed.), Stochastic Optimization. Proceedings, 1990. VII, 182 pages. 1992.

Vol. 380: J. Odelstad, Invariance and Structural Dependence. XII, 245 pages. 1992.

Vol. 381: C. Giannini, Topics in Structural VAR Econometrics. XI, 131 pages. 1992.

Vol. 382: W. Oettli, D. Pallaschke (Eds.), Advances in Optimization. Proceedings, 1991. X, 527 pages. 1992.

Vol. 383: J. Vartiainen, Capital Accumulation in a Corporatist Economy. VII, 177 pages. 1992.

Vol. 384: A. Martina, Lectures on the Economic Theory of Taxation. XII, 313 pages. 1992.

Vol. 385: J. Gardeazabal, M. Regúlez, The Monetary Model of Exchange Rates and Cointegration. X, 194 pages. 1992.

Vol. 386: M. Desrochers, J.-M. Rousseau (Eds.), Computer-Aided Transit Scheduling. Proceedings, 1990. XIII, 432 pages. 1992.

Vol. 387: W. Gaertner, M. Klemisch-Ahlert, Social Choice and Bargaining Perspectives on Distributive Justice. VIII, 131 pages. 1992.

Vol. 388: D. Bartmann, M. J. Beckmann, Inventory Control. XV, 252 pages. 1992.

Vol. 389: B. Dutta, D. Mookherjee, T. Parthasarathy, T. Raghavan, D. Ray, S. Tijs (Eds.), Game Theory and Economic Applications. Proceedings, 1990. IX, 454 pages. 1992.

Vol. 390: G. Sorger, Minimum Impatience Theorem for Recursive Economic Models. X, 162 pages. 1992.

Vol. 391: C. Keser, Experimental Duopoly Markets with Demand Inertia. X, 150 pages. 1992.

Vol. 392: K. Frauendorfer, Stochastic Two-Stage Programming. VIII, 228 pages. 1992.

Vol. 393: B. Lucke, Price Stabilization on World Agricultural Markets. XI, 274 pages. 1992.

Vol. 394: Y.-J. Lai, C.-L. Hwang, Fuzzy Mathematical Programming. XIII, 301 pages. 1992.

Vol. 395: G. Haag, U. Mueller, K. G. Troitzsch (Eds.), Economic Evolution and Demographic Change. XVI, 409 pages. 1992.

Vol. 396: R. V. V. Vidal (Ed.), Applied Simulated Annealing. VIII, 358 pages. 1992.

Vol. 397: J. Wessels, A. P. Wierzbicki (Eds.), User-Oriented Methodology and Techniques of Decision Analysis and Support. Proceedings, 1991. XII, 295 pages. 1993.

Vol. 398: J.-P. Urbain, Exogeneity in Error Correction Models. XI, 189 pages. 1993.

Vol. 399: F. Gori, L. Geronazzo, M. Galeotti (Eds.), Nonlinear Dynamics in Economics and Social Sciences. Proceedings, 1991. VIII, 367 pages. 1993.

Vol. 400: H. Tanizaki, Nonlinear Filters. XII, 203 pages. 1993.

Vol. 401: K. Mosler, M. Scarsini, Stochastic Orders and Applications. V, 379 pages. 1993.

Vol. 402: A. van den Elzen, Adjustment Processes for Exchange Economies and Noncooperative Games. VII, 146 pages. 1993.

Vol. 403: G. Brennscheidt, Predictive Behavior. VI, 227 pages. 1993.

Vol. 404: Y.-J. Lai, Ch.-L. Hwang, Fuzzy Multiple Objective Decision Making. XIV, 475 pages. 1994.

Vol. 405: S. Komlósi, T. Rapcsák, S. Schaible (Eds.), Generalized Convexity. Proceedings, 1992. VIII, 404 pages. 1994.

Vol. 406: N. M. Hung, N. V. Quyen, Dynamic Timing Decisions Under Uncertainty. X, 194 pages. 1994.

Vol. 407: M. Ooms, Empirical Vector Autoregressive Modeling. XIII, 380 pages. 1994.

Vol. 408: K. Haase, Lotsizing and Scheduling for Production Planning. VIII, 118 pages. 1994.

Vol. 409: A. Sprecher, Resource-Constrained Project Scheduling. XII, 142 pages. 1994.

Vol. 410: R. Winkelmann, Count Data Models. XI, 213 pages. 1994.

Vol. 411: S. Dauzère-Péres, J.-B. Lasserre, An Integrated Approach in Production Planning and Scheduling. XVI, 137 pages. 1994.

Vol. 412: B. Kuon, Two-Person Bargaining Experiments with Incomplete Information. IX, 293 pages. 1994.

Vol. 413: R. Fiorito (Ed.), Inventory, Business Cycles and Monetary Transmission. VI, 287 pages. 1994.

Vol. 414: Y. Crama, A. Oerlemans, F. Spieksma, Production Planning in Automated Manufacturing. X, 210 pages. 1994.

Vol. 415: P. C. Nicola, Imperfect General Equilibrium. XI, 167 pages. 1994.

Vol. 416: H. S. J. Cesar, Control and Game Models of the Greenhouse Effect. XI, 225 pages. 1994.

Vol. 417: B. Ran, D. E. Boyce, Dynamic Urban Transportation Network Models. XV, 391 pages. 1994.

Vol. 418: P. Bogetoft, Non-Cooperative Planning Theory. XI, 309 pages. 1994.

Vol. 419: T. Maruyama, W. Takahashi (Eds.), Nonlinear and Convex Analysis in Economic Theory. VIII, 306 pages. 1995.

Vol. 420: M. Peeters, Time-To-Build. Interrelated Investment and Labour Demand Modelling. With Applications to Six OECD Countries. IX, 204 pages. 1995.

Vol. 421: C. Dang, Triangulations and Simplicial Methods. IX, 196 pages. 1995.

Vol. 422: D. S. Bridges, G. B. Mehta, Representations of Preference Orderings. X, 165 pages. 1995.

Vol. 423: K. Marti, P. Kall (Eds.), Stochastic Programming. Numerical Techniques and Engineering Applications. VIII, 351 pages. 1995.

Vol. 424: G. A. Heuer, U. Leopold-Wildburger, Silverman's Game. X, 283 pages. 1995.

Vol. 425: J. Kohlas, P.-A. Monney, A Mathematical Theory of Hints. XIII, 419 pages, 1995.

Vol. 426: B. Finkenstädt, Nonlinear Dynamics in Economics. IX, 156 pages. 1995.

Vol. 427: F. W. van Tongeren, Microsimulation Modelling of the Corporate Firm. XVII, 275 pages. 1995.

Vol. 428: A. A. Powell, Ch. W. Murphy, Inside a Modern Macroeconometric Model. XVIII, 424 pages. 1995.

Vol. 429: R. Durier, C. Michelot, Recent Developments in Optimization. VIII, 356 pages. 1995.

Vol. 430: J. R. Daduna, I. Branco, J. M. Pinto Paixão (Eds.), Computer-Aided Transit Scheduling. XIV, 374 pages. 1995.

Vol. 431: A. Aulin, Causal and Stochastic Elements in Business Cycles. XI, 116 pages. 1996.

Vol. 432: M. Tamiz (Ed.), Multi-Objective Programming and Goal Programming. VI, 359 pages. 1996.

Vol. 433: J. Menon, Exchange Rates and Prices. XIV, 313 pages. 1996.

Vol. 434: M. W. J. Blok, Dynamic Models of the Firm. VII, 193 pages. 1996.

Vol. 435: L. Chen, Interest Rate Dynamics, Derivatives Pricing, and Risk Management. XII, 149 pages. 1996.

Vol. 436: M. Klemisch-Ahlert, Bargaining in Economic and Ethical Environments. IX, 155 pages. 1996.

Vol. 437: C. Jordan, Batching and Scheduling. IX, 178 pages. 1996.

Vol. 438: A. Villar, General Equilibrium with Increasing Returns. XIII, 164 pages. 1996.

Vol. 439: M. Zenner, Learning to Become Rational. VII, 201 pages. 1996.

Vol. 440: W. Ryll, Litigation and Settlement in a Game with Incomplete Information. VIII, 174 pages. 1996.

Vol. 441: H. Dawid, Adaptive Learning by Genetic Algorithms. IX, 166 pages.1996.

Vol. 442: L. Corchón, Theories of Imperfectly Competitive Markets. XIII, 163 pages. 1996.

Vol. 443: G. Lang, On Overlapping Generations Models with Productive Capital. X, 98 pages. 1996.

Vol. 444: S. Jørgensen, G. Zaccour (Eds.), Dynamic Competitive Analysis in Marketing. X, 285 pages. 1996.

Vol. 445: A. H. Christer, S. Osaki, L. C. Thomas (Eds.), Stochastic Modelling in Innovative Manufactoring. X, 361 pages. 1997.

Vol. 446: G. Dhaene, Encompassing. X, 160 pages. 1997.

Vol. 447: A. Artale, Rings in Auctions. X, 172 pages. 1997.

Vol. 448: G. Fandel, T. Gal (Eds.), Multiple Criteria Decision Making. XII, 678 pages. 1997.

Vol. 449: F. Fang, M. Sanglier (Eds.), Complexity and Self-Organization in Social and Economic Systems. IX, 317 pages, 1997.

Vol. 450: P. M. Pardalos, D. W. Hearn, W. W. Hager, (Eds.), Network Optimization. VIII, 485 pages, 1997.

Vol. 451: M. Salge, Rational Bubbles. Theoretical Basis, Economic Relevance, and Empirical Evidence with a Special Emphasis on the German Stock Market.IX, 265 pages. 1997.

Vol. 452: P. Gritzmann, R. Horst, E. Sachs, R. Tichatschke (Eds.), Recent Advances in Optimization. VIII, 379 pages. 1997.

Vol. 453: A. S. Tangian, J. Gruber (Eds.), Constructing Scalar-Valued Objective Functions. VIII, 298 pages. 1997.

Vol. 454: H.-M. Krolzig, Markov-Switching Vector Autoregressions. XIV, 358 pages. 1997.

Vol. 455: R. Caballero, F. Ruiz, R. E. Steuer (Eds.), Advances in Multiple Objective and Goal Programming. VIII, 391 pages. 1997.

Vol. 456: R. Conte, R. Hegselmann, P. Terna (Eds.), Simulating Social Phenomena. VIII, 536 pages. 1997.

Vol. 457: C. Hsu, Volume and the Nonlinear Dynamics of Stock Returns. VIII, 133 pages. 1998.

Vol. 458: K. Marti, P. Kall (Eds.), Stochastic Programming Methods and Technical Applications. X, 437 pages. 1998.

Vol. 459: H. K. Ryu, D. J. Slottje, Measuring Trends in U.S. Income Inequality. XI, 195 pages. 1998.

Vol. 460: B. Fleischmann, J. A. E. E. van Nunen, M. G. Speranza, P. Stähly, Advances in Distribution Logistic. XI, 535 pages. 1998.

Vol. 461: U. Schmidt, Axiomatic Utility Theory under Risk. XV, 201 pages. 1998.

Vol. 462: L. von Auer, Dynamic Preferences, Choise Mechanisms, and Welfare. XII, 226 pages. 1998.

Vol. 463: G. Abraham-Frois (Ed.), Non-Linear Dynamics and Endogenous Cycles. VI, 204 pages. 1998.

Vol. 464: A. Aulin, The Impact of Science on Economic Growth and its Cycles. IX, 204 pages. 1998.

Vol. 465: T. J. Stewart, R. C. van den Honert (Eds.), Trends in Multicriteria Decision Making. X, 448 pages. 1998.

Vol. 466: A. Sadrieh, The Alternating Double Auction Market. VII, 350 pages. 1998.

Vol. 467: H. Hennig-Schmidt, Gargaining in a Video Experiment. Determinants of Boundedly Rational Behavior. XII, 221 pages. 1999.

Vol. 468: A. Ziegler, A Game Theory Analysis of Options. XIV, 145 pages. 1999.

Vol. 469: M. P. Vogel, Environmental Kuznets Curves. XIII, 197 pages. 1999.

GPSR Compliance

The European Union's (EU) General Product Safety Regulation (GPSR) is a set of rules that requires consumer products to be safe and our obligations to ensure this.

If you have any concerns about our products, you can contact us on ProductSafety@springernature.com

In case Publisher is established outside the EU, the EU authorized representative is:

Springer Nature Customer Service Center GmbH
Europaplatz 3
69115 Heidelberg, Germany

Batch number: 10844675

Printed by Printforce, the Netherlands